D0340544

DISCARD

The Jane Austen Writers' Club

ALSO BY REBECCA SMITH

Fiction

The Bluebird Café
Happy Birthday and All That
A Bit of Earth

Non-fiction

Jane Austen's Guide to Modern Life's Dilemmas

The Jane Austen Writers' Club

Inspiration and Advice from the World's Best-Loved Novelist

REBECCA SMITH

Illustrations by Sarah J Coleman

BLOOMSBURY

NEW YORK · LONDON · OXFORD · NEW DELHI · SYDNEY

Bloomsbury USA
An imprint of Bloomsbury Publishing Plc

1385 Broadway   50 Bedford Square
New York   London
NY 10018   WC1B 3DP
USA   UK

www.bloomsbury.com

BLOOMSBURY and the Diana logo are trademarks of Bloomsbury Publishing Plc

First published in Great Britain 2016
First U.S. edition 2016

© Rebecca Smith, 2016

Every reasonable effort has been made to trace copyright holders of material
reproduced in this book, but if any have been inadvertently overlooked the publishers
would be glad to hear from them.

All rights reserved. No part of this publication may be reproduced or transmitted
in any form or by any means, electronic or mechanical, including photocopying,
recording, or any information storage or retrieval system, without prior permission in
writing from the publishers.

No responsibility for loss caused to any individual or organization acting on or
refraining from action as a result of the material in this publication can be accepted by
Bloomsbury or the author.

ISBN: HB: 978-1-63286-588-5
EPUB: 978-1-63286-590-8

Library of Congress Cataloging-in-Publication Data is available.

2 4 6 8 10 9 7 5 3 1

Typeset by Newgen Knowledge Works (P) Ltd., Chennai, India
Printed and bound in the U.S.A. by Berryville Graphics Inc., Berryville, Virginia

To find out more about our authors and books visit www.bloomsbury.com.
Here you will find extracts, author interviews, details of forthcoming events, and the
option to sign up for our newsletters.

Bloomsbury books may be purchased for business or promotional use.
For information on bulk purchases please contact Macmillan Corporate and
Premium Sales Department at specialmarkets@macmillan.com.

For the staff, volunteers and trustees, past and present,
of Jane Austen's House Museum

CONTENTS

CONTENTS

A NOTE FROM THE AUTHOR

I have been following Jane Austen around for a long
time. Like so many people I was introduced to her work
at school – *Pride and Prejudice* when I was fourteen, the
perfect age. The school was in Dorking, or 'the Town
of D—' as Jane Austen puts it in *The Watsons*. It was a
short walk from Box Hill, site of the disastrous picnic in
Emma. I didn't notice any Mr Darcys or Mr Knightleys in
Form 4A, but there were plenty of aspiring heroines like
Catherine Morland. *Pride and Prejudice* was one of the
first novels for adults that I fell in love with. It transported
me from a world of boys who tortured wasps to Pemberley.
I remember reading it in the garden of our house, which

was in Reigate, not Dorking, in the company of a neighbour's disreputable frog-killing ginger tom. I called him Ginger Wickham.

I am Jane Austen's five-times-great-niece. It is a nice thing to be but no claim to fame. Jane Austen's brothers had thirty-three children between them, so two hundred years on there must be thousands of Austen descendants. But when I visited my great-aunt in Winchester I loved looking at some little portraits of Jane Austen's sailor brothers, Francis (my ancestor) and Charles, and what turned out to be a rare depiction of her father, the Reverend George Austen. These portraits are now on display at Jane Austen's House Museum in Chawton, Hampshire so I can visit them there.

I went to university in Southampton and still live in the city and teach creative writing at the university. There are still traces of the Southampton Jane Austen knew when it was her home before she finally settled at Chawton. The sea has been pushed back from where it once came up to the city walls so that she could see it from the garden she created with Francis's family, her sister Cassandra and her mother. She liked the city – there was and is much more to it than the stinking fish mentioned in *Love and Freindship*.

From 2009 to 2010 I had the immense good fortune to be the writer-in-residence at Jane Austen's House Museum. I reread all Jane's works and her letters and had a wonderful year with the staff and volunteers, talking to visitors, running writing workshops, visiting schools, generally getting lost in Austen and working on my fifth novel. On Jane Austen's 234th birthday, 16 December

2009, I was one of the first in the house. I remember going to open the shutters in Jane's bedroom and desperately hoping that I'd catch a glimpse of her. I didn't, but this book had its genesis during that year. Spending so much time where Jane Austen lived, where she wrote *Mansfield Park*, *Emma* and *Persuasion* and revised her three earlier novels, walking where she did and seeing the views from her windows was magical and inspiring. The museum isn't haunted, but many of the staff, volunteers and visitors testify to its healing atmosphere. I have now run many writing workshops at Jane Austen's House Museum and elsewhere, using Jane's work and methods to inspire writers working in all genres. I'm so grateful to the museum for the opportunities it has given me and to the writers who have come to the workshops, sharing their writing, ideas and experiences.

I thought of those writers as I worked on this book. I hope it will be useful to them and to writers around the world who love Jane Austen or are less familiar with her work, and to readers, teachers and Janeites everywhere.

I hope this book will help you, whether you are writing a novel, concentrating on short stories or working in another form. People love Jane Austen's work for so many reasons – the comedy, her sparkling dialogue, the unforgettable characters, the accuracy of her observations, her neat and satisfying plots, her use of language, the way she writes relationships, and how she captures what it is to be in love, lonely, bullied, wrong, disappointed, to be part of a family . . . The list goes on and on. Her letters give us wonderful insights into her life, and in them she gives advice on writing; I have included that too.

One of the most difficult aspects of writing this book was deciding which extracts to use and then having to limit their length. I hope you find the advice and exercises useful. I'm sure that the quotations will send you back to Jane Austen's novels and letters themselves. There is no better place to go.

Rebecca Smith
Spring 2016

Plan of a novel

Planning, plotting and getting started

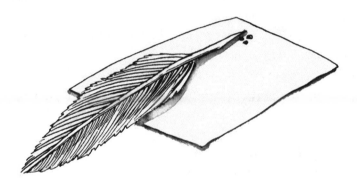

T HIS CHAPTER IS ABOUT planning a novel and the things you can do to set out in the right direction and stay on track. You can't plan everything. Unless you are doing something truly formulaic, such as writing as an anonymous jobbing author for a series, you should leave room to surprise yourself, for creativity and for those moments of alchemy and inspiration which have the power to lift and transform your work.

It's probably easier to suggest how *not* to write a novel. Jane Austen knew exactly what she *didn't* want to write. Her *Plan of a Novel according to hints from various quarters* dates from 1816, when she was corresponding with James Stanier Clarke, the Prince Regent's chaplain and librarian at Carlton House. He was clearly rather taken with her but couldn't resist making lots of 'helpful' suggestions for her work. Perhaps he hoped to make himself indispensable to her. Dream on, Mr Stanier Clarke. Her letters to Mr Clarke and her *Plan of a Novel* show us what she definitely *wouldn't* do. She included in the margins the names of people whose hints she was not going to take. His name was there.

Incidentally, one of the most likely but unauthenticated portraits of Jane Austen is a watercolour by James Stanier Clarke preserved in his *Friendship Book*. This lovely portrait of an elegant woman is very likely Jane. She had been 'invited' to dedicate her next novel (*Emma*) to the Prince Regent, who was a fan. She wasn't a fan of his but had no choice but to comply.

Here is Jane's *Plan of a Novel*.[1]

SCENE to be in the Country, Heroine the Daughter of a Clergyman, one who after having lived much in the World had retired from it and settled in a Curacy with a very small fortune of his own. – He, the most excellent Man that can be imagined, perfect in Character, Temper, and Manners – without the smallest drawback or peculiarity to prevent his being the most delightful companion to his Daughter from one year's end to the other. – Heroine a faultless Character herself, – perfectly good, with much tenderness and sentiment, and not the least Wit – very highly accomplished, understanding modern Languages and (generally speaking) everything that the most accomplished young Women learn, but particularly excelling in Music – her favourite pursuit – and playing equally well on the PianoForte and Harp – and singing in the first stile. Her Person quite beautiful – dark eyes and plump cheeks. – Book to open with the description of Father and Daughter – who are to converse in long speeches, elegant Language – and a tone of high serious sentiment. – The Father to be induced, at his Daughter's earnest request, to relate to her the past events of his Life. This Narrative will reach through the greatest part of the first volume – as besides all the circumstances of his attachment to her Mother and their Marriage, it will comprehend his going to sea as Chaplain to a distinguished naval character about the Court, his going afterwards to Court himself, which introduced him to a great variety of Characters and involved him in many interesting situations, concluding with his opinions on the Benefits to result from Tithes being done away, and his having buried his own Mother (Heroine's lamented Grandmother) in consequence of the High Priest of the Parish in which she died refusing to pay her Remains the respect due to them. The Father to be of a very literary turn, an Enthusiast in Literature, nobody's Enemy but his own – at the same time most zealous in discharge of his Pastoral Duties, the model of an exemplary Parish

Priest. – The heroine's friendship to be sought after by a young woman in the same Neighbourhood, of Talents and Shrewdness, with light eyes and a fair skin, but having a considerable degree of Wit, Heroine shall shrink from the acquaintance.

From this outset, the Story will proceed, and contain a striking variety of adventures. Heroine and her Father never above a fortnight together in one place, *he* being driven from his Curacy by the vile arts of some totally unprincipled and heart-less young Man, desperately in love with the Heroine, and pursuing her with unrelenting passion. – No sooner settled in one Country of Europe than they are necessitated to quit it and retire to another – always making new acquaintance, and always obliged to leave them. – This will of course exhibit a wide variety of Characters – but there will be no mixture; the scene will be for ever shifting from one Set of People to another – but All the Good will be unexceptionable in every respect – and there will be no foibles or weaknesses but with the Wicked, who will be completely depraved and infamous, hardly a resemblance of humanity left in them. – Early in her career, in the progress of her first removals, Heroine must meet with the Hero – all perfection of course – and only prevented from paying his addresses to her by some excess of refinement. – Wherever she goes, somebody falls in love with her, and she receives repeated offers of Marriage – which she refers wholly to her Father, exceedingly angry that *he* should not be first applied to. – Often carried away by the anti-hero, but rescued either by her Father or by the Hero – often reduced to support herself and her

Father by her Talents and work for her Bread; continually cheated and defrauded of her hire, worn down to a Skeleton, and now and then starved to death. – At last, hunted out of civilized Society, denied the poor Shelter of the humblest Cottage, they are compelled to retreat into Kamschatka[2] where the poor Father, quite worn down, finding his end approaching, throws himself on the Ground, and after 4 or 5 hours of tender advice and parental Admonition to his miserable Child, expires in a fine burst of Literary Enthusiasm, intermingled with Invectives against holders of Tithes. – Heroine inconsolable for some time – but afterwards crawls back towards her former Country – having at least 20 narrow escapes from falling into the hands of the Anti-hero – and at last in the very nick of time, turning a corner to avoid him, runs into the arms of the Hero himself, who having just shaken off the scruples which fetter'd him before, was at the very moment setting off in pursuit of her. – The Tenderest and completest Eclaircissement takes place, and they are happily united. – Throughout the whole work, Heroine to be in the most elegant Society and living in high style. The name of the work *not* to be *Emma*, but of the same sort as *S. & S.* and *P. & P.*

So, drawn from that, here are some of Jane Austen's tips on how not to write a novel.

1. Have leading characters who are perfect in every way.

2. Make sure that your villains are evil through and through.

3. Open with a long description of the characters and have them converse in long and implausibly elegant speeches. (Make all your dialogue like that.)

4. Continue with a huge wodge of backstory. This should take about a third of the book before the actual story starts.

5. Keep your story jumping about in seemingly random directions.

6. Keep introducing new sets of characters whom you then forget about in the next scene.

7. Keep up a series of implausible events.

8. Make sure that any really important scene is bogged down with boring irrelevancies.

9. Make sure that your plot is full of inconsistencies. It doesn't much matter what happens or how things are connected as long as you just keep going for a really, really long time.

10. The ending should be completely predictable but nevertheless precipitated by a coincidence or by something that has developed without the reader having any knowledge of it.

These mistakes might seem obvious, but agents see aspiring writers fall into such tar pits again and again. Jane Austen gently pointed out some of these things to her niece, Anna Austen – later Anna Lefroy, the eldest daughter of her brother James – for instance telling her,

'Your Aunt C. does not like desultory novels, and is rather afraid yours will be too much so, that there will be too frequently a change from one set of people to another, and that circumstances will be introduced of apparent consequence which will lead to nothing. It will not be so great an objection to *me* if it does. I allow much more latitude than she does, and think nature and spirit cover many sins of a wandering story.'[3]

I suspect that Jane shared Cassandra's reservations but wanted to be tactful, giving many more detailed criticisms and suggestions in this and other letters. Jane and her mother and sister read Anna's work and returned it with comments and suggested cuts. Anna clearly had potential. Although her novel, *Which One Is the Heroine?* or *Enthusiasm*, was never published, and the manuscript doesn't seem to have survived, we can discern quite a lot about it from Jane's letters. Jane Austen gave advice to Anna's younger siblings, Caroline and James Edward, who were also aspiring writers. She was a patient aunt and helpful critic. Here are some of the key things Jane advised apprentice writers to do.

Read

We know that Jane Austen was a voracious and omnivorous reader, not just from the evidence of her novels but from her letters and the records we have of her family's collections of books. She was a member of the Chawton Book Society (in the way that so many people are members of book clubs today) and a dedicated library user. The members of the Chawton Book Society clubbed together to buy and share books.

And, when Jane Austen was only weeks away from death, she wrote to her niece Caroline to stress that if she wanted to be a writer, she had to be a reader. Caroline recalled this in her reminiscences.

As I grew older, my aunt would talk to me more seriously of my reading and my amusements. I had taken early to writing verses and stories, and I am sorry to think how I troubled her with reading them. She was very kind about it, and always had some praise to bestow, but at last she warned me against spending too much time upon them. She said – how well I recollect it! – that she knew writing stories was a great amusement, and – she thought – a harmless one, though many people, she was aware, thought otherwise; but that at my age it would be bad for me to be much taken up with my own compositions. Later still – it was after she had gone to Winchester – she sent me a message to this effect, that if I would take her advice I should cease writing till I was sixteen; that she had herself often wished she had read more, and written less in the corresponding years of her own life.[4]

Many aspiring writers are so busy thinking about their own work and dreaming of fame and fortune that they don't spend nearly enough time reading. Reading is the education, the food and drink, the work and repose of the writer. Jane may have thought that she should have read more and written less when she was young, but I'm guessing she read rather more than Caroline, and I'm very glad that her early efforts have survived – they are so full of joy and jokes and show her responding to her reading. But Jane Austen knew that however much a writer reads, it is never enough.

Write about things you understand

This isn't the oft-given advice, 'Write what you know.' Jane Austen hadn't experienced what it was like to be asked to marry Mr Darcy or be as rich as Emma Woodhouse, but she could imagine. What she did was set her work in a society that she understood. She wrote to Anna in August and September 1814, 'we [Cassandra and herself] think you had better not leave England. Let the Portmans go to Ireland, but as you know nothing of the manners there, you had better not go with them. Stick to Bath and the Foresters. There you will be quite at home.'

Anna hadn't been to Ireland and would have got things wrong if she'd tried to write about it. It wasn't just that Anna didn't know the locations; she didn't know enough about the way society operated there and wouldn't have been able to capture the voices convincingly. Anna's characters could be sent there, but what happened in Ireland should stay offstage. Jane Austen captured voices that she knew – the rich and snobby that she mixed with, for instance when she stayed with her brother Edward or was in Bath, and people like Nancy Steele with her West Country accent. Jane Austen must have met more than her fair share of pompous clergymen, and through her sailor brothers was able to create the nautical characters for *Persuasion* and *Mansfield Park*. It isn't 'Write what you know;' it's 'Use what you know.'

Get things right or readers will lose faith with you

If a reader notices something and thinks, *'That wouldn't happen like that!'* you have lost them. Here is Jane pointing this out to Anna on 9 September 1814.

My Dear Anna,

We have been very much amused by your three books,[5] but I have a good many criticisms to make, more than you will like. We are not satisfied with Mrs Forester settling herself as tenant and near neighbour to such a man as Sir Thomas, without having some other inducement to go there. She ought to have some friend living thereabouts to tempt her. A woman going with two girls just growing up into a neighbourhood where she knows nobody but one man of not very good character, is an awkwardness which so prudent a woman as Mrs F. would not be likely to fall into. Remember she *is* very prudent. You must not let her act inconsistently. Give her a friend, and let that friend be invited by Sir Thomas H. to meet her, and we shall have no objection to her dining at the Priory as she does; but otherwise a woman in her situation would hardly go there before she had been visited by other families. I like the scene itself, the Miss Leslie, Lady Anne, and the music very much. Leslie *is* a noble name. Sir Thomas H. you always do very well. I have only taken the liberty of expunging one phrase of his which would not be allowable – 'Bless my heart!' It is too familiar and inelegant. Your grandmother is more disturbed at Mrs Forester's not returning the Egertons' visit sooner than by anything else. They ought to have called at the Parsonage before Sunday . . .

Get to know your characters properly

Make sure they are consistent. Readers will soon notice if you seem to be making them up as the novel progresses. Jane's letter of 9 September 1814 continues:

> Mrs Forester is not careful enough of Susan's health. Susan ought not to be walking out so soon after heavy rains, taking long walks in the dirt. An anxious mother would not suffer it. I like your Susan very much, she is a sweet creature, her playfulness of fancy is very delightful. I like her as she is *now* exceedingly, but I am not quite so well satisfied with her behaviour to George R. At first she seems all over attachment and feeling, and afterwards to have none at all; she is so extremely confused at the ball and so well satisfied apparently with Mr Morgan. She seems to have changed her character.

Readers today can see how influenced Anna was by her aunt's novels. A mother of girls who moves to a neighbourhood where she knows hardly anybody sounds rather like Mrs Dashwood in *Sense and Sensibility*. Jane suggests that Anna cut a section that utilizes a play (probably too much like *Mansfield Park*), and as for that lively heroine who goes out walking in the mud ... But Anna was clearly learning from her reading.

Don't clutter your work with unnecessary detail; cut and edit

This is from the same letter: 'You describe a sweet place, but your descriptions are often more minute than will be liked. You give too many particulars of right hand & left.'

Jane understood that for a setting to come across as convincing, its creator needs to have all this information in her head but not all of it should appear on the page. Even if you are writing about a cluttered room, readers don't want cluttered prose and overlong descriptions. Anna needed to fix on the correct key details to use in the pictures she was painting.

It may have happened in real life, but that doesn't mean it will work in a novel

'I have scratched out Sir Thos. from walking with the other men to the stables, &c. the very day after his breaking his arm – for, though I find your papa *did* walk out immediately after *his* arm was set, I think it can be so little usual as to *appear* unnatural in a book.'

Aspiring novelists often feel that the events of their lives will work well in novels. This is not always so.

And don't respond to criticism by saying, 'Yes, but . . . '

With the broken-arm incident Jane anticipates Anna saying, 'Yes, but my father did that.' 'Yes, but . . . ' doesn't cut any ice with readers. Writers who keep saying 'Yes, but' don't write the best stories.

Think about the scale of your story and the best thing to tackle when you are starting out

Jane Austen's famous description of her work as being painted onto a 'little bit (two inches wide) of ivory' was in a letter to her nephew, James Edward, an aspiring novelist who was to become her biographer. He had just left Winchester College, so was still a teenager, but Jane writes to him as though they are labouring in the same field and his efforts are as important as hers:

Chawton, Monday, Dec. 16th (1816)

My Dear E.

One reason for my writing to you now is, that I may have the pleasure of directing to you Esqre. I give you joy of having left Winchester. Now you may own how miserable you were there; now it will gradually all come out, your crimes and your miseries – how often you went up by the Mail to London and threw away fifty guineas at a tavern, and how often you were on the point of hanging yourself, restrained only, as some ill-natured aspersion upon poor old Winton has it, by the want of a tree within some miles of the city . . .

Uncle Henry writes very superior sermons. You and I must try to get hold of one or two, and put them into our novels: it would be a fine help to a volume; and we could make our heroine read it aloud on a Sunday evening, just as well as Isabella Wardour, in the 'Antiquary', is made to read the 'History of the Hartz Demon' in the ruins of St Ruth, though I believe, on recollection, Lovell is the reader. By the bye, my dear E., I am quite concerned for the loss your mother mentions in her letter. Two chapters and a half to be missing is monstrous! It is well that _I_ have not been at Steventon lately, and therefore cannot be suspected of purloining them: two strong twigs and a half towards a nest of my own would have been something. I do not think however, that any theft of that sort would be really very useful to me. What should I do with your strong, manly, spirited sketches, full of variety and glow? How could I possibly join them on to the little bit (two inches wide) of ivory on which I work with so fine a brush, as produces little effect after much labour?

So poor James Edward (the family called him Edward) had lost two and a half chapters of his novel. I'm sure his aunt was smiling when she wrote about his 'strong, manly, spirited sketches, full of variety and glow', but she was always encouraging to young writers. I think she was also quietly suggesting that he might want to tone his writing down a bit.

Funny is good

The things that Jane Austen praises most in Anna's writing (about which we hear the most) are the jokes and the things that will make a reader smile.

I should like to have had more of Devereux. I do not feel enough acquainted with him. You were afraid of meddling with him I dare say. I like your sketch of Lord Clanmurray, and your picture of the two young girls' enjoyment is very good. I have not noticed St Julian's serious conversation with Cecilia, but I like it exceedingly. What he says about the madness of otherwise sensible women on the subject of their daughters coming out is worth its weight in gold.

I do not perceive that the language sinks. Pray go on.[6]

Beware of overwriting and clichés

Overwriting is all too easy when you are carried away by the joy of writing a first draft, but it must be cut. Jane Austen told Anna, 'Devereux Forester's [one of Anna's characters] being ruined by his vanity is extremely good, but I wish you would not let him plunge into a "vortex of dissipation". I do not object to the thing, but I cannot bear the expression; it is such thorough novel slang, and so old that I daresay Adam met with it in the first novel he opened.'[7]

Edit meticulously

Jane wrote to Cassandra that 'an artist cannot do any thing slovenly'.[8] Check your prose for infelicities and repetitions. Jane noticed these in whatever she was reading, joking to Cassandra when she was writing from London in spring 1811, 'It gives me sincere pleasure to hear of Mrs Knight's having had a tolerable night at last, but upon this occasion I wish she had another name, for the two *nights* jingle very much.'

Editing will take you longer than composition. There were many years between Jane Austen starting writing and her first novel being published. Expect your own path to be just as long and stony.

PLANNING YOUR NOVEL

Think about the stories that you are working with and the stories that underpin those stories.

Be aware of the archetypal narrative(s) you are working with and the power and potential that those have. It's well worth reading up on this.[9] Think about the novels, plays, poems, paintings, films, pieces of music, etc. that have influenced you and that are particularly resonant for what you are working on. Readers have spotted many different things underpinning Jane's work. For example, in *Mansfield Park* we can see echoes of *King Lear*, *Les Liaisons dangereuses* and *Cinderella*.

Plotting

Start by being as succinct as possible. Answer these questions in one sentence each.

1. What is the problem that must be solved in your novel?

2. What happens?

3. What is the outcome? [10]

If you were writing *Mansfield Park*, your answers might be:

1. Fanny Price is bullied and neglected.

2. She stays true to what she believes in.

3. Her worth is acknowledged and the villains are vanquished.

This is actually very similar to *Cinderella*. Now, again in one sentence:

4. Sum up your story – the truth at the heart of it, not the plot.

5. What universal truth (assuming there is such a thing) does your novel prove?

Your *Mansfield Park* answers might be:

4. Fanny Price finds love and the place where she belongs.

5. Virtue will be rewarded.

Don't worry if your final answer sounds a bit like the motto from a fortune cookie.

Mansfield Park is the easiest of Jane Austen's novels to do this with because it has a moral plot and is so like *Cinderella*, but even *Mansfield Park* can be looked at in different ways. Henry Crawford is masquerading as a prince but is really a frog; Mrs Norris is the wicked stepmother who must be banished, and there are the love triangles to boot. The important thing is to know what your story is really about and to keep that in mind. You should look at each scene you write and ask yourself how it advances the plot and how readers will see the characters develop. Ask as many questions of your work as you can: Might readers find any of my characters too annoying? Where might my story drag?

Autobiographies for your characters

When you start out, write a short autobiography for each character. *Auto*biography is best because it will help you find and capture the character's voice. Each one need only be a page long. This is the sort of work that will probably stay in your notebook. It is clear from the novels how well Jane Austen knew her characters. She often included snippets of information which demonstrated that she knew what had happened to them before the opening of the novel. Some of this information would be made known to the reader as the novel progressed, but other things just stayed in Jane's head. She also knew what would happen to the characters after the novel closed, and talked to family and friends about this. Poor Jane Fairfax, for instance, was to die after a couple of years' marriage to Frank Churchill.

For your characters' autobiographies, think about their backgrounds, their families, their situations in society, etc. What might they have lost? What will they be longing for? Here are some snippets from Jane Austen's backstories, which show how well she knew her creations.

From Mr Darcy's letter to Elizabeth in Chapter 35 of *Pride and Prejudice* after she has turned down his first offer of marriage:

> Mr Wickham is the son of a very respectable man, who had for many years the management of all the Pemberley estates, and whose good conduct in the discharge of his trust naturally inclined my father to be of service to him; and on George Wickham, who was his godson, his kindness was therefore liberally bestowed [. . .]
>
> My excellent father died about five years ago; and his attachment to Mr Wickham was to the last so steady, that in his will he particularly recommended it to me, to promote his advancement in the best manner that his profession might allow – and if he took orders, desired that a valuable family living might be his as soon as it became vacant. There was also a legacy of one thousand pounds. His own father did not long survive mine,

and within half a year from these events, Mr Wickham wrote to inform me that, having finally resolved against taking orders, he hoped I should not think it unreasonable for him to expect some more immediate pecuniary advantage, in lieu of the preferment, by which he could not be benefited. He had some intention, he added, of studying the law, and I must be aware that the interest of one thousand pounds would be a very insufficient support therein. I rather wished than believed him to be sincere; but, at any rate, was perfectly ready to accede to his proposal. I knew that Mr Wickham ought not to be a clergyman; the business was therefore soon settled – he resigned all claim to assistance in the church, were it possible that he could ever be in a situation to receive it, and accepted in return three thousand pounds. All connexion between us seemed now dissolved. I thought too ill of him to invite him to Pemberley, or admit his society in town. In town I believe he chiefly lived, but his studying the law was a mere pretence, and being now free from all restraint, his life was a life of idleness and dissipation. For about three years I heard little of him; but on the decease of the incumbent of the living which had been designed for him, he applied to me again by letter for the presentation. His circumstances, he assured me, and I had no difficulty in believing it, were exceedingly bad. He had found the law a most unprofitable study, and was now absolutely resolved on being ordained, if I would present him to the living in question – of which he trusted there could be little doubt, as he was well assured that I had no other person to provide for, and I could not have forgotten my revered father's intentions. You will hardly blame me for refusing to comply with this entreaty, or for resisting every repetition of it. His resentment was in proportion to the distress of his circumstances – and he was doubtless as violent in his abuse of me to others as in his reproaches to myself. After this period every appearance of acquaintance was dropt. How he lived I know not. But last summer he was again most painfully obtruded on my notice.

I must now mention a circumstance which I would wish to forget myself, and which no obligation less than the present should induce me to unfold to any human being. Having said thus much, I feel no doubt of your secrecy. My sister, who is more than ten years my junior, was left to the guardianship of my mother's nephew, Colonel Fitzwilliam, and myself. About a year ago, she was taken from school, and an establishment formed for her in London; and last summer she went with the lady who presided over it, to Ramsgate; and thither also went Mr Wickham, undoubtedly by design; for there proved to have been a prior acquaintance between him and Mrs Younge, in whose character we were most unhappily deceived; and by her connivance and aid he so far recommended himself to Georgiana, whose affectionate heart retained a strong impression of his kindness to her as a child, that she was persuaded to believe herself in love, and to consent to an elopement. She was then but fifteen, which must be her excuse; and after stating her imprudence, I am happy to add that I owed the knowledge of it to herself. I joined them unexpectedly a day or two before the intended elopement, and then

Georgiana, unable to support the idea of grieving and offending a brother whom she almost looked up to as a father, acknowledged the whole to me. You may imagine what I felt and how I acted. Regard for my sister's credit and feelings prevented any public exposure, but I wrote to Mr Wickham, who left the place immediately, and Mrs Younge was of course removed from her charge. Mr Wickham's chief object was unquestionably my sister's fortune, which is thirty thousand pounds; but I cannot help supposing that the hope of revenging himself on me was a strong inducement. His revenge would have been complete indeed.

In the opening chapter of *Mansfield Park* we are given the story of three sisters, one of them Fanny Price's poor mother. What is really interesting here is that it was Mrs Norris who provoked the sisters' falling-out.

About thirty years ago Miss Maria Ward, of Huntingdon, with only seven thousand pounds, had the good luck to captivate Sir Thomas Bertram, of Mansfield Park, in the county of Northampton, and to be thereby raised to the rank of a baronet's lady, with all the comforts and consequences of an handsome house and large income. All Huntingdon exclaimed on the greatness of the match, and her uncle, the lawyer, himself, allowed her to be at least three thousand pounds short of any equitable claim to it. She had two sisters to be benefited by her elevation; and such of their acquaintance as thought Miss Ward and Miss Frances quite as handsome as Miss Maria, did not scruple to predict their marrying with almost equal advantage. But there certainly are not so many men of large fortune in the world as there are pretty women to deserve them. Miss Ward, at the end of half a dozen years, found herself obliged to be attached to the Rev. Mr Norris, a friend of her brother-in-law, with scarcely any private fortune, and Miss Frances fared yet worse. Miss Ward's match, indeed, when it came to the point, was not contemptible: Sir Thomas being happily able to give his friend an income in the living of Mansfield; and Mr and Mrs Norris began their career of conjugal felicity with very little less than a thousand a year. But Miss Frances married, in the common phrase, to disoblige her family, and by fixing on a lieutenant of marines, without education, fortune, or connexions, did it very thoroughly. She could hardly have made a more untoward choice. Sir Thomas Bertram had interest, which, from principle as well as pride – from a general wish of doing right, and a desire of seeing all that were connected with him in situations of respectability, he would have been glad to exert for the advantage of Lady Bertram's sister; but her husband's profession was such as no interest could reach; and before he had time to devise any other method of assisting them, an absolute breach between the sisters had taken place. It was the natural result of the conduct of each party, and such as a very imprudent marriage almost always produces. To save herself from useless remonstrance, Mrs Price never wrote to her family on the subject till actually married. Lady Bertram, who was a woman of very tranquil feelings, and a temper remarkably easy and indolent, would have contented herself with merely giving up her sister, and thinking no more of the matter; but

Mrs Norris had a spirit of activity, which could not be satisfied till she had written a long and angry letter to Fanny, to point out the folly of her conduct, and threaten her with all its possible ill consequences. Mrs Price, in her turn, was injured and angry; and an answer, which comprehended each sister in its bitterness, and bestowed such very disrespectful reflections on the pride of Sir Thomas as Mrs Norris could not possibly keep to herself, put an end to all intercourse between them for a considerable period.

EXERCISES

1. Write an autobiography for each of your characters. You must choose a point in time from which each one will be speaking; I'd suggest just before the moment when you plan to open the novel.

2. Write a scene in which we see one of your characters *before* the main action of the novel. This kind of work will remain in your notebook, never to be seen by a reader, but you should be prepared to do this sort of thing.

THINKING ABOUT YOUR SETTING

Remember that setting means time as well as place. You should know exactly when your novel is set as well as where. Don't think that you can make the novel 'timeless' or 'universal' as your assumptions and those of the characters will make this impossible. Readers want to be taken to particular places and to see them at a specific time. Jane Austen very deliberately told us where and when her novels were set, and when *Northanger Abbey* was published more than a decade after it was written, she deemed it necessary to explain the delay so that readers had the correct context for the work.

> This little work was finished in the year 1803, and intended for immediate publication. It was disposed of to a bookseller, it was even advertised, and why the business proceeded no farther, the author has never been able to learn. That any bookseller should think it worth-while to purchase what he did not think it worth-while to publish seems extraordinary. But with this, neither the author nor the public have any other concern than as some observation is necessary upon those parts of the work which thirteen years have made comparatively obsolete. The public are entreated to bear in mind that thirteen years have passed since it was finished, many more since it was begun, and that during that period, places, manners, books, and opinions have undergone considerable changes.[11]

Researchers have been able to work out that Jane Austen used the calendar of a particular year as she plotted and wrote each novel. Doing this makes the story work for readers, who won't be distracted by thoughts such as '*But I thought it was autumn!*' or '*I thought she was twenty-six!*' and also makes it much easier for the writer to keep everything under control.

It's important to know and establish your locations properly too. There's more to help you with locations later on, but this is to get you started. Fans of Austen's work are often keen to identify the 'real' Pemberley or the 'real' 'Meryton'. However, I believe that she, like so many writers, combined elements of different places while adding details of her own invention. She also often used a technique that filmmakers employ – giving the reader a long shot or panorama of a place as well as an interior, where we see things much closer up.

Here are some of these shots – or perhaps we should use the language of painting for Georgian novels – from *Sense and Sensibility*. The reader travels with Mrs Dashwood and her daughters to their new home in Devonshire and then walks with them around the house before the eye is allowed to linger on some particular things: Marianne's piano being unpacked and pictures by Elinor being hung on the walls. Marianne is the musician and so likes to perform and make a noise – 'her sorrows, her joys, could have no moderation'. Elinor is the quieter one, 'who possessed a strength of understanding, and coolness of judgment, which qualified her, though only nineteen, to be the counsellor of her mother'. Her expertise lies in observation.

We get additional pictures with the arrival of Sir John Middleton, who gives them 'a large basket full of garden stuff and fruit' from the park, which is followed before the end of the day by 'a present of game'; he also 'sends them his newspaper every day'. We already know it is September so can imagine the harvest-festival-style basket of goodies. These details contrast starkly with what we have seen of the staggering meanness of John and Fanny Dashwood, Mrs Dashwood's stepson and his wife, in the opening chapters. These pictures, then, are not just about the setting but establish the characters too.

The first part of their journey was performed in too melancholy a disposition to be otherwise than tedious and unpleasant. But as they drew towards the end of it, their interest in the appearance of a country which they were to inhabit overcame their dejection, and a view of Barton Valley as they entered it gave them cheerfulness. It was a pleasant fertile spot, well wooded, and rich in pasture. After winding along it for more than a mile, they reached their own house. A small green court was the whole of its demesne in front; and a neat wicket gate admitted them into it.

As a house, Barton Cottage, though small, was comfortable and compact; but as a cottage it was defective, for the building was regular, the roof was tiled, the window shutters were not painted green, nor were the walls covered with honeysuckles. A narrow passage led directly through the house into the garden behind. On each side of the entrance was a sitting room, about sixteen feet square; and beyond them were the offices and the stairs. Four bed-rooms and two garrets formed the rest of the house. It had not been built many years and was in good repair. In comparison of Norland, it was poor and small indeed! – but the tears which recollection called forth as they entered the house were soon dried away. They were cheered by the joy of the servants on their arrival, and each for the sake of the others resolved to appear happy. It was very early in September; the season was fine, and from first seeing the place under the advantage of good weather, they received an impression in its favour which was of material service in recommending it to their lasting approbation.

The situation of the house was good. High hills rose immediately behind, and at no great distance on each side; some of which were open downs, the others cultivated and woody. The village of Barton was chiefly on one of these hills, and formed a pleasant view from the cottage windows. The prospect in front was more extensive; it commanded the whole of the valley, and reached into the country beyond. The hills which surrounded the cottage terminated the valley in that direction; under another name, and in another course, it branched out again between two of the steepest of them.

With the size and furniture of the house Mrs Dashwood was upon the whole well satisfied; for though her former style of life rendered many additions to the latter indispensable, yet to add and improve was a delight to her; and she had at this time ready money enough to supply all that was wanted of greater elegance to the apartments. 'As for the house itself, to be sure,' said she, 'it is too small for our family, but we will make ourselves tolerably comfortable for the present, as it is too late in the year for improvements. Perhaps in the spring, if I have plenty of money, as I dare say I shall, we may think about building. These parlors are both too small for such parties of our friends as I hope to see often collected here; and I have some thoughts of throwing the passage into one of them with perhaps a part of the other, and so leave the remainder of that other for an entrance; this, with a new drawing-room which may be easily added, and a bed-chamber and garret above, will make it a very snug little cottage. I could wish the stairs were handsome. But one must not expect everything; though I suppose it would be no difficult matter to widen them. I shall see how much I am before-hand with the world in the spring, and we will plan our improvements accordingly.'

In the mean time, till all these alterations could be made from the savings of an income of five hundred a-year by a woman who never saved in her life, they were wise enough to be contented with the house as it was; and each of them was busy in arranging their particular concerns, and endeavouring, by placing around them books and other possessions, to form themselves a home. Marianne's pianoforte was unpacked and properly disposed of; and Elinor's drawings were affixed to the walls of their sitting room.

EXERCISE: PANORAMAS, LONG SHOTS,
INTERIORS AND DETAILS

Write a scene that gives us a long shot or panorama of your location and a scene that gives us a close-up of an important room or place. You may want to include characters in these scenes. Think about the point of view. It often works well to have somebody new to the place observing things so that they are seen with fresh eyes.

THINKING ABOUT CENTRAL IMAGES

Think about a novel that you love but haven't read for a while. Which things have really stayed in your mind?

Which aspects of *your* work will be the most memorable? When you are starting out it's useful to think about the scenes and images that you hope will stay in your readers' minds. In Jane Austen's work these are often the marriage proposals (of course) but also the scenes of drama (Louisa Musgrove's fall from the Cobb) and the times when she focuses on particular objects. Harriet Smith's treasures associated with her crush on Mr Elton (*Emma*, Chapter 40) stay with the reader as they are so pathetic and emblematic; Henry Crawford's barouche with its front seat ideal for flirting, the silver knife quarrelled over by Susan and Betsey Price and Fanny Price's amber cross all fix themselves in readers' minds.

Fanny loves the amber cross her brother gives her, but wearing it to her first ball causes her terrible anguish as first of all she has no chain to wear it on, and then she has to choose which of two chains to wear – one pressed on her by Mary Crawford, which comes with strings attached, or the one given to her by her beloved Edmund. Here is Fanny before the rival chains are given to her (*Mansfield Park*, Chapter 26).

> The ball was now a settled thing, and before the evening a proclaimed thing to all whom it concerned. Invitations were sent with despatch, and many a young lady went to bed that night with her head full of happy cares as well as Fanny. To her the cares were sometimes almost beyond the happiness; for young and inexperienced, with small

means of choice and no confidence in her own taste, the 'how she should be dressed' was a point of painful solicitude; and the almost solitary ornament in her possession, a very pretty amber cross which William had brought her from Sicily, was the greatest distress of all, for she had nothing but a bit of ribbon to fasten it to; and though she had worn it in that manner once, would it be allowable at such a time in the midst of all the rich ornaments which she supposed all the other young ladies would appear in? And yet not to wear it! William had wanted to buy her a gold chain too, but the purchase had been beyond his means, and therefore not to wear the cross might be mortifying him. These were anxious considerations; enough to sober her spirits even under the prospect of a ball given principally for her gratification.

The episode continues with Fanny being given a chain by Mary Crawford. When she finds out that it was a gift from Henry, she feels she has been tricked into accepting it. Edmund then appears with a chain that he has bought for Fanny. The Crawfords' chain is too big for the cross's eyelet, but Edmund's is a perfect fit.

EXERCISE: TREASURED OR SIGNATURE POSSESSIONS

Write about a character's treasured or signature possession – for example, Fanny's cross, Henry Crawford's barouche with its front seat ideal for flirting, or the silver knife quarrelled over by Susan and Betsey Price, Isabella Thorpe's hideous purple hat, John Thorpe's gig. Keep hold of this piece of writing and think about how this and other key images will work within your novel.

THINKING ABOUT KEY SCENES

Of course all of your scenes must be important, whether they are quiet or explosive; they should all progress the plot and our understanding of the characters. Avoid having chapters or scenes where people just think about things and go over what has happened so far.

When you are starting a novel, you will probably have some idea of what the really key scenes will be. It doesn't matter when you are starting out if you don't know everything that will happen; lots of things will develop and occur to you when you are writing and then editing. I think it's helpful to have a go at some of your key scenes, or even just one of them, very early on in the process. Having a key scene done (even if only sketchily) will help you get to the end of that all-important first draft. It will give you a place to aim for and act as a staging post.

We don't know if Jane Austen wrote her novels in a linear, chronological way, but that seems likely, given the way she wrote in little homemade books, and as is evidenced by the pieces of her manuscripts that have survived. Kathryn Sutherland in *Jane Austen's Textual Lives* talks about her as being an 'imminent' writer, one who tended to get things down in a close-to-finished state straight away. The many long walks Jane Austen took and the times when she couldn't write because she was too busy looking after visiting relatives also make this way of working more likely. The times when you aren't actually writing but are thinking (imaginatively or critically) about your work should help you work all the faster when you finally sit down with your quill or laptop.

Word-processing software means writers can now edit and rearrange their work much more easily than in the Regency period. However we know from the fragments of Jane Austen's manuscripts that have survived (once a novel was sent to the presses the writer's manuscript was thrown away) that her cutting and pasting was exactly that. She added little patches, pinning them to her pages. Most of her writing took place during wartime, and paper was expensive; a thrifty woman like Jane Austen would not have wanted to waste any. She wrote up to the margins and clearly didn't expect to make major changes to her work.

However, not everybody is an imminent writer. You may be more the sort who constantly changes their mind, writes far too much and cuts most of it, but whichever sort you are, it will help if you get some of your key scenes down on paper.

We don't know which scenes Jane Austen already had plans for when she started each of her novels, but you can still look at her key scenes and start planning your own. I knew even before I started writing *Happy Birthday and All That* that the novel was going to end with my character Frank drifting away in a hot-air balloon; writing that scene before much of the rest of the book helped to keep me on track, although of course I edited and worked on aspects of it later.

Jane Austen sends the *Mansfield Park* characters on a day out to Sotherton, home of Maria's fiancé, Mr Rushworth. The day is redolent of so much that is important in the novel – Henry Crawford flirting with both Maria and Julia; Fanny being abandoned by Mary Crawford and Edmund; Mrs Norris 'sponging' (we might say scrounging) a very curious specimen of heath, four pheasant eggs to hatch at home[12] and a cream cheese; Fanny being the quiet bystander, listening and observing (sometimes unseen) what everybody else is up to; the chapel at Sotherton, which has fallen into disuse.

Have a look at this key moment when, watched by a horrified Fanny Price who cannot restrain them, Maria Bertram and Henry Crawford cross a boundary.

A quarter of an hour, twenty minutes, passed away, and Fanny was still thinking of Edmund, Miss Crawford, and herself, without interruption from any one. She began to be surprised at being left so long, and to listen with an anxious desire of hearing their steps and their voices again. She listened, and at length she heard; she heard voices and feet approaching; but she had just satisfied herself that it was not those she wanted, when Miss Bertram, Mr Rushworth, and Mr Crawford issued from the same path which she had trod herself, and were before her.

'Miss Price all alone' and 'My dear Fanny, how comes this?' were the first salutations. She told her story. 'Poor dear Fanny,' cried her cousin, 'how ill you have been used by them! You had better have staid with us.'

Then seating herself with a gentleman on each side, she resumed the conversation which had engaged them before, and discussed the possibility of improvements with much animation. Nothing was fixed on; but Henry Crawford was full of ideas and projects, and, generally speaking, whatever he proposed was immediately approved, first by her, and then by Mr Rushworth, whose principal business seemed to be to hear the others, and who scarcely risked an original thought of his own beyond a wish that they had seen his friend Smith's place.

After some minutes spent in this way, Miss Bertram, observing the iron gate, expressed a wish of passing through it into the park, that their views and their plans might be more comprehensive. It was the very thing of all others to be wished, it was the best, it was the only way of proceeding with any advantage, in Henry Crawford's opinion; and he directly saw a knoll not half a mile off, which would give them exactly the requisite command of the house. Go therefore they must to that knoll, and through that gate; but the gate was locked. Mr Rushworth wished he had brought the key; he had been very near thinking whether he should not bring the key; he was determined he would never come without the key again; but still this did not remove the present evil. They could not get through; and as Miss Bertram's inclination for so doing did by no means lessen, it ended in Mr Rushworth's declaring outright that he would go and fetch the key. He set off accordingly.

'It is undoubtedly the best thing we can do now, as we are so far from the house already,' said Mr Crawford, when he was gone.

'Yes, there is nothing else to be done. But now, sincerely, do not you find the place altogether worse than you expected?'

'No, indeed, far otherwise. I find it better, grander, more complete in its style, though that style may not be the best. And to tell you the truth,' speaking rather lower, 'I do not think that *I* shall ever see Sotherton again with so much pleasure as I do now. Another summer will hardly improve it to me.'

After a moment's embarrassment the lady replied, 'You are too much a man of the world not to see with the eyes of the world. If other people think Sotherton improved, I have no doubt that you will.'

'I am afraid I am not quite so much the man of the world as might be good for me in some points. My feelings are not quite so evanescent, nor my memory of the past under such easy dominion as one finds to be the case with men of the world.'

This was followed by a short silence. Miss Bertram began again. 'You seemed to enjoy your drive here very much this morning. I was glad to see you so well entertained. You and Julia were laughing the whole way.'

'Were we? Yes, I believe we were; but I have not the least recollection at what. Oh! I believe I was relating to her some ridiculous stories of an old Irish groom of my uncle's. Your sister loves to laugh.'

'You think her more light-hearted than I am?'

'More easily amused,' he replied; 'consequently, you know,' smiling, 'better company. I could not have hoped to entertain you with Irish anecdotes during a ten miles' drive.'

'Naturally, I believe, I am as lively as Julia, but I have more to think of now.'

'You have, undoubtedly; and there are situations in which very high spirits would denote insensibility. Your prospects, however, are too fair to justify want of spirits. You have a very smiling scene before you.'

'Do you mean literally or figuratively? Literally, I conclude. Yes, certainly, the sun shines, and the park looks very cheerful. But unluckily that iron gate, that ha-ha, give me a feeling of restraint and hardship. "I cannot get out," as the starling said.' As she spoke, and it was with expression, she walked to the gate: he followed her. 'Mr Rushworth is so long fetching this key!'

'And for the world you would not get out without the key and without Mr Rushworth's authority and protection, or I think you might with little difficulty pass round the edge of the gate, here, with my assistance; I think it might be done, if you really wished to be more at large, and could allow yourself to think it not prohibited.'

'Prohibited! nonsense! I certainly can get out that way, and I will. Mr Rushworth will be here in a moment, you know; we shall not be out of sight.'

'Or if we are, Miss Price will be so good as to tell him that he will find us near that knoll: the grove of oak on the knoll.'

Fanny, feeling all this to be wrong, could not help making an effort to prevent it. 'You will hurt yourself, Miss Bertram,' she cried; 'you will certainly hurt yourself against those spikes; you will tear your gown; you will be in danger of slipping into the ha-ha. You had better not go.'

Her cousin was safe on the other side while these words were spoken, and, smiling with all the good-humour of success, she said, 'Thank you, my dear Fanny, but I and my gown are alive and well, and so good-bye.'

Fanny watches them go, and it seems they are not heading towards where they said Mr Rushworth would find them. Julia follows where her sister leads and also crosses the boundary.

THINKING ABOUT BALANCE AND SUBPLOTS

When starting out you should also think about the things that will eventually make your novel seem rich and complete. You may not even know who all your characters are when you begin, but you should have strong feelings about some of them and about your theme. Readers delight in the way that Jane Austen works with the different themes in her novels. We see characters facing similar dilemmas and quandaries and responding in contrasting ways. The consequences of the choices they make keep us pondering the questions Jane poses.

In *Emma*, for instance, she asks what it means to be a woman with and without money. What is it like to be an Emma Woodhouse, a Jane Fairfax, a Harriet Smith or a Miss Bates? We see the questions posed and consequences played out in intriguing and contrasting ways. The way that Jane works with these permutations and reflections makes her work so interesting and satisfying to the reader. She achieves a balance of plots and subplots, dilemmas and consequences.

Her novels work like pieces of music: the story weaves around the themes, returning to develop the refrains and always building to a satisfying conclusion. We know that Jane Austen loved music and got up early each day to practise the piano. She worried about her piano when she was away, writing to remind Cassandra that none of her visiting nephews and nieces should be allowed to put anything on top of it. Seventeen music books (collections of pieces copied out and printed sheet music) that belonged to Jane Austen and her female relations have survived; they give us a wonderful insight into the way the family enjoyed and made music at home.[13]

We see the musician's mind at work in Jane Austen's plotting and in how she achieves balance and utilizes reflections. This is something you can aim for in even the simplest of stories. In picture books (which are often works of art worthy of their precious audience) we frequently see subplots played out in the illustrations when there is no room for them in the text. Think about the way you can achieve similar effects in your own stories.

In good novels we are offered different possibilities to consider and see different characters exploring them. The whole of *Sense and Sensibility* is constructed like this – sense versus sensibility, Elinor versus Marianne, Edward versus Robert, Colonel Brandon versus Willoughby, John Dashwood versus Sir John Middleton, Elinor versus Lucy Steele, Lucy versus Nancy Steele, Marianne versus Nancy Steele (they are both enamoured with ideas of love), Fanny Dashwood versus Mrs Jennings, the differences between Mr and Mrs Palmer, Marianne's fate contrasted with that of Colonel Brandon's ward. The contrasts and reflections develop the theme and give rise to drama, irony and comedy. The plot is driven by the differences and conflicts between the characters.

Mansfield Park is concerned with three sisters (Lady Bertram, Mrs Norris and Mrs Price), two sets of three cousins (Maria, Julia and Fanny, and Tom, Edmund and William)[14] and four pairs of siblings, Maria and Julia, Fanny and Susan, Tom and Edmund, and Mary and Henry. We see siblings working together and against each other. There are echoes here of *King Lear* and *Cinderella*. We are also given other pairs of characters to consider: Henry Crawford and Edmund Bertram, Henry Crawford and Mr Rushworth, Mary Crawford and Fanny Price.

In *Pride and Prejudice* we can compare the actions and destinies of sisters such as Lizzy and Lydia, and parents – for example, Mr and Mrs Bennet or Mr Bennet versus Mr Gardiner – or the actions of friends like Lizzy and Charlotte Lucas. We also see characters' different approaches to people or situations – for example, Caroline Bingley's behaviour towards Mr Darcy compared to Lizzy Bennet's.

Across Jane Austen's oeuvre we see consideration of the same themes again and again – themes that speak to each new generation of readers. You might not quite know what it is you are writing about until you get going – often we write to find out what we think – but keep thinking about music, themes, reflections and balance as you work.

EXERCISES

1. Clever use of minor characters will propel your plot and add texture. Think about the way that you can use subplots and more minor characters to add tension, and develop your theme(s). The way you use your minor characters can transform your work, adding humour, surprises and choices. Add perfect prose and you'll have nothing to worry about . . .

   Write a scene in which the actions of a more minor character have huge implications for the central character(s) and the plot. Here are some of many examples from Jane Austen's work to inspire you: Mrs Norris decides that one of her impoverished sister's children should be brought to Mansfield Park; Tom Bertram's debts mean that the Crawfords will come to the Parsonage (*Mansfield Park*); the presence of some poultry thieves means that Emma and Mr Knightley can bring their nuptials forward (*Emma*); Colonel Forster's wife invites Lydia to Brighton and Mr and Mrs Gardiner invite Lizzy to go to the Lake District (*Pride and Prejudice*).

2. Think about the web of relationships that will grow in your novel. Draw a map of the relationships, showing how they are when the novel opens and also how they will develop. This map should be a working document; having it in front of you will suggest other possibilities and show where things may be lacking. It might help to use different-coloured lines to represent different things like 'in love with', 'friends with', 'cousin of', 'jealous of', 'in debt to', 'childhood friend of', etc. Remember to take account of the characters' backstories in your diagram.

AND FINALLY

You need not leave deciding on the ending until the end. Knowing where you are going and even writing your final scene in advance can be really helpful. You may not know *how* you are going to get there, or *exactly* what the destination will be, but visualizing and planning the way that your novel will close can make the journey earlier. This is how the final chapter of *Mansfield Park* opens.

Let other pens dwell on guilt and misery. I quit such odious subjects as soon as I can, impatient to restore everybody, not greatly in fault themselves, to tolerable comfort, and to have done with all the rest.

My Fanny, indeed, at this very time, I have the satisfaction of knowing, must have been happy in spite of everything. She must have been a happy creature in spite of all that she felt, or thought she felt, for the distress of those around her. She had sources of delight that must force their way. She was returned to Mansfield Park, she was useful, she was beloved; she was safe from Mr Crawford; and when Sir Thomas came back she had every proof that could be given in his then melancholy state of spirits, of his perfect approbation and increased regard; and happy as all this must make her, she would still have been happy without any of it, for Edmund was no longer the dupe of Miss Crawford.

Jane's six completed novels end with weddings, the happy endings the reader has been longing for. Her heroines find love and security. The details aren't as predictable: Maria Bertram is treated particularly harshly, expelled from Mansfield Park and condemned to live out her days with her Aunt Norris, while in *Pride and Prejudice* Wickham (apart from being married to Lydia) pretty much gets away with things and will be able to keep sponging off his sisters-in-law, even if he isn't received at Pemberley.

Who knows how Jane would have ended other novels if she hadn't died such a tragically early death, but we can be sure that she would have continued innovating and working at her craft. Her writing was continually evolving. There is scheming in *Persuasion* (between Mrs Clay and William Elliot), perhaps not fully developed due to Jane's declining health. Jane also seemed to be setting something similar up in *Sanditon*. Or perhaps she would have gone in another direction. Whatever she did, though, we can be sure that her endings would have been satisfying and involved the reversal (of fortune, good to bad or bad to good) and recognition (the character(s) comprehending the significance of what has occurred) that Aristotle said was essential to a complex plot. Jane understood the need for each novel to feel complete.

EXERCISE: A STAB AT AN ENDING

Write your ending or a scene from very near the end of your novel. The ending of *Mansfield Park* is preceded by this uncomfortable scene in Chapter 47 between Edmund Bertram and Mary Crawford. The reader doesn't see it in real time, but is given Edmund's account of it to Fanny. Edmund and Mary have what amounts to a terrible row. He is appalled that she thinks the sins committed by her brother and his sister can be glossed over. Poor Mary Crawford – after Edmund walks out she tries to entice him back, but he does not return. Jane Austen doesn't need to spell out what Mary Crawford was hoping would happen.

'She was astonished [Edmund tells Fanny], exceedingly astonished – more than astonished. I saw her change countenance. She turned extremely red. I imagined I saw a mixture of many feelings: a great, though short struggle; half a wish of yielding to truths, half a sense of shame, but habit, habit carried it. She would have laughed if she could. It was a sort of laugh, as she answered, "A pretty good lecture, upon my word. Was it part of your last sermon? At this rate you will soon reform everybody at Mansfield and Thornton Lacey; and when I hear of you next, it may be as a celebrated preacher in some great society of Methodists, or as a missionary into foreign parts." She tried to speak carelessly, but she was not so careless as she wanted to appear. I only said in reply, that from my heart I wished her well, and earnestly hoped that she might soon learn to think more justly, and not owe the most valuable knowledge we could any of us acquire, the knowledge of ourselves and of our duty, to the lessons of affliction, and immediately left the room. I had gone a few steps, Fanny, when I heard the door open behind me. "Mr Bertram," said she. I looked back. "Mr Bertram," said she, with a smile; but it was a smile ill-suited to the conversation that had passed, a saucy playful smile, seeming to invite in order to subdue me; at least it appeared so to me. I resisted; it was the impulse of the moment to resist, and still walked on. I have since, sometimes, for a moment, regretted that I did not go back, but I know I was right, and such has been the end of our acquaintance. And what an acquaintance has it been! How have I been deceived! Equally in brother and sister deceived! I thank you for your patience, Fanny. This has been the greatest relief, and now we will have done.'

[. . .] Fanny's friendship was all that he had to cling to.

We can imagine how Mary and Henry Crawford would have felt, some time later, when they found out that the virtuous cousins they had been in love with had married each other.

'Intricate characters are the most amusing'

Creating and developing your characters

THIS CHAPTER IS ABOUT the thing that makes writing and reading such good fun – creating and developing characters. My advice to writers starting out is to forget about plot; concentrate on character, and everything else will follow. Here we will look at some of Jane Austen's immortal characters and how she created and used them.

In *Pride and Prejudice* Mrs Bennet is visiting Netherfield, where Jane is staying, having been taken ill.

'I am sure,' she [Mrs Bennet] added, 'if it was not for such good friends, I do not know what would become of her, for she is very ill indeed, and suffers a vast deal, though with the greatest patience in the world – which is always the way with her, for she has, without exception, the sweetest temper I ever met with. I often tell my other girls they are nothing to *her*. You have a sweet room here, Mr Bingley, and a charming prospect over that gravel walk. I do not know a place in the country that is equal to Netherfield. You will not think of quitting it in a hurry, I hope, though you have but a short lease.'

'Whatever I do is done in a hurry,' replied he; 'and therefore if I should resolve to quit Netherfield, I should probably be off in five minutes. At present, however, I consider myself as quite fixed here.'

'That is exactly what I should have supposed of you,' said Elizabeth.

'You begin to comprehend me, do you?' cried he, turning towards her.

'Oh! yes – I understand you perfectly.'

'I wish I might take this for a compliment; but to be so easily seen through, I am afraid, is pitiful.'

'That is as it happens. It does not necessarily follow that a deep, intricate character is more or less estimable than such a one as yours.'

'Lizzy,' cried her mother, 'remember where you are, and do not run on in the wild manner that you are suffered to do at home.'

'I did not know before,' continued Bingley immediately, 'that you were a studier of character. It must be an amusing study.'

'Yes; but intricate characters are the *most* amusing. They have at least that advantage.'

'The country,' said Darcy, 'can in general supply but few subjects for such a study. In a country neighbourhood you move in a very confined and unvarying society.'

'But people themselves alter so much, that there is something new to be observed in them for ever.'

INTRODUCING YOUR CHARACTERS

Study the different ways that Jane Austen introduces her characters and experiment with the method that will work best for your story. Here are some of her techniques:

Show your characters doing the thing they most love doing

In the opening scene of *Persuasion* we see Sir Walter Elliot doing the Regency equivalent of googling himself.

Sir Walter Elliot, of Kellynch Hall, in Somersetshire, was a man who, for his own amusement, never took up any book but the Baronetage; there he found occupation for an idle hour, and consolation in a distressed one; there his faculties were roused into admiration and respect, by contemplating the limited remnant of the earliest patents; there any unwelcome sensations, arising from domestic affairs changed naturally into pity and contempt as he turned over the almost endless creations of the last century; and there, if every other leaf were powerless, he could read his own history with an interest which never failed. This was the page at which the favourite volume always opened:

'ELLIOT OF KELLYNCH HALL.

'Walter Elliot, born March 1, 1760, married, July 15, 1784, Elizabeth, daughter of James Stevenson, Esq. of South Park, in the county of Gloucester, by which lady (who died 1800) he has issue Elizabeth, born June 1, 1785; Anne, born August 9, 1787; a stillborn son, November 5, 1789; Mary, born November 20, 1791.'

EXERCISE: THE SIR WALTER ELLIOT METHOD

Introduce a character by showing them doing whatever it is they love to do or something that they do when they are alone. This might be something quite mundane in real life but which in fiction can be made enthralling. Make sure readers know how your characters spend their time, including idle moments.

Let your hero or heroine be discovered by the reader

The Austen heroine isn't always in the spotlight straight away. Jane sometimes wanted to establish a character's world and predicament before placing her centre stage. She did this with Anne Elliot, whom we are told was 'only Anne'. Fanny Price doesn't make her entrance until Chapter 2 of *Mansfield Park.*

> Fanny Price was at this time just ten years old, and though there might not be much in her first appearance to captivate, there was, at least, nothing to disgust her relations. She was small of her age, with no glow of complexion, nor any other striking beauty; exceedingly timid and shy, and shrinking from notice; but her air, though awkward, was not vulgar, her voice was sweet, and when she spoke her countenance was pretty. Sir Thomas and Lady Bertram received her very kindly.

The benefits of this strategy are obvious when the heroine is quiet or neglected, but even Elizabeth Bennet is introduced in this way, and of course Mr Darcy makes a sulky first appearance. The world of your story can seem more real if readers are led into it and then discover the central character there. An opening like this can feel like going to a party and only after a while finding that the most interesting person, the one that you will lose your heart to, is that one over there in the corner. Only slowly focusing on the central character will keep your readers on their toes and leave you able to spring surprises and take the story in unexpected directions. The downside of this strategy is that impatient readers may not get the immediate focus they want.

EXERCISE: LETTING THE READER DISCOVER
THE HERO OR HEROINE

Write or recast an opening so that a principal character is not immediately centre stage. Open *in media res*, with action and dialogue. A variation on this is to open with some sort of graphic element, or a letter, newspaper article or piece of non-fiction, that will intrigue while establishing the tone and contributing texture.

Be upfront with the introductions

Sometimes Jane Austen introduces her heroine to the reader straight away. She does this with Catherine Morland of *Northanger Abbey* and with Emma Woodhouse. She is quick to point out the faults and foibles of both heroines.

'Emma Woodhouse, handsome, clever, and rich, with a comfortable home and happy disposition, seemed to unite some of the best blessings of existence; and had lived nearly twenty-one years in the world with very little to distress or vex her.' But just a few lines later we learn that 'The real evils indeed of Emma's situation were the power of having rather too much her own way, and a disposition to think a little too well of herself; these were the disadvantages which threatened alloy to her many enjoyments. The danger, however, was at present so unperceived, that they did not by any means rank as misfortunes with her.'

Here Jane sets up her plot – the danger is at present unperceived but we realize that all will not remain well in the village of Highbury.

Writing to her niece, Fanny Knight, in March 1816, Jane remarked 'pictures of perfection, as you know, make me sick and wicked'. Make sure your characters don't cause your readers to feel like that. Readers don't have to *like* your characters, but they do have to find them intriguing. When Jane Austen was writing *Emma* she said that she was working with 'a heroine whom no-one but myself will much like'. And here is the opening of *Northanger Abbey*:

No one who had ever seen Catherine Morland in her infancy would have supposed her born to be an heroine. Her situation in life, the character of her father and mother, her own person and disposition, were all equally against her. Her father was a clergyman, without being neglected, or poor, and a very respectable man, though his name was Richard – and he had never been handsome. He had a considerable independence besides two good livings – and he was not in the least addicted to locking up his daughters. Her mother was a woman of useful plain sense, with a good temper, and, what is more remarkable, with a good constitution. She had three sons before Catherine was born; and instead of dying in bringing the latter into the world, as anybody might expect, she still lived on – lived to have six children more – to see them growing up around her, and to enjoy excellent health herself. A family of ten children will be always called a fine family, where there are heads and arms and legs enough for the number; but the Morlands had little other right to the word, for they were in general very plain, and Catherine, for many years of her life, as plain as any. She had a thin awkward figure, a sallow skin without colour, dark lank hair, and strong features – so much for her person; and not less unpropitious for heroism seemed her mind. She was fond of all boy's plays, and greatly preferred cricket not merely to dolls, but to the more heroic enjoyments of infancy, nursing a dormouse, feeding a canary-bird, or watering a rose-bush. Indeed she had no taste for a garden; and if she gathered flowers at all, it was chiefly for the pleasure of mischief – at least so it was conjectured from her always preferring those which she was forbidden to take. Such were her propensities – her abilities were quite as extraordinary. She never could learn or understand anything before she was taught; and sometimes not even then, for she was often inattentive, and occasionally stupid. Her mother was three months in teaching her only to repeat the 'Beggar's Petition'; and after all, her next sister, Sally, could say it better than she did. Not that Catherine was always stupid – by no means; she learnt the fable of 'The Hare and Many Friends' as quickly as any girl in England. Her mother wished her to learn music; and Catherine was sure she should like it, for she was very fond of tinkling the keys of the old forlorn spinnet; so, at eight years old she began. She learnt a year, and could not bear it; and Mrs Morland, who did not insist on her daughters being accomplished in spite of incapacity or distaste, allowed her to leave off. The day which dismissed the music-master was one of the happiest of Catherine's life. Her taste for drawing was not superior; though whenever she could obtain the outside of a letter from her mother or seize upon any other odd piece of paper, she did what she could in that way, by drawing houses and trees, hens and chickens, all very much like one another. Writing and accounts she was taught by her father; French by her mother: her proficiency in either was not remarkable, and she shirked her lessons in both whenever she could. What a strange, unaccountable character! – for with all these symptoms of profligacy at ten years old, she had neither a bad heart nor a bad temper, was seldom stubborn, scarcely ever quarrelsome, and very kind to the little ones, with few interruptions of tyranny; she was moreover noisy and wild, hated confinement and cleanliness, and loved nothing so well in the world as rolling down the green slope at the back of the house.

EXERCISE: BE UPFRONT

Have a look at the openings of *Emma* and *Northanger Abbey* (above) and then write one of your own, in which you are upfront with an introduction, making sure that the reader starts seeing the character's faults, oddities and idiosyncrasies straight away. Begin showing your central character's complexity from the very first page.

Let your characters introduce themselves

Sometimes the best way of introducing your characters is to hand things over to them. Whether you are writing in the first or the third person, make sure that your characters' voices are heard from early on. It may be that you want to show a particular point of view from the very first page, or have your characters argue or involved in a conflict immediately. In *Sense and Sensibility* the first thing we learn about sensible Elinor Dashwood is that she can stop her mother acting rashly.

You might like to let a character take over the narration completely. In *Lady Susan* we are given almost nothing but the characters' voices as the novel consists of letters. Even if you don't want to tell the whole of your story in this way (or through diary entries, emails or whatever), you can use some of these forms as conduits for characters' voices. The white space around one of these communications on the page of a book is pleasing to the eye, and readers will find that your novel is more of a page-turner if you use them – the pages really will be turned more quickly. Introducing a character through a letter also means that you are crediting the reader with enough intelligence to read between the lines. Of course you can use this method of introduction later on in a novel too. You can be subtle and sly and really have some fun.

Here is Mr Collins's first letter to the Bennets.

Hunsford, near Westerham, Kent,
15th October.

DEAR SIR, – The disagreement subsisting between yourself and my late honoured father always gave me much uneasiness, and since I have had the misfortune to lose him I have frequently wished to heal the breach; but for some time I was kept back by my own doubts, fearing lest it might seem disrespectful to his memory for me to be on good terms with any one with whom it had always pleased him to be at variance. [. . .] My mind however is now made up on the subject, for having received ordination at

Easter, I have been so fortunate as to be distinguished by the patronage of the Right Honourable Lady Catherine de Bourgh, widow of Sir Lewis de Bourgh, whose bounty and beneficence has preferred me to the valuable rectory of this parish, where it shall be my earnest endeavour to demean myself with grateful respect towards her ladyship, and be ever ready to perform those rites and ceremonies which are instituted by the Church of England. As a clergyman, moreover, I feel it my duty to promote and establish the blessing of peace in all families within the reach of my influence; and on these grounds I flatter myself that my present overtures of good-will are highly commendable, and that the circumstance of my being next in the entail of Longbourn estate will be kindly overlooked on your side, and not lead you to reject the offered olive branch. I cannot be otherwise than concerned at being the means of injuring your amiable daughters, and beg leave to apologize for it, as well as to assure you of my readiness to make them every possible amends, – but of this hereafter. If you should have no objection to receive me into your house, I propose myself the satisfaction of waiting on you and your family, Monday, November 18th, by four o'clock, and shall probably trespass on your hospitality till the Saturday se'nnight following, which I can do without any inconvenience, as Lady Catherine is far from objecting to my occasional absence on a Sunday, provided that some other clergyman is engaged to do the duty of the day. I remain, dear sir, with respectful compliments to your lady and daughters, your well-wisher and friend,

William Collins.

SHOW THE READER WHAT'S BEEN LOST AND WHAT'S AT STAKE

In the opening of *Persuasion*, as well as showing readers what it is that Sir Walter most cares about, Jane Austen cleverly gives a miniature history of the Elliots. She goes on to reveal (in a subtle way) what the future may hold for them and what one of the central issues of the novel will be. Writers often slip this sort of information into their opening scenes. Readers need to know what most concerns the characters, what the characters care about and what they long for. Characters have often lost something. Sir Walter's son and heir was stillborn and his wife is dead. What will become of the Elliots and Kellynch Hall?

Make sure you don't delay when it comes to telling your readers what's at risk. You can be subtle about it and slip it in the way Jane Austen does in *Persuasion* – the last novel she finished – or be more overt, following the model of *Sense and Sensibility*, her first published work, in which readers discover what has been lost *and* get little sketches of Elinor, Marianne, Margaret and their mother all in the first couple of pages. By evoking feelings and ideas of loss you can make readers care about your characters straight away.

EXERCISES

1. *What's been lost.* All readers will have a vivid memory of a time when they lost something. It might be a person, a place, a thing or a version of a former self. When he was about four my son lost a new spade at

the beach. It was a sharp blue metal one with a sturdy wooden handle. Although we bought an identical one the next day, he carried on mourning the loss of the original, and the spade has become family shorthand for situations of minor tragedy.

Think about a time when you or somebody you know lost something. It is probably easier not to focus on the death of a loved one; rather think about an object, a place or a childhood friend you lost touch with. Write about that time. Carry on for a few paragraphs and see where it takes you. Once you have something on paper, experiment with recasting it in the third or second person; more distance between you and the memory may help you craft better fiction. What you write could become part of a novel opening, a short story or a passage that gives readers a subtle insight into one of your characters.

2. *What is longed for.* Good novelists ensure that we know what characters most want. The fun starts when desires conflict. Mr Bennet wants to be left alone in his study/library: 'In his library he had been always sure of leisure and tranquillity; and though prepared, as he told Elizabeth, to meet with folly and conceit in every other room in the house, he was used to be free from them there.'[1] Mrs Bennet wants security for herself and her five daughters: 'The business of her life was to get her daughters married; its solace was visiting and news.'[2] And who can blame her?

Write a scene in which you show through dialogue and action what it is that one of your key characters longs for. Try to be subtle. Repeat this for each of your major players. Don't expect everything you write to end up in your finished work; just use this exercise to get to the heart of what each character wants.

3. *What is found.* Later on in your story your characters may find what they had lost or a replacement for it. They may or may not get what they have longed for. Will they find it for themselves or with the help of somebody else? Perhaps your hero or heroine will give something to somebody else. In *Mansfield Park* Fanny becomes the agent of her own destiny when we see her buying a replacement silver knife for the one that her sister Susan has lost. Lost objects can act as symbols. That knife is an emblem of discord and unfair treatment in the Price family. Mr Darcy finds Lydia and restores the Bennets' respectability. But sometimes the attempt to restore something can be indicative of thoughtlessness and show that a character is, as Mr Woodhouse puts it, 'not quite the thing'. Willoughby tries to give Marianne a horse to replace the one she lost along with the family home and fortune. It is a present that she cannot accept. The Dashwoods cannot afford to keep a horse, and she should not accept a gift from a man so recently known to them. Later on, Marianne has the use of Colonel Brandon's library and then becomes the

mistress of his lovely home, finding a replacement for Norland, which she loved so much. She'll have plenty of horses too.

Write a scene that shows a character trying to replace something (not necessarily a physical thing) that another character has lost by giving them a present. How will the gift be received? This probably won't be a scene for your story's opening as readers will most likely need to understand the characters and what has befallen them before this happens.

UNLIKELY HEROES AND SURPRISING HEROINES

Jane Austen continually challenged herself and her readers by creating intriguing and surprising characters. With the successes of *Sense and Sensibility* and *Pride and Prejudice* under her belt, she must have felt confident during the writing of *Mansfield Park*. She approached it determined to try something new, and in Fanny Price she gives us a heroine who contrasts strongly with Lizzy Bennet. *Mansfield Park* would have surprised readers who had anticipated a 'marriage plot'; this is a much more complex novel, one that would have defied expectations.

Many people find *Mansfield Park* the least appealing of Austen's novels. Even if you're one of those, you'll still be able to take inspiration from it and its rich cast of charming, bad, dangerous, feckless, dim, determined, scheming, ineffectual, vulgar, good and completely believable characters.

Finding your characters

Characters can be found in different places and different ways. In *Mansfield Park*, as in the other novels, we can spot echoes of people that Jane Austen knew, but a special writerly alchemy of observation and imagination was required to transform and shape aspects of those people into a cast of characters.

Eliza de Feuillide was Jane Austen's cousin, the daughter of her father's sister Philadelphia, who had gone to India, like so many women of the time, to find a husband. Eliza fluttered into the Steventon family like an exotic butterfly among the cabbage whites of Hampshire. Her first marriage was to a French count; he was guillotined in 1794. Eliza took part in the family's theatricals, and after she was widowed both James, Jane's eldest brother (also a widower), and Henry (younger and more dashing) pursued her. Eliza was fourteen years older than Jane and an important influence on her. Jane's early work *Henry and Eliza* seems to be about Henry Austen and Eliza's romance (they later married); *Love and Freindship* was dedicated to Eliza, and there seem to be elements of Eliza's life in *Lady Susan* too. There are certainly echoes of Eliza in Mary Crawford.

On 13 December 1796 Eliza wrote to another cousin, Phylly Walter, of the current situation with James Austen:

I am glad to find you have made up your mind to visiting the Rectory, but at the same time, and in spite of all your conjectures and belief, I do assert that Preliminaries are so far from settled that I do not believe the parties ever will come together, not however that they have quarrelled, but one of them cannot bring her mind to give up dear Liberty, and yet dearer flirtation – After a few months stay in the Country she sometimes thinks it possible to undertake sober Matrimony, but a few weeks stay in London convinces her how little the state suits her taste – Lord S's card has this moment been brought me which I think very ominous considering I was talking of Matrimony, but it does not signify, I shall certainly escape both Peer and Parson.

And on 3 May 1797 (also to Phylly Walter) she wrote of Henry Austen: 'Captain Austen has just spent a few days in Town; I suppose you know that our Cousin Henry is now Captain, Pay Master and Adjudant [*sic*]. He is a very lucky young Man and bids fair to possess a considerable Share of Riches and Honours; I believe he has now given up all thoughts of the Church, and he is right for he certainly is not so fit for a Parson as a Soldier.'[3]

Eliza was pretty, amiable and an accomplished flirt. She and Jane were clearly very fond of each other, and later on, when Eliza had married Henry Austen, Jane would stay with them in London, going to parties, the theatre, the circus and galleries as well as using their home as a base when she was working on her proofs.

Think about a person who made a strong impression on you, perhaps somebody who seemed glamorous or odd, was a bully, a square peg or particularly attractive, or someone you really disliked. (This exercise works best if you choose somebody that you have lost touch with.) Write a sketch of this person or a short scene in which they do something that you recall. This might be when you first met them. Use particular details. What were their oddities or distinguishing features? Can you remember particular phrases that they used, what they wore or particular possessions of theirs?

Now move this person either forward or back in time. What would they be or have been like at fifteen or twenty-five, forty-five, or eighty-five? Pick the age for them that seems most interesting. What job would they have? Would they be rich or poor, single or in a relationship? What would their clothes be like? Would they have a car? Where might they have moved to? What would their house be like? What would their ambitions be and what might they long for? What would they have failed at? You could write a CV for them, but include all the things they had left unfinished or failed at too.

Now write a sketch of this character at this age.

Now write an internal monologue for them. Concentrate on really capturing their voice.

Finally, writing in the first or the third person, whichever you prefer, send them out somewhere and see what happens.

THE WRITER AS SADIST

> 'Be a Sadist. No matter how sweet and
> innocent your leading characters, make awful
> things happen to them in order that the reader
> may see what they are made of.'
>
> Kurt Vonnegut[5]

Jane Austen was very good at making dreadful things happen or *almost* happen to her characters. The way that they are brought low is always completely plausible; the calamities that befall them are nothing like the ones that she joked about in her *Plan of a Novel according to hints from various quarters*. In this the heroine is 'continually cheated and defrauded of her hire, worn down to a Skeleton, and now and then starved to death'.

In *Sense and Sensibility* the Dashwood sisters and their mother go from riches to (relative) rags; in *Pride and Prejudice* Lizzy Bennet is threatened with marriage to Mr Collins and then, when Lydia runs away with Wickham, the whole family faces being plunged into the outer darkness of social ostracism. Just when Lizzy has met Mr Darcy at Pemberley and things are going swimmingly, everything seems to be snatched away; her sister Jane has already seemingly lost Mr Bingley. In *Persuasion* Anne Elliot has had years of sadness and regret at the loss of Captain Wentworth. In *Emma* Jane's eponymous heroine is berated by Mr Knightley, and then, when she begins to realise that she is in love with him, thinks he is in love with Harriet Smith. Catherine Morland is expelled from Northanger Abbey.

But here we'll look at the dreadful treatment that Jane Austen metes out to poor little Fanny Price. Removed from her home to the initially terrifying world of Mansfield Park, Fanny is homesick for Portsmouth, but when back at Portsmouth she longs for Mansfield. She is bullied by her cousins Maria and Julia and her evil Aunt Norris, falls in love with Edmund but has to watch in silence while he falls for the glamorous Mary Crawford, a woman who is everything that Fanny is not. Worst of all, she is almost forced into marriage with Henry Crawford, a man whom she can never respect or love. By refusing Henry Crawford she seems to throw back in her uncle's face everything that he has ever done for her, and Fanny, always so eager to do what is right, hates to be seen as obstinate, disobedient and ungrateful.

This is from *Mansfield Park*, Chapter 32.

'Sit down, my dear. I must speak to you for a few minutes, but I will not detain you long.'

Fanny obeyed, with eyes cast down and colour rising. After a moment's pause, Sir Thomas, trying to suppress a smile, went on.

'You are not aware, perhaps, that I have had a visitor this morning. I had not been long in my own room, after breakfast, when Mr Crawford was shewn in. His errand you may probably conjecture.'

Fanny's colour grew deeper and deeper; and her uncle, perceiving that she was embarrassed to a degree that made either speaking or looking up quite impossible, turned away his own eyes, and without any farther pause proceeded in his account of Mr Crawford's visit.

Mr Crawford's business had been to declare himself the lover of Fanny, make decided proposals for her, and entreat the sanction of the uncle, who seemed to stand in the place of her parents; and he had done it all so well, so openly, so liberally, so properly, that Sir Thomas, feeling, moreover, his own replies, and his own remarks to have been very much to the purpose, was exceedingly happy to give the particulars of their conversation; and little aware of what was passing in his niece's mind, conceived that by such details he must be gratifying her far more than himself. He talked, therefore, for several minutes without Fanny's daring to interrupt him. She had hardly even attained the wish to do it. Her mind was in too much confusion. She had changed her position; and, with her eyes fixed intently on one of the windows, was listening to her uncle in the utmost perturbation and dismay. For a moment he ceased, but she had barely become conscious of it, when, rising from his chair, he said, 'And now, Fanny, having performed one part of my commission, and shewn you everything placed on a basis the most assured and satisfactory, I may execute the remainder by prevailing on you to accompany me downstairs, where, though I cannot but presume on having been no unacceptable companion myself, I must submit to your finding one still better worth listening to. Mr Crawford, as you have perhaps foreseen, is yet in the house. He is in my room, and hoping to see you there.'

There was a look, a start, an exclamation on hearing this, which astonished Sir Thomas; but what was his increase of astonishment on hearing her exclaim – 'Oh!

no, sir, I cannot, indeed I cannot go down to him. Mr Crawford ought to know – he must know that: I told him enough yesterday to convince him; he spoke to me on this subject yesterday, and I told him without disguise that it was very disagreeable to me, and quite out of my power to return his good opinion.'

'I do not catch your meaning,' said Sir Thomas, sitting down again. 'Out of your power to return his good opinion? What is all this? I know he spoke to you yesterday, and (as far as I understand) received as much encouragement to proceed as a well-judging young woman could permit herself to give. I was very much pleased with what I collected to have been your behaviour on the occasion; it shewed a discretion highly to be commended. But now, when he has made his overtures so properly, and honourably – what are your scruples *now*?'

'You are mistaken, sir,' cried Fanny, forced by the anxiety of the moment even to tell her uncle that he was wrong; 'you are quite mistaken. How could Mr Crawford say such a thing? I gave him no encouragement yesterday. On the contrary, I told him, I cannot recollect my exact words, but I am sure I told him that I would not listen to him, that it was very unpleasant to me in every respect, and that I begged him never to talk to me in that manner again. I am sure I said as much as that and more; and I should have said still more, if I had been quite certain of his meaning anything seriously; but I did not like to be, I could not bear to be, imputing more than might be intended. I thought it might all pass for nothing with *him*.'

She could say no more; her breath was almost gone.

'Am I to understand,' said Sir Thomas, after a few moments' silence, 'that you mean to *refuse* Mr Crawford?'

'Yes, sir.'

'Refuse him?'

'Yes, sir.'

[...]

Sir Thomas came towards the table where she sat in trembling wretchedness, and with a good deal of cold sternness, said, 'It is of no use, I perceive, to talk to you. We had better put an end to this most mortifying conference. Mr Crawford must not be kept longer waiting. I will, therefore, only add, as thinking it my duty to mark my opinion of your conduct, that you have disappointed every expectation I had formed, and proved yourself of a character the very reverse of what I had supposed. For I *had*, Fanny, as I think my behaviour must have shewn, formed a very favourable opinion of you from the period of my return to England. I had thought you peculiarly free from wilfulness of temper, self-conceit, and every tendency to that independence of spirit which prevails so much in modern days, even in young women, and which in young women is offensive and disgusting beyond all common offence. But you have now shewn me that you can be wilful and perverse; that you can and will decide for yourself, without any consideration or deference for those who have surely some right to guide you, without even asking their advice. You have shewn yourself very, very different from anything that

I had imagined. The advantage or disadvantage of your family, of your parents, your brothers and sisters, never seems to have had a moment's share in your thoughts on this occasion. How *they* might be benefited, how *they* must rejoice in such an establishment for you, is nothing to *you*. You think only of yourself, and because you do not feel for Mr Crawford exactly what a young heated fancy imagines to be necessary for happiness, you resolve to refuse him at once, without wishing even for a little time to consider of it, a little more time for cool consideration, and for really examining your own inclinations; and are, in a wild fit of folly, throwing away from you such an opportunity of being settled in life, eligibly, honourably, nobly settled, as will, probably, never occur to you again. Here is a young man of sense, of character, of temper, of manners, and of fortune, exceedingly attached to you, and seeking your hand in the most handsome and disinterested way; and let me tell you, Fanny, that you may live eighteen years longer in the world without being addressed by a man of half Mr Crawford's estate, or a tenth part of his merits. [. . .] After half a moment's pause: 'And I should have been very much surprised had either of my daughters, on receiving a proposal of marriage at any time which might carry with it only *half* the eligibility of *this*, immediately and peremptorily, and without paying my opinion or my regard the compliment of any consultation, put a decided negative on it. I should have been much surprised and much hurt by such a proceeding. I should have thought it a gross violation of duty and respect. *You* are not to be judged by the same rule. You do not owe me the duty of a child. But, Fanny, if your heart can acquit you of *ingratitude*—'

He ceased. Fanny was by this time crying so bitterly that, angry as he was, he would not press that article farther. Her heart was almost broke by such a picture of what she appeared to him; by such accusations, so heavy, so multiplied, so rising in dreadful gradation! Self-willed, obstinate, selfish, and ungrateful. He thought her all this. She had deceived his expectations; she had lost his good opinion. What was to become of her?

'I am very sorry,' said she inarticulately, through her tears, 'I am very sorry indeed.'

'Sorry! yes, I hope you are sorry; and you will probably have reason to be long sorry for this day's transactions.'

Henry Crawford is offering Fanny financial security for herself and her struggling family at a level they would barely have dreamed of. He has also been responsible for the advancement of her beloved brother's career, but she cannot bear to accept him as she knows what he is really like. Mousey little Fanny stands up for herself, and as the onslaught continues we see what she is really made of. Her family will come to realize how right she is to reject Henry, but not for some time. Mansfield Park's Cinderella rejects the prince because she knows he is really a frog, or, to mix the fairy tales, a wolf. She is subsequently rewarded with her true prince and sees her enemy Aunt Norris banished at last.

Think about what you can hurl at your characters. In a good plot, just when the reader thinks that things can't get any worse, they do.

Here is Fanny Price standing firm in extracts from Chapter 35. How galling that Edmund says that she is not being rational when she disagrees with him but is saying what she actually thinks and wants.

'Oh! never, never, never! he never will succeed with me.' And she spoke with a warmth which quite astonished Edmund, and which she blushed at the recollection of herself, when she saw his look, and heard him reply,

'Never! Fanny! – so very determined and positive! This is not like yourself, your rational self.'

'I mean,' she cried, sorrowfully correcting herself, 'that I *think* I never shall, as far as the future can be answered for; I think I never shall return his regard.' [...]

'We are so totally unlike,' said Fanny, avoiding a direct answer, 'we are so very, very different in all our inclinations and ways, that I consider it as quite impossible we should ever be tolerably happy together, even if I *could* like him. There never were two people more dissimilar. We have not one taste in common. We should be miserable' [...]

'It is not merely in *temper* that I consider him as totally unsuited to myself; though, in *that* respect, I think the difference between us too great, infinitely too great: his spirits often oppress me; but there is something in him which I object to still more. I must say, cousin, that I cannot approve his character. I have not thought well of him from the time of the play. I then saw him behaving, as it appeared to me, so very improperly and unfeelingly – I may speak of it now because it is all over – so improperly by poor Mr Rushworth, not seeming to care how he exposed or hurt him, and paying attentions to my cousin Maria, which – in short, at the time of the play, I received an impression which will never be got over' [...] 'As a bystander,' said Fanny, 'perhaps I saw more than you did.'

DEMONSTRATING HEROICS – AND SOME MORE THOUGHTS ON HORSES

Willoughby's gift horse to Marianne has to be looked in the mouth. It's a different matter when Fanny Price's old grey pony dies (*Mansfield Park*, Chapter 4).

The ensuing spring deprived her of her valued friend, the old grey pony; and for some time she was in danger of feeling the loss in her health as well as in her affections; for in spite of the acknowledged importance of her riding on horse-back, no measures were taken for mounting her again, 'because,' as it was observed by her aunts, 'she might ride one of her cousin's horses at any time when they did not want them,' and as the Miss Bertrams regularly wanted their horses every fine day, and had no idea of carrying their obliging manners to the sacrifice of any real pleasure, that time, of course, never came. They took their cheerful rides in the fine mornings of April and May; and Fanny either sat at home the whole day with one aunt, or walked beyond her strength at the instigation of the other: Lady Bertram holding exercise to be as unnecessary for everybody as it was unpleasant to herself; and Mrs Norris, who was walking all day, thinking everybody ought to walk as much.

Edmund is away when this happens. He has already been established as the kind cousin, the one who comforted Fanny when she was homesick, but his insistence that 'she have a horse' and the way he gets one for her, cleverly circumnavigating the objections of his horrible aunt and lazy mother, makes him even more of a hero to Fanny. It is then even more significant when Mary Crawford, at Edmund's instigation, borrows Fanny's horse and again she is deprived of it. The Mansfield Park coachman ensures that Fanny knows how superior a horsewoman Mary Crawford is: 'It is a pleasure to see a lady with such a good heart for riding!' said he. 'I never see one sit a horse better. She did not seem to have a thought of fear. Very different from you, miss, when you first began, six years ago come next Easter. Lord bless you! how you did tremble when Sir Thomas first had you put on!'

EXERCISE

Write a scene in which a small action by one of your characters advances your plot and changes or reinforces the way that the reader will feel about them.

BAD PEOPLE DOING GOOD THINGS

If you want your novel to be 'like life' then the things that your characters do and the impressions that they give shouldn't be straightforward. Actions must be open to different interpretations. Complicate things and make your characters seem real by ensuring that they act in the sort of complex ways that people do in real life.

Fanny Price is almost on the point of believing that Henry Crawford has changed when he comes to visit her in Portsmouth and behaves so nicely, displaying such good manners towards her less-than-ideal family. Here they are out for a Sunday morning walk (Chapter 41).

> When Mr Price and his friend had seen all that they wished, or had time for, the others were ready to return; and in the course of their walk back, Mr Crawford contrived a minute's privacy for telling Fanny that his only business in Portsmouth was to see her; that he was come down for a couple of days on her account, and hers only, and because he could not endure a longer total separation. She was sorry, really sorry; and yet in spite of this and the two or three other things which she wished he had not said, she thought him altogether improved since she had seen him; he was much more gentle, obliging, and attentive to other people's feelings than he had ever been at Mansfield; she had never seen him so agreeable – so *near* being agreeable; his behaviour to her father could not offend, and there was something particularly kind and proper in the notice he took of Susan. He was decidedly improved.

In *Pride and Prejudice* even the horrible Caroline Bingley tries to behave nicely towards Elizabeth by warning her against Wickham. Caroline doesn't know all the details of Wickham's villainy, and Lizzy is determined not to think anything bad of him.

Miss Bingley came towards her, and with an expression of civil disdain thus accosted her: – 'So, Miss Eliza, I hear you are quite delighted with George Wickham! – Your sister has been talking to me about him, and asking me a thousand questions; and I find that the young man forgot to tell you, among his other communications, that he was the son of old Wickham, the late Mr Darcy's steward. Let me recommend you, however, as a friend, not to give implicit confidence to all his assertions; for as to Mr Darcy's using him ill, it is perfectly false; for, on the contrary, he has been always remarkably kind to him, though George Wickham has treated Mr Darcy in a most infamous manner. I do not know the particulars, but I know very well that Mr Darcy is not in the least to blame, that he cannot bear to hear George Wickham mentioned, and that though my brother thought he could not well avoid including him in his invitation to the officers, he was excessively glad to find that he had taken himself out of the way. His coming into the country at all is a most insolent thing indeed, and I wonder how he could presume to do it. I pity you, Miss Eliza, for this discovery of your favourite's guilt; but really, considering his descent, one could not expect much better.'

'His guilt and his descent appear by your account to be the same,' said Elizabeth angrily; 'for I have heard you accuse him of nothing worse than of being the son of Mr Darcy's steward, and of *that*, I can assure you, he informed me himself.'

'I beg your pardon,' replied Miss Bingley, turning away with a sneer. 'Excuse my interference: it was kindly meant.'

Elizabeth decides that Caroline Bingley's criticism of Wickham is based on snobbery and dislikes Caroline too much to see anything else. If she had thought a little harder she might have wondered why Caroline, who is trying to snare Mr Darcy, would be warning her off Wickham. It's interesting that Caroline Bingley calls her 'Miss Eliza', choosing to use a form of her name that seems more 'below stairs' than 'Elizabeth'. I can't imagine her using 'Lizzy', which is more the Bennet family's pet name for her. The Lucases and Gardiners also occasionally use 'Eliza' but never with Caroline Bingley's tone.

EXERCISES: MORE IDEAS FOR USEFUL SCENES
AND DEVELOPMENTS

1. Write a scene in which a seemingly small action or decision will show the reader new aspects of a character and prove or reveal what they are really like. Such incidents can be of huge significance in your stories.

2. Show a character acting heroically or unheroically or describe one of your characters acting in a way that will

show them in all their complexity. Think about how you want readers and the other characters to perceive their action. Things shouldn't be straightforward; remember that even the horrible Caroline Bingley tried to warn Elizabeth about Wickham. Mary Crawford is beautiful when she plays the harp and is often kind to Fanny, but is manipulative and unprincipled.

3. Do as Kurt Vonnegut advises and make something awful happen to one of your characters. This is likely to be at the heart of your story. Sometimes making a character *think* that something awful has happened can work really well too. The scene at the end of *Sense and Sensibility* in which Elinor thinks that Edward has married Lucy Steele just before he reveals that he has come to ask her to marry him is a powerful example of this.[6]

4. Show your characters acting in tandem as well as in opposition to each other. Think about the way that brothers and sisters behave when they are together. Show how people can unite, squabble, be rivals, etc. Think about how Maria and Julia Bertram behave together and towards each other, and the ways that Tom and Edmund Bertram treat each other.

5. Show your characters making assumptions. Mary Crawford is aghast that there are no locals willing to lend her a horse and cart to transport her harp; Edmund understands that at harvest time nothing can be spared.

WRITING CHILDREN

There is a myth that Jane Austen didn't like children because there are so many badly behaved ones in her novels. The little Middletons are some of the most annoying. In *Sense and Sensibility* (Chapter 21) Lucy Steele says in her ingratiating way,

> 'I never saw such fine children in my life. – I declare I quite doat upon them already, and indeed I am always distractedly fond of children.'
>
> 'I should guess so,' said Elinor with a smile, 'from what I have witnessed this morning.'
>
> 'I have a notion,' said Lucy, 'you think the little Middletons rather too much indulged; perhaps they may be the outside of enough; but it is so natural in Lady Middleton; and for my part, I love to see children full of life and spirits; I cannot bear them if they are tame and quiet.'
>
> 'I confess,' replied Elinor, 'that while I am at Barton Park, I never think of tame and quiet children with any abhorrence.'

When children and teenagers behave badly in Jane Austen's work it is because their parents ignore them, overindulge them or set them bad examples.

Jane Austen loved children. She was very close to many of her nephews and nieces, often mentions what she is doing with them and writes about them and other children in the most affectionate terms. Her description of the young Catherine Morland in Chapter 1 of *Northanger*

Abbey shows how well she understood children and appreciated their need to be themselves.

> The day which dismissed the music-master was one of the happiest of Catherine's life. Her taste for drawing was not superior; though whenever she could obtain the outside of a letter from her mother or seize upon any other odd piece of paper, she did what she could in that way, by drawing houses and trees, hens and chickens, all very much like one another. Writing and accounts she was taught by her father; French by her mother: her proficiency in either was not remarkable, and she shirked her lessons in both whenever she could. What a strange, unaccountable character! – for with all these symptoms of profligacy at ten years old, she had neither a bad heart nor a bad temper, was seldom stubborn, scarcely ever quarrelsome, and very kind to the little ones, with few interruptions of tyranny; she was moreover noisy and wild, hated confinement and cleanliness, and loved nothing so well in the world as rolling down the green slope at the back of the house.

It's also important to point out that many of Jane Austen's heroines and key characters are extremely young and would not be thought of as adults today. The behaviour of Georgiana Darcy, Marianne Dashwood, Lydia and Kitty Bennet and Catherine Morland is easier to understand when we remember that they are just teenagers. Fanny Price is introduced as a timid little girl.

The children in Jane Austen's novels often have important roles in her plots or in key scenes. In *Persuasion*

the nephews that Anne Elliot spends so much time looking after show the reader and Captain Wentworth what
a lovely person she is. It is Anne who stays with little
Charles Musgrove when he dislocates his collarbone
while his parents go out to dinner. And when Charles's
brother Walter, 'a remarkable stout, forward child, of two
years old', climbs all over Anne and practically strangles
her, it is Captain Wentworth who strides in and removes
him in what becomes a highly charged scene. Such sudden
proximity to the man she is in love with leaves Anne
speechless. Afterwards she feels 'ashamed of herself, quite
ashamed of being so nervous, so overcome by such a trifle;
but so it was, and it required a long application of solitude
and reflection to recover her'.[7]

In *Sense and Sensibility* (Chapter 12) Margaret
Dashwood tells Elinor that she saw Marianne giving
Willoughby a lock of her hair, and then tells Mrs Jennings
that Elinor has also lost her heart to somebody.

'Oh, Elinor!' she cried, 'I have such a secret to tell you
about Marianne. I am sure she will be married to Mr
Willoughby very soon.'

'You have said so,' replied Elinor, 'almost every day
since they first met on High-church Down; and they
had not known each other a week, I believe, before you
were certain that Marianne wore his picture round her
neck; but it turned out to be only the miniature of our
great uncle.'

'But indeed this is quite another thing. I am sure
they will be married very soon, for he has got a lock of
her hair.'

'Take care, Margaret. It may be only the hair of some great uncle of *his*.'

'But, indeed, Elinor, it is Marianne's. I am almost sure it is, for I saw him cut it off. Last night after tea, when you and mama went out of the room, they were whispering and talking together as fast as could be, and he seemed to be begging something of her, and presently he took up her scissors and cut off a long lock of her hair, for it was all tumbled down her back; and he kissed it, and folded it up in a piece of white paper; and put it into his pocketbook.'

From such particulars, stated on such authority, Elinor could not withhold her credit; nor was she disposed to it, for the circumstance was in perfect unison with what she had heard and seen herself.

Margaret's sagacity was not always displayed in a way so satisfactory to her sister. When Mrs Jennings attacked her one evening at the Park, to give the name of the young man who was Elinor's particular favourite, which had been long a matter of great curiosity to her, Margaret answered by looking at her sister, and saying, 'I must not tell, may I, Elinor?'

This of course made everybody laugh; and Elinor tried to laugh too. But the effort was painful. She was convinced that Margaret had fixed on a person, whose name she could not bear with composure to become a standing joke with Mrs Jennings. Marianne felt for her most sincerely; but she did more harm than good to the cause, by turning very red, and saying in an angry manner to Margaret,

'Remember that whatever your conjectures may be, you have no right to repeat them.'

'I never had any conjectures about it,' replied Margaret; 'it was you who told me of it yourself.'

This increased the mirth of the company, and Margaret was eagerly pressed to say something more.

'Oh! pray, Miss Margaret, let us know all about it,' said Mrs Jennings. 'What is the gentleman's name?'

'I must not tell, ma'am. But I know very well what it is; and I know where he is too.'

'Yes, yes, we can guess where he is; at his own house at Norland to be sure. He is the curate of the parish I dare say.'

'No, *that* he is not. He is of no profession at all.'

'Margaret,' said Marianne, with great warmth, 'you know that all this is an invention of your own, and that there is no such person in existence.'

'Well, then, he is lately dead, Marianne, for I am sure there was such a man once, and his name begins with an F.'

In the closing lines of *Sense and Sensibility* Margaret's future is made clear:

And fortunately for Sir John and Mrs Jennings, when Marianne was taken from them, Margaret had reached an age highly suitable for dancing, and not very ineligible for being supposed to have a lover.

Between Barton and Delaford, there was that constant communication which strong family affection would naturally dictate; – and among the merits and the happiness of Elinor and Marianne, let it not be ranked as the least considerable, that though sisters, and living almost within sight of each other, they could live without disagreement between themselves, or producing coolness between their husbands.

In *The Watsons* (Part 1) we have a completely charming little boy; Emma Watson dancing with him is the inciting incident, the event that precipitates the action of the story. This child is the most appealing person in a roomful of boring, stuffy and preoccupied adults.

At the conclusion of the two dances, Emma found herself, she knew not how, seated among the Osborne set; and she was immediately struck with the fine countenance and animated gestures of the little boy, as he was standing before his mother, wondering when they should begin.

'You will not be surprised at Charles' impatience,' said Mrs Blake, a lively, pleasant-looking little woman of five or six and thirty, to a lady who was standing near her, 'when you know what a partner he is to have. Miss Osborne has been so very kind as to promise to dance the two first dances with him.'

'Oh, yes! we have been engaged this week,' cried the boy, 'and we are to dance down every couple.'

On the other side of Emma, Miss Osborne, Miss Carr, and a party of young men were standing engaged in very lively consultation; and soon afterwards she saw the smartest officer of the set walking off to the orchestra to order the dance, while Miss Osborne, passing before her to her little expecting partner, hastily said: 'Charles, I beg your pardon for not keeping my engagement, but I am going to dance these two dances with Colonel Beresford. I know you will excuse me, and I will certainly dance with you after tea'; and without staying for an answer, she turned again to Miss Carr, and in another minute was led by Colonel Beresford to begin the set. If the poor little boy's face had in its happiness been interesting to Emma, it was infinitely more so under this sudden reverse; he stood the picture of disappointment, with crimsoned cheeks, quivering lips, and eyes bent on the floor. His mother, stifling her own mortification, tried to soothe his with the prospect of Miss Osborne's second promise; but though he contrived to utter, with an effort of boyish bravery, 'Oh, I do not mind it!' it was very evident, by the unceasing agitation of his features, that he minded it as much as ever.

EXERCISE: THINKING ABOUT
YOUR CHILD CHARACTERS

Look at the children in your work. Are there enough to make the world seem real? What roles do they play in the plot? Could you do more with them? Do your minor child characters (excuse the pun) seem real and complex enough to spawn future novels of their own? Look at how your child characters develop throughout your story and ensure that they have proper arcs of their own.

Write a scene in which you use the actions of one of your child characters to progress the plot. They might blurt something out, like Margaret Dashwood; or something they get up to (think Charles Musgrove, Junior) might bring people together or show them in their true colours. You can use the actions of a child character to send your story in a surprising new direction.

WORKING WITH ANIMALS

There are very few cats in Jane Austen's work, though there must have been cats wherever Jane lived and it's impossible to imagine the Chawton cottage without at least one. Dogs and horses feature far more often. We know that Jane's brothers hunted (an aspect of my family history I would rather forget). Willoughby, we learn in the final chapter of *Sense and Sensibility*, finds solace with his equine and canine companions after he has lost Marianne.

Willoughby could not hear of her marriage without a pang; and his punishment was soon afterwards complete in the voluntary forgiveness of Mrs. Smith, who, by stating his marriage with a woman of character, as the source of her clemency, gave him reason for believing that had he behaved with honour towards Marianne, he might at once have been happy and rich [...] His wife was not always out of humour, nor his home always uncomfortable; and in his breed of horses and dogs, and in sporting of every kind, he found no inconsiderable degree of domestic felicity.

Jane's most memorable animal character is Lady Bertram's beloved pug. Pug is present throughout *Mansfield Park* – as Lady Bertram's constant companion on her sofa and a witness to Fanny's many sorrows. In Chapter 2:

> The little visitor meanwhile was as unhappy as possible. Afraid of everybody, ashamed of herself, and longing for the home she had left, she knew not how to look up, and could scarcely speak to be heard, or without crying. Mrs Norris had been talking to her the whole way from Northampton of her wonderful good fortune, and the extraordinary degree of gratitude and good behaviour which it ought to produce, and her consciousness of misery was therefore increased by the idea of its being a wicked thing for her not to be happy. The fatigue, too, of so long a journey, became soon no trifling evil. In vain were the well-meant condescensions of Sir Thomas, and all the officious prognostications of Mrs Norris that she would be a good girl; in vain did Lady Bertram smile and make her sit on the sofa with herself and pug, and vain was even the sight of a gooseberry tart towards giving her comfort; she could scarcely swallow two mouthfuls before tears interrupted her, and sleep seeming to be her likeliest friend, she was taken to finish her sorrows in bed.

Later in the novel, in Chapter 33, Lady Bertram is so impressed that Henry Crawford wants to marry Fanny that she plans to bestow an honour on her that not even Maria received when she married Mr Rushworth: 'And I will tell you what, Fanny, which is more than I did for Maria: the next time Pug has a litter you shall have a puppy.' Even this offer isn't enough to sway Fanny's resolve.

EXERCISE

Think about the animals that should be in your stories. What will your characters' attitudes and behaviour towards them tell the reader? How might they be used to advance the plot? An encounter with a creature (wild or domesticated) can also be a useful way of bringing an unexpected event into a story in a plausible way. Give a character a pet and take it from there.

THE CLOTHES SECTION

Jane Austen doesn't tell us much about her characters' appearances, usually just giving us a line or two of description when they are introduced. Here is Mr Collins arriving in Chapter 13 of *Pride and Prejudice*:

> Mr Collins was punctual to his time, and was received with great politeness by the whole family. Mr Bennet, indeed, said little; but the ladies were ready enough to talk, and Mr Collins seemed neither in need of encouragement, nor inclined to be silent himself. He was a tall, heavy-looking young man of five-and-twenty. His air was grave and stately, and his manners were very formal. He had not been long seated before he complimented Mrs Bennet on having so fine a family of daughters.

And here is Elizabeth's first view of Lady Catherine and her daughter (Chapter 29):

> Lady Catherine was a tall, large woman, with strongly marked features, which might once have been handsome. Her air was not conciliating, nor was her manner of receiving them such as to make her visitors forget their inferior rank. She was not rendered formidable by silence; but whatever she said was spoken in so authoritative a tone as marked her self-importance [...] When, after examining the mother, in whose countenance and deportment she soon found some resemblance of Mr Darcy, she turned her eyes on the daughter, she could almost have joined in Maria's astonishment at her being so thin and so small. There was neither in

figure nor face any likeness between the ladies. Miss de Bourgh was pale and sickly; her features, though not plain, were insignificant; and she spoke very little, except in a low voice.

Jane Austen uses key details about appearance, manner and style of speaking to quickly establish her characters. She has a particular interest in eyes (of which, more later). It is her characters' clothes that she really has fun with.

Most writers dress in a modern-day equivalent of what Jo March in *Little Women* called her 'scribbling suit'. Jo had a black pinafore that could absorb ink stains; twenty-first-century writers are more likely to favour some daytime approximation of pyjamas, the better to be undistracted by itchy fabrics, stiff collars or belts that dig in. I do this but worry that I'm not abiding by the Pringle Principle, which I established when I was writing my second novel. This is that I should be clad in something that wouldn't mean dying of shame if my editor Alexandra Pringle suddenly appeared at my door – a highly unlikely event as I live in Southampton. Jane Austen's scribbling suit would have been a 'morning gown'. There's a replica on display at Jane Austen's House Museum. This comfortable, loose dress would have been made from muslin or wool and been worn at home until dinner. It wouldn't have been as comfortable as harem pants, a T-shirt and an M & S man's cardigan (my preferred writing garb) as it would have been worn with stays – the corset of the time.

Jane Austen's letters provide lots of intriguing details about her attitudes to clothes and the way people dressed. Sometimes we get the impression that she is really interested in appearances, but at other times she is impatient with what she sees as time-consuming trivialities. Many of Jane's surviving letters to her sister Cassandra were written when one of them was away and shopping for whatever the other one needed, so the precise details of what to buy had to be included. Here is Jane writing to Cassandra on 25 January 1801.

I shall want two new coloured gowns for the summer, for my pink one will not do more than clear me from Steventon. I shall not trouble you, however, to get more than one of them, and that is to be a plain brown cambric muslin, for morning wear; the other, which is to be a very pretty yellow and white cloud, I mean to buy in Bath. Buy two brown ones, if you please, and both of a length, but one longer than the other – it is for a tall woman. Seven yards for my mother, seven yards and a half for me; a dark brown, but the kind of brown is left to your own choice, and I had rather they were different, as it will be always something to say, to dispute about which is the prettiest. They must be cambric muslin.

And this from 18 April 1811 when she is staying with Henry and Eliza and shopping in London.

I am sorry to tell you that I am getting very extravagant, and spending all my money, and, what is worse for *you*, I have been spending yours too; for in a linen-draper's shop to which I went for checked muslin, and for which I was obliged to give seven shillings a yard, I was tempted by a pretty-coloured muslin, and bought ten yards of it on the chance of your liking it; but, at the same time, if it should not suit you, you must not think yourself at all obliged to take it; it is only 3*s*. 6*d*. per yard, and I should not in the least mind keeping the whole. In texture it is just what we prefer, but its resemblance to green crewels, I must own, is not great, for the pattern is a small red spot. And now I believe I have done all my commissions except Wedgwood.

I liked my walk very much; it was shorter than I had expected, and the weather was delightful. We set off immediately after breakfast, and must have reached Grafton House by half-past 11; but when we entered the shop the whole counter was thronged, and we waited *full* half an hour before we could be attended to. When we were served, however, I was very well satisfied with my purchases – my bugle trimming at 2*s*. 4*d*. and three pair silk stockings for a little less than 12*s*. a pair.

Perhaps Jane saw someone like the dreadful Robert Ferrars (*Sense and Sensibility*) choosing a fancy toothpick case while she was waiting. If she was reporting on a ball or evening out the details of what had been worn couldn't be omitted.

MY DEAR CASSANDRA [she wrote from London during the same stay]

I had sent off my letter yesterday before yours came, which I was sorry for; but as Eliza has been so good as to get me a frank, your questions shall be answered without much further expense to you.

The best direction to Henry at Oxford will be The Blue Boar, Cornmarket.

I do not mean to provide another trimming for my pelisse, for I am determined to spend no more money; so I shall wear it as it is, longer than I ought, and then – I do not know. My head-dress was a bugle-band like the border to my gown, and a flower of Mrs Tilson's. I depended upon hearing something of the evening from Mr W. K., and am very well satisfied with his notice of me – 'A pleasing-looking young woman' – that must do; one cannot pretend to anything better now; thankful to have it continued a few years longer!

In the novels we aren't given very much information about people's clothes, so when Jane Austen tells us something about someone's attire we know that her decision to do so is *very* deliberate. *Northanger Abbey* contains more about dress than any of the other novels. Its Bath location, where people went to shop and to see and be seen, and the heroine's youth makes this fitting. There is a running joke about Mrs Allen's preoccupation with her dresses, and one of the first things we learn about the lovely Henry Tilney is that he is knowledgeable about dresses and fabrics and whether they will wash well. It shows his sense of humour and his kindness. This is from Chapter 3.

They were interrupted by Mrs Allen: 'My dear Catherine,' said she, 'do take this pin out of my sleeve; I am afraid it has torn a hole already; I shall be quite sorry if it has, for this is a favourite gown, though it cost but nine shillings a yard.'

'That is exactly what I should have guessed it, madam,' said Mr Tilney, looking at the muslin.

'Do you understand muslins, sir?'

'Particularly well; I always buy my own cravats, and am allowed to be an excellent judge; and my sister has often trusted me in the choice of a gown. I bought one for her the other day, and it was pronounced to be a prodigious bargain by every lady who saw it. I gave but five shillings a yard for it, and a true Indian muslin.'

Mrs Allen was quite struck by his genius. 'Men commonly take so little notice of those things,' said she; 'I can never get Mr Allen to know one of my gowns from another. You must be a great comfort to your sister, sir.'

'I hope I am, madam.'

'And pray, sir, what do you think of Miss Morland's gown?'

'It is very pretty, madam,' said he, gravely examining it; 'but I do not think it will wash well; I am afraid it will fray.'

'How can you,' said Catherine, laughing, 'be so—' She had almost said 'strange'.

'I am quite of your opinion, sir,' replied Mrs Allen; 'and so I told Miss Morland when she bought it.'

'But then you know, madam, muslin always turns to some account or other; Miss Morland will get enough out of it for a handkerchief, or a cap, or a cloak. Muslin can never be said to be wasted. I have heard my sister say so forty times, when she has been extravagant in buying more than she wanted, or careless in cutting it to pieces.'

'Bath is a charming place, sir; there are so many good shops here. We are sadly off in the country; not but what we have very good shops in Salisbury, but it is so far to go – eight miles is a long way; Mr Allen says it is nine, measured nine; but I am sure it cannot be more than eight; and it is such a fag – I come back tired to death. Now, here one can step out of doors and get a thing in five minutes.'

Mr Tilney was polite enough to seem interested in what she said; and she kept him on the subject of muslins till the dancing recommenced. Catherine feared, as she listened to their discourse, that he indulged himself a little too much with the foibles of others.

When Jane Austen tells us about Catherine's attitude to clothes, we see how the heroine's attitudes are very typical of a young woman falling in love, but despite this, Catherine is too sensible to spend a huge amount of time worrying about which dress to wear. She only lies awake wondering which dress to wear for ten minutes (Chapter 10):

The evening of the following day was now the object of expectation, the future good. What gown and what head-dress she should wear on the occasion became her chief concern. She cannot be justified in it. Dress is at all times a frivolous distinction, and excessive solicitude about it often destroys its own aim. Catherine knew all this very well; her great aunt had read her a lecture on the subject only the Christmas before; and yet she lay awake ten minutes on Wednesday night debating between her spotted and her tamboured muslin, and nothing but the shortness of the time prevented her buying a new one for the evening. This would have been an error in judgment, great though not uncommon, from which one of the other sex rather than her own, a brother rather than a great aunt, might have warned her, for man only can be aware of the insensibility of man towards a new gown. It would be mortifying to the feelings of many ladies, could they be made to understand how little the heart of man is affected by what is costly or new in their attire; how little it is biased by the texture of their muslin, and how unsusceptible of peculiar tenderness towards the spotted, the sprigged, the mull, or the jackonet. Woman is fine for her own satisfaction alone. No man will admire her the more, no woman will like her the better for it. Neatness and fashion are enough for the former, and a something of shabbiness or impropriety will be most endearing to the latter. But not one of these grave reflections troubled the tranquillity of Catherine.

Jane Austen uses choices about clothes in *Northanger Abbey* to show us the contrast between Catherine Morland's two friends Eleanor Tilney and Isabella Thorpe. The vain, shallow coquette Isabella Thorpe writes to Catherine in Chapter 27, 'I wear nothing but purple now: I know I look hideous in it, but no matter – it is your dear brother's favourite colour.' Whereas in Chapter 8 Eleanor Tilney's dress is much more elegant:

Miss Tilney had a good figure, a pretty face, and a very agreeable countenance; and her air, though it had not all the decided pretension, the resolute stylishness of Miss Thorpe's, had more real elegance. Her manners showed good sense and good breeding; they were neither shy nor affectedly open; and she seemed capable of being young, attractive, and at a ball without wanting to fix the attention of every man near her, and without exaggerated feelings of ecstatic delight or inconceivable vexation on every little trifling occurrence.

And in Chapter 12:

'Mrs Allen,' said Catherine the next morning, 'will there be any harm in my calling on Miss Tilney today? I shall not be easy till I have explained everything.'

'Go, by all means, my dear; only put on a white gown; Miss Tilney always wears white.'

Catherine cheerfully complied.

In *Pride and Prejudice* (Chapter 39) Lydia Bennet demonstrates her silliness with the impulse buy of an ugly bonnet:

Then shewing her purchases: 'Look here, I have bought this bonnet. I do not think it is very pretty; but I thought I might as well buy it as not. I shall pull it to pieces as soon as I get home, and see if I can make it up any better.'

And when her sisters abused it as ugly, she added, with perfect unconcern, 'Oh! but there were two or three much uglier in the shop; and when I have bought some prettier-coloured satin to trim it with fresh, I think it will be very tolerable. Besides, it will not much signify what one wears this summer, after the ——shire have left Meryton, and they are going in a fortnight.'

Dressing your male characters is just as important. It isn't simply about appearance; it's about attitudes – the attitudes of the person wearing the clothes and the person observing. Catherine Morland thinks Henry Tilney completely dreamy in the greatcoat he wears when he's driving her in his curricle to Northanger Abbey; in *Pride and Prejudice* (Chapter 8) Caroline Bingley and Louisa Hurst are swift to notice Lizzy Bennet's muddy petticoat, something that doesn't signify with Mr Bingley or Mr Darcy.

'She has nothing, in short, to recommend her, but being an excellent walker. I shall never forget her appearance this morning. She really looked almost wild.'

'She did indeed, Louisa. I could hardly keep my countenance. Very nonsensical to come at all! Why must *she* be scampering about the country, because her sister had a cold? Her hair, so untidy, so blowsy!'

'Yes, and her petticoat; I hope you saw her petticoat, six inches deep in mud, I am absolutely certain; and the gown which had been let down to hide it, not doing its office.'

'Your picture may be very exact, Louisa,' said Bingley; 'but this was all lost upon me. I thought Miss Elizabeth Bennet looked remarkably well, when she came into the room this morning. Her dirty petticoat quite escaped my notice.'

'*You* observed it, Mr Darcy, I am sure,' said Miss Bingley; 'and I am inclined to think that you would not wish to see *your sister* make such an exhibition.'

'Certainly not.'

'To walk three miles, or four miles, or five miles, or whatever it is, above her ancles in dirt, and alone, quite alone! what could she mean by it? It seems to me to shew an abominable sort of conceited independence, a most country-town indifference to decorum.'

'It shews an affection for her sister that is very pleasing,' said Bingley.

'I am afraid, Mr Darcy,' observed Miss Bingley, in a half-whisper, 'that this adventure has rather affected your admiration of her fine eyes.'

'Not at all,' he replied; 'they were brightened by the exercise.'

Of course your characters can't always wear what they would like. You can use their clothes to indicate that they are struggling for money or don't fit in. Who hasn't experienced the feeling of wearing the wrong thing – of being over- or underdressed, having the wrong school uniform or being forced to wear something that a parent said 'would do perfectly well'? Conversely, another way to develop your characters through their clothes is to give them the opportunity to wear exactly what they would like, their fantasy outfit. Poor Mr Rushworth in *Mansfield Park* (Chapter 15) cannot hide how pleased he is with his silly costume for the theatricals:

'We have got a play,' said he. 'It is to be *Lovers' Vows*; and I am to be Count Cassel, and am to come in first with a blue dress and a pink satin cloak, and afterwards am to have another fine fancy suit, by way of a shooting-dress. I do not know how I shall like it.'

Fanny's eyes followed Edmund, and her heart beat for him as she heard this speech, and saw his look, and felt what his sensations must be.

'Lovers' Vows!' in a tone of the greatest amazement, was his only reply to Mr Rushworth, and he turned towards his brother and sisters as if hardly doubting a contradiction [...]

Mr Rushworth followed him to say, 'I come in three times, and have two-and-forty speeches. That's something, is not it? But I do not much like the idea of being so fine. I shall hardly know myself in a blue dress and a pink satin cloak.'

Edmund could not answer him.

EXERCISES

1. Put a character in a situation where they can choose exactly what to wear, perhaps for a party, a wedding or a part in a play. What would they dream of wearing? You could also try sending them on a date, to a job interview or to meet prospective in-laws.

2. Send a character out wearing something that they have no choice about or something that will be disapproved of or get the wrong sort of attention. Develop the characters of the observers too.

Building the village of your story

Creating and utilizing your setting

JANE AUSTEN TOLD HER niece Anna, an aspiring writer, that 'three or four families in a country village is the very thing to work on',[1] and there's something particularly interesting and satisfying about the scale and dynamics of a village. Two hundred years since the publication of *Emma*, thinking about the 'village' of your story can help you with plotting, managing your cast of characters, building tension and creating a sense of place, whether your setting is inner-city or rural, contemporary, historical or futuristic. The exercises in this chapter will help you to lead your readers into a convincing world.

When I got married in my late twenties I was part of a group of friends from university all doing the same thing within the same couple of years. Everybody seemed to have the same number of guests or at least people that they felt they should invite. We joked about how people's 'social capacity' seemed to be identical. Weddings in Jane Austen's time were smaller affairs and took place in the morning. In *Emma* (Chapter 55) Mrs Elton criticizes Miss Woodhouse and Mr Knightley's wedding 'from the particulars detailed by her husband' (she didn't get to go) and thought it all extremely shabby, and very inferior to her own. 'Very little white satin, very few lace veils; a most pitiful business!'

What I now know is that my own and my friends' guest lists were about equal to Dunbar's Number, which is around one hundred and fifty. Anthropologist Robin Dunbar found that this is the ideal size for a community, whether a military unit, an Amish village, a business or a group of friends (the sort who are actual friends and relations) on Facebook.[2] Villages in eighteenth-century England were around this size, just as they had been at the time of the Domesday Book.

The idea of building the village of your story occurred to me when I was rereading *Emma*. It is the quintessential village novel. If you are writing a story about a quest or 'a voyage and return' then the village model won't apply so much to you, but if you are penning something set in a particular community, whether it is a neighbourhood, a school, an office, a Brownie pack or whatever, thinking about the village of your story should help.

BOUNDARIES AND CONTAINMENT

It is easy to map Highbury. Jane Austen may have done this herself and certainly had a functioning map in her head. We are given plenty of information so that readers can picture the village, its layout and position: London is sixteen miles away; Mr Knightley can easily walk the mile from his home to Emma's; the Westons live only half a mile from Emma's home, Hartfield; and we are told what Emma sees from the doorway of Ford's, exactly where the Gypsies are camped, what one passes on the way to the vicarage and much more. Emma rarely leaves Highbury, but other people, particularly men, come and go. Frank Churchill is able to leave on a whim to get his hair cut – and secretly buy a piano. At the end of the novel Emma is at last able to leave the village and go to the seaside.

EXERCISE: MAPPING THE VILLAGE OF YOUR STORY

Start a map as soon as you start your story. Keep it in the front of your notebook or pinned above your desk, adding to it and amending it as your story progresses. Readers will be able to tell if your 'village' isn't properly worked out. They will feel jolted out of the story if the geography doesn't make sense. Interiors of buildings are important too. Draw plans of these. Readers might need to know if a person upstairs can hear what is going on in the kitchen and what a visitor will see when the front door is opened.

A map of Highbury

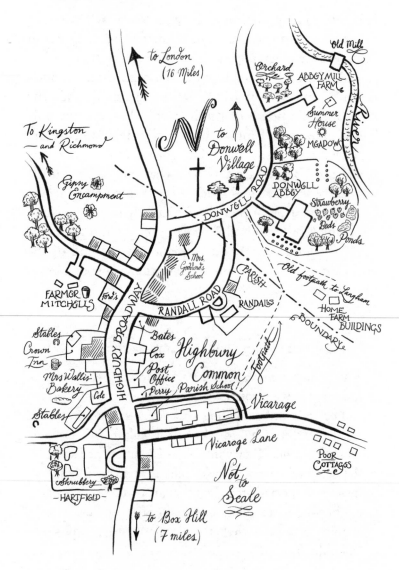

PRIVATE SPACES, SHARED SPACES, PUBLIC SPACES[3]

In *Emma* we see the characters at church, meeting in and around the village, at balls and at Ford's, which is 'the principal woollen-draper, linen-draper, and haberdasher's shop united; the shop first in size and fashion in the place' and the site of significant meetings. In Chapter 24 Frank Churchill shows that he understands the importance of Ford's.

At this moment they were approaching Ford's, and he hastily exclaimed, 'Ha! this must be the very shop that every body attends every day of their lives, as my father informs me. He comes to Highbury himself, he says, six days out of the seven, and has always business at Ford's. If it be not inconvenient to you, pray let us go in, that I may prove myself to belong to the place, to be a true citizen of Highbury. I must buy something at Ford's. It will be taking out my freedom. – I dare say they sell gloves.'

'Oh! yes, gloves and every thing. I do admire your patriotism. You will be adored in Highbury. You were very popular before you came, because you were Mr Weston's son – but lay out half a guinea at Ford's, and your popularity will stand upon your own virtues.'

How well do you know the spaces in your story?

EXERCISE: MAKE A LIST OF THE DIFFERENT SPACES IN YOUR STORY

This list may grow as the work progresses. A character's private space may be their bedroom, car, shed or perhaps just a locker if they are at school or in hospital. Shared spaces might be the areas between the beds in a dormitory, shared hallways and drives, communal areas where bins are kept and so on. Public spaces are invaluable for the writer – that's why there are so many launderettes, cafes, pubs and squares in soap operas and sitcoms. A space may be controlled by an individual such as a pub landlord or be owned by certain people but still function as a public area.

Existing in public and shared space

The picnic at Box Hill in *Emma* Chapter 43 is an example of characters being let loose in a public space. Jane Austen's readers might well have been familiar with images of Box Hill, and the outing is much anticipated in the novel: 'Emma had never been to Box Hill; she wished to see what every body found so well worth seeing.'

They had a very fine day for Box Hill; and all the other outward circumstances of arrangement, accommodation, and punctuality, were in favour of a pleasant party. Mr Weston directed the whole, officiating safely between Hartfield and the Vicarage, and every body was in good time. Emma and Harriet went together; Miss Bates and her niece, with the Eltons; the gentlemen on horseback. Mrs Weston remained with Mr Woodhouse. Nothing was wanting but to be happy when they got there. Seven miles were travelled in expectation of enjoyment, and every body had a burst of admiration on first arriving;

but in the general amount of the day there was deficiency. There was a languor, a want of spirits, a want of union, which could not be got over. They separated too much into parties. The Eltons walked together; Mr Knightley took charge of Miss Bates and Jane; and Emma and Harriet belonged to Frank Churchill. And Mr Weston tried, in vain, to make them harmonize better. It seemed at first an accidental division, but it never materially varied. Mr and Mrs Elton, indeed, shewed no unwillingness to mix, and be as agreeable as they could; but during the two whole hours that were spent on the hill, there seemed a principle of separation, between the other parties, too strong for any fine prospects, or any cold collation, or any cheerful Mr Weston, to remove.

It's significant that Jane Fairfax isn't mentioned by name in the list of who sets out – she is just 'Miss Bates' niece' – and a person reading the novel for the first time would, like Emma, probably pay little attention to her presence or realize that Frank Churchill's behaviour is more to do with Jane Fairfax than Emma, the one he flirts with.

At first it was downright dullness to Emma. She had never seen Frank Churchill so silent and stupid. He said nothing worth hearing – looked without seeing – admired without intelligence – listened without knowing what she said. While he was so dull, it was no wonder that Harriet should be dull likewise, and they were both insufferable.

When they all sat down it was better; to her taste a great deal better, for Frank Churchill grew talkative and gay, making her his first object. Every distinguishing attention that could be paid, was paid to her. To amuse her, and be agreeable in her eyes, seemed all that he cared for – and Emma, glad to be enlivened, not sorry to be flattered, was gay and easy too, and gave him all the friendly encouragement, the admission to be gallant, which she had ever given in the first and most animating period of their acquaintance; but which now, in her own estimation, meant nothing, though in the judgment of most people looking on it must have had such an appearance as no English word but flirtation could very well describe. 'Mr Frank Churchill and Miss Woodhouse flirted together excessively.' They were laying themselves open to that very phrase – and to having it sent off in a letter to Maple Grove by one lady, to Ireland by another.

The drama of a landscape can enhance a scene. There is also something about letting characters loose in a public space that can lead to them behaving in unanticipated ways. Normal expectations are removed. Characters may have conflicting expectations and feelings about the ownership of spaces and events. How will your public and shared spaces impact on your plot? You can also use them to introduce new characters. Who else might be encountered in these places? Think of the way that in *Persuasion*, Chapter 12, Anne Elliot and William Elliot see each other in Lyme:

When they came to the steps, leading upwards from the beach, a gentleman, at the same moment preparing to come down, politely drew back, and stopped to give them way. They ascended and passed him; and as they passed, Anne's face caught his eye, and he looked at her with a degree of earnest admiration which she could not be insensible of. She was looking remarkably well; her very regular, very pretty features, having the bloom and freshness of youth restored by the fine wind which had been blowing on her complexion, and by the animations of eye which it had also produced. It was evident that the gentleman, (completely a gentleman in manner) admired her exceedingly. Captain Wentworth looked round at her instantly in a way which shewed his noticing of it. He gave her a momentary glance, a glance of brightness, which seemed to say, 'That man is struck with you, and even I, at this moment, see something like Anne Elliot again.'

The seaside, for Jane Austen, is a place for romance, adventure, chance meetings and, in the cases of Lydia Bennet and Georgiana Darcy, misadventure. When characters are removed from their usual spheres, anything might happen.

In another important scene in *Emma* we see the characters literally negotiating the use of space. Frank Churchill and Emma are determined to have a ball, and when the Westons' house is deemed not suitable, Frank Churchill has the idea of using the Crown Inn. We see the characters' reactions to the space and their machinations to ensure that they all get what they want. Mr Woodhouse shows himself to be more astute and a better judge of character than many might give him credit for; he can see that because Frank Churchill is inclined to open windows and leave doors gaping, he is 'not quite the thing', something that it takes Emma a lot longer to realize.

Here are the residents of Highbury planning a ball (from *Emma*, Chapter 29):

> It may be possible to do without dancing entirely. Instances have been known of young people passing many, many months successively, without being at any ball of any description, and no material injury accrue either to body or mind; – but when a beginning is made – when the felicities of rapid motion have once been, though slightly, felt – it must be a very heavy set that does not ask for more.
>
> Frank Churchill had danced once at Highbury, and longed to dance again; and the last half-hour of an evening which Mr Woodhouse was persuaded to spend with his daughter at Randalls, was passed by the two young people in schemes on the subject. Frank's was the first idea; and his the greatest zeal in pursuing it; for the lady was the best judge of the difficulties, and the most solicitous for accommodation and appearance.

They first think of having the ball at Randalls, the Westons' house.

> The doors of the two rooms were just opposite each other. 'Might not they use both rooms, and dance across the passage?' It seemed the best scheme; and yet it was not so good but that many of them wanted a better.

Emma said it would be awkward; Mrs Weston was in distress about the supper; and Mr Woodhouse opposed it earnestly, on the score of health. It made him so very unhappy, indeed, that it could not be persevered in.

'Oh! no,' said he; 'it would be the extreme of imprudence. I could not bear it for Emma! – Emma is not strong. She would catch a dreadful cold. So would poor little Harriet. So would you all. Mrs Weston, you would be quite laid up; do not let them talk of such a wild thing. Pray do not let them talk of it. That young man (speaking lower) is very thoughtless. Do not tell his father, but that young man is not quite the thing. He has been opening the doors very often this evening, and keeping them open very inconsiderately. He does not think of the draught. I do not mean to set you against him, but indeed he is not quite the thing!' [...]

Before the middle of the next day, he [Frank Churchill] was at Hartfield; and he entered the room with such an agreeable smile as certified the continuance of the scheme. It soon appeared that he came to announce an improvement.

'Well, Miss Woodhouse,' he almost immediately began, 'your inclination for dancing has not been quite frightened away, I hope, by the terrors of my father's little rooms. I bring a new proposal on the subject: – a thought of my father's, which waits only your approbation to be acted upon. May I hope for the honour of your hand for the two first dances of this little projected ball, to be given, not at Randalls, but at the Crown Inn?'

'The Crown!'

'Yes; if you and Mr Woodhouse see no objection, and I trust you cannot, my father hopes his friends will be so kind as to visit him there. Better accommodations, he can promise them, and not a less grateful welcome than at Randalls. It is his own idea. Mrs Weston sees no objection to it, provided you are satisfied. This is what we all feel. Oh! you were perfectly right! Ten couple, in either of the Randalls rooms, would have been insufferable! – Dreadful! – I felt how right you were the whole time, but was too anxious for securing *any thing* to like to yield. Is not it a good exchange? – You consent – I hope you consent?'

'It appears to me a plan that nobody can object to, if Mr and Mrs Weston do not. I think it admirable; and, as far as I can answer for myself, shall be most happy – It seems the only improvement that could be. Papa, do you not think it an excellent improvement?'

She was obliged to repeat and explain it, before it was fully comprehended; and then, being quite new, further representations were necessary to make it acceptable.

'No; he thought it very far from an improvement – a very bad plan – much worse than the other. A room at an inn was always damp and dangerous; never properly aired, or fit to be inhabited. If they must dance, they had better dance at Randalls. He had never been in the room at the Crown in his life – did not know the people who kept it by sight. – Oh! no – a very bad plan. They would catch worse colds at the Crown than anywhere.' [. . .]

'From the very circumstance of its being larger, sir. We shall have no occasion to open the windows at all – not once the whole evening; and it is that dreadful habit of opening the windows, letting in cold air upon heated bodies, which (as you well know, sir) does the mischief.'

'Open the windows! – but surely, Mr Churchill, nobody would think of opening the windows at Randalls. Nobody could be so imprudent! I never heard of such a thing. Dancing with open windows! – I am sure, neither your father nor Mrs Weston (poor Miss Taylor that was) would suffer it.'

EXERCISE: NEGOTIATING AND USING PUBLIC AND SHARED SPACE

Write a scene which involves characters in public or shared space. What conflicts, feuds, romances or friendships will arise? How will people's behaviour be judged by others? The space needn't be outdoors. How does being in public or shared space affect the dialogue and the scene as a whole?

Thinking about your characters in their private space

In *Emma*, Chapter 42, faced with leaving Highbury to become a governess and unable to be with the man she secretly loves, Jane Fairfax confides a little of how she feels. She has almost no private space and longs for just a few moments by herself.

Jane Fairfax appeared, coming quickly in from the garden, and with a look of escape. – Little expecting to meet Miss Woodhouse so soon, there was a start at first; but Miss Woodhouse was the very person she was in quest of.

'Will you be so kind,' said she, 'when I am missed, as to say that I am gone home? – I am going this moment. My aunt is not aware how late it is, nor how long we have been absent – but I am sure we shall be wanted, and I am determined to go directly. – I have said nothing about it to any body. It would only be giving trouble and distress. Some are gone to the ponds, and some to the lime walk. Till they all come in I shall not be missed; and when they do, will you have the goodness to say that I am gone?'

'Certainly, if you wish it; – but you are not going to walk to Highbury alone?'

'Yes – what should hurt me? – I walk fast. I shall be at home in twenty minutes.'

'But it is too far, indeed it is, to be walking quite alone. Let my father's servant go with you. – Let me order the carriage. It can be round in five minutes.'

'Thank you, thank you – but on no account. – I would rather walk. – And for *me* to be afraid of walking alone! – I, who may so soon have to guard others!'

She spoke with great agitation; and Emma very feelingly replied, 'That can be no reason for your being exposed to danger now. I must order the carriage. The heat even would be danger. – You are fatigued already.'

'I am,' – she answered, – 'I am fatigued; but it is not the sort of fatigue – quick walking will refresh me. – Miss Woodhouse, we all know at times what it is to be wearied in spirits. Mine, I confess, are exhausted. The greatest kindness you can shew me, will be to let me have my own way, and only say that I am gone when it is necessary.'

Emma had not another word to oppose. She saw it all; and entering into her feelings, promoted her quitting the house immediately, and watched her safely off with the zeal of a friend. Her parting look was grateful – and her parting words, 'Oh! Miss Woodhouse, the comfort of being sometimes alone!' – seemed to burst from an overcharged heart, and to describe somewhat of the continual endurance to be practised by her, even towards some of those who loved her best.

In *Pride and Prejudice* Mr Bennet retreats to his library – sometimes pursued by Mr Collins. In *Sense and Sensibility* the Dashwood sisters and their mother lose their home, Norland Park. In *Mansfield Park* (Chapter 19) an invasion of the private space of Lord Bertram's study is emblematic of the wrongness of the theatricals and the way that the Bertrams, Crawfords and Mr Yates have been moving the normal boundaries of their previously ordered existence. 'Sir Thomas had been a good deal surprised to find candles burning in his room; and on casting his eye round it, to see other symptoms of recent habitation and a general air of confusion in the furniture. The removal of the bookcase from before the billiard-room door struck him especially.'

EXERCISE

Write about a character whose private space is invaded or threatened, or about an attempt to annexe a character's private space.

RULES, CODES, TRADITIONS

Emma is a snob and has a very particular view of Highbury society and her place within it. Readers see how the village functions and how things and attitudes change. At the start of the novel there are people she will not mix with, and she tells Harriet Smith that she will not be able to continue their friendship if Harriet marries Robert Martin. All villages have their spoken and unspoken rules, codes and traditions. These might determine who is in charge of what, who parks where, what sort of present is or isn't acceptable for a schoolteacher at the end of term, etc.

Think about how the society you are writing about operates. How do different characters feel about the rules, codes and traditions of your village? The fun starts when somebody threatens to break the rules. In one of my favourite films, *Serial Mom*, which stars Kathleen Turner, wearing white shoes after Labor Day or failing to sort your recycling has fatal consequences.

EXERCISES

1. Write the Ten Commandments of your village.

2. Now write a scene in which somebody breaks one or more of the rules; this could be from the point of view of a rule breaker, a rule enforcer or a bystander.

Strangers coming to town

All literature, in an axiom attributed to Tolstoy, is either a man goes on a journey or a stranger comes to town. This certainly seems true in the work of Jane Austen. In *Emma* the arrivals of Frank Churchill, Jane Fairfax and Mrs Elton are catalysts for change, comedy, romance and drama. In Austen's novels readers see many characters setting out on journeys (Catherine Morland and Anne Elliot are prime examples) and strangers coming to town (Mr Bingley, Mr Darcy, Mr Collins, Wickham, the Crawfords).

More on journeys later, but for now think about the way that a stranger coming into the village of your novel can be your inciting incident or move your plot in a new direction. In Jane Austen's work it is striking how often women wait for news, for things to happen and for people to arrive, a situation that Jane must have known only too well, for example waiting for news of her sailor brothers. Here she is writing to Cassandra in November 1801.

We have at last heard from Frank; a letter from him to you came yesterday, and I mean to send it on as soon as I can ... *En attendant,* you must rest satisfied with knowing that on the 8th of July the 'Petterel,' with the rest of the Egyptian squadron, was off the Isle of Cyprus, whither they went from Jaffa for provisions, &c., and whence they were to sail in a day or two for Alexandria, there to wait the result of the English proposals for the evacuation of Egypt. The rest of the letter, according to the present fashionable style of composition, is chiefly descriptive. Of his promotion he knows nothing.

Austen's readers often come across heroines looking out of windows, longing for people to arrive or being surprised by sudden arrivals or communications. This is from Chapter 53 of *Pride and Prejudice.*

The housekeeper at Netherfield had received orders to prepare for the arrival of her master, who was coming down in a day or two, to shoot there for several weeks. Mrs Bennet was quite in the fidgets. She looked at Jane, and smiled and shook her head by turns.

'Well, well, and so Mr Bingley is coming down, sister,' (for Mrs Philips first brought her the news). 'Well, so much the better. Not that I care about it, though. He is nothing to us, you know, and I am sure *I* never want to see him again. But, however, he is very welcome to come to Netherfield, if he likes it. And who knows what *may* happen? But that is nothing to us. You know, sister, we agreed long ago never to mention a word about it. And so, is it quite certain he is coming?'

'You may depend on it,' replied the other, 'for Mrs Nicholls was in Meryton last night; I saw her passing by, and went out myself on purpose to know the truth of it; and she told me that it was certain true. He comes down on Thursday at the latest, very likely on Wednesday. She was going to the butcher's, she told me, on purpose to order in some meat on Wednesday, and she has got three couple of ducks just fit to be killed.'

Miss Bennet had not been able to hear of his coming without changing colour. It was many months since she had mentioned his name to Elizabeth; but now, as soon as they were alone together, she said,

'I saw you look at me today, Lizzy, when my aunt told us of the present report; and I know I appeared distressed. But don't imagine it was from any silly cause. I was only confused for the moment, because I felt that I *should* be looked at. I do assure you, that the news does not affect me either with pleasure or pain. I am glad of one thing, that he comes alone; because we shall see the less of him. Not that I am afraid of *myself*, but I dread other people's remarks.'

Elizabeth did not know what to make of it. Had she not seen him in Derbyshire, she might have supposed him capable of coming there with no other view than what was acknowledged; but she still thought him partial to Jane, and she wavered as to the greater probability of his coming there *with* his friend's permission, or being bold enough to come without it.

'Yet it is hard,' she sometimes thought, 'that this poor man cannot come to a house which he has legally hired, without raising all this speculation! I *will* leave him to himself.'

In spite of what her sister declared, and really believed to be her feelings in the expectation of his arrival, Elizabeth could easily perceive that her spirits were affected by it. They were more disturbed, more unequal, than she had often seen them.

The subject which had been so warmly canvassed between their parents, about a twelvemonth ago, was now brought forward again.

'As soon as ever Mr Bingley comes, my dear,' said Mrs Bennet, 'you will wait on him of course.'

'No, no. You forced me into visiting him last year, and promised, if I went to see him, he should marry one of my daughters. But it ended in nothing, and I will not be sent on a fool's errand again.'

His wife represented to him how absolutely necessary such an attention would be from all the neighbouring gentlemen, on his returning to Netherfield.

"Tis an etiquette I despise,' said he. 'If he wants our society, let him seek it. He knows where we live. I will not spend *my* hours in running after my neighbours every time they go away and come back again.'

'Well, all I know is, that it will be abominably rude if you do not wait on him. But, however, that shan't prevent my asking him to dine here, I am determined. We must have Mrs Long and the Gouldings soon. That will make thirteen with ourselves, so there will be just room at the table for him.'

Consoled by this resolution, she was the better able to bear her husband's incivility; though it was very mortifying to know that her neighbours might all see

Mr Bingley, in consequence of it, before *they* did. As the day of his arrival drew near,

'I begin to be sorry that he comes at all,' said Jane to her sister. 'It would be nothing: I could see him with perfect indifference, but I can hardly bear to hear it thus perpetually talked of. My mother means well; but she does not know, no one can know, how much I suffer from what she says. Happy shall I be when his stay at Netherfield is over!'

'I wish I could say anything to comfort you,' replied Elizabeth; 'but it is wholly out of my power. You must feel it; and the usual satisfaction of preaching patience to a sufferer is denied me, because you have always so much.'

Mr Bingley arrived. Mrs Bennet, through the assistance of servants, contrived to have the earliest tidings of it, that the period of anxiety and fretfulness on her side might be as long as it could. She counted the days that must intervene before their invitation could be sent; hopeless of seeing him before. But on the third morning after his arrival in Hertfordshire, she saw him, from her dressing-room window, enter the paddock and ride towards the house.

Her daughters were eagerly called to partake of her joy. Jane resolutely kept her place at the table; but Elizabeth, to satisfy her mother, went to the window – she looked, – she saw Mr Darcy with him, and sat down again by her sister.

'There is a gentleman with him, mamma,' said Kitty; 'who can it be?'

'Some acquaintance or other, my dear, I suppose; I am sure I do not know.'

'La!' replied Kitty, 'it looks just like that man that used to be with him before. Mr what's-his-name. That tall, proud man.'

EXERCISE

Write a departure or an arrival scene – somebody going on a journey or a stranger coming to town.

Outsiders, outlaws and those who cross boundaries

As well as new arrivals, Jane Austen makes good use of outsiders, outlaws and people who can cross the boundaries of society. There would be many other unnamed characters too, the sort of characters that Jo Baker made such clever and interesting use of in *Longbourn,* which imagines the lives of those below stairs and behind the scenes in *Pride and Prejudice.*

In *Emma* (Chapter 55) we have the Gypsies who frighten Harriet Smith, Mr Perry the apothecary, and the poultry thieves whose return Emma and Mr Knightley use to hasten their nuptials.

Mrs Weston's poultry-house was robbed one night of all her turkeys – evidently by the ingenuity of man. Other poultry-yards in the neighbourhood also suffered. – Pilfering was *housebreaking* to Mr Woodhouse's fears. – He was very uneasy [. . .]

The result of this distress was, that, with a much more voluntary, cheerful consent than his daughter had ever presumed to hope for at the moment, she was able to fix her wedding-day.

Outlaws and boundary crossers may not be human. In Inga Moore's delightful picture book *Six Dinner Sid* the actions of a boundary-crossing cat bring together the residents of a street, a group of people who have never spoken to each other before. Sid has six different names and behaves in six different ways for his six different 'owners'[4] so that he can have six different dinners every day. All is well until one day he gets a cough. The vet finds it strange that six residents of the same street have identical black cats with the same problem . . .

EXERCISE

Think about how outsiders, outlaws and those who cross boundaries will exist in the world of your story. You can use them to deepen our understanding of the other characters and the setting, to heighten tension or to effect change. They might be foxes, cats, rats or people – perhaps somebody who sees into other people's lives, for example a cleaner, health visitor, doctor, priest or gardener.

Write a scene that centres on the actions of a stranger, outsider, outlaw or somebody who can cross boundaries. How can the actions of a seemingly less significant character influence events in your story? How do different characters feel about and respond to the outsider or boundary-crosser? The whole plot can turn on the actions of one of these people or creatures. Write from any point of view.

CHARACTERS' ROOMS

Fanny Price sleeps in a little white attic at Mansfield Park. Attic bedrooms were usually occupied by servants, and readers can imagine how much grander her cousins' bedrooms were. Fanny's other sanctuary is the East room, a chamber that nobody else uses any more. It is described in Chapter 16.

It had been their school-room; so called till the Miss Bertrams would not allow it to be called so any longer, and inhabited as such to a later period. There Miss Lee had lived, and there they had read and written, and talked and laughed, till within the last three years, when she had quitted them. The room had then become useless, and for some time was quite deserted, except by Fanny, when she visited her plants, or wanted one of the books, which she was still glad to keep there, from the deficiency of space and accommodation in her little chamber above: but gradually, as her value for the comforts of it increased, she had added to her possessions, and spent more of her time there; and having nothing to oppose her, had so naturally and so artlessly worked herself into it, that it was now generally admitted to be hers. The East room, as it had been called ever since Maria Bertram was sixteen, was now considered Fanny's, almost as decidedly as the white attic: the smallness of the one making the use of the other so evidently reasonable that the Miss Bertrams, with every superiority in their own apartments which their own sense of superiority could demand, were entirely approving it; and Mrs Norris, having stipulated for there never being a fire in it on Fanny's account, was tolerably resigned to her having the use of what nobody else wanted, though the terms in which she sometimes spoke of the indulgence seemed to imply that it was the best room in the house.

The aspect was so favourable that even without a fire it was habitable in many an early spring and late autumn morning to such a willing mind as Fanny's; and while there was a gleam of sunshine she hoped not to be driven from it entirely, even when winter came. The comfort of it in her hours of leisure was extreme. She could go there after anything unpleasant below, and find immediate consolation in some pursuit, or some train of thought at hand. Her plants, her books – of which she had been a collector from the first hour of her commanding a shilling – her writing-desk, and her works of charity and ingenuity, were all within her reach; or if indisposed for employment, if nothing but musing would do, she could scarcely see an object in that room which had not an interesting remembrance connected with it. Everything was a friend, or bore her thoughts to a friend; and though there had been some- times much of suffering to her; though her motives had often been misunderstood, her feelings disregarded, and her comprehension undervalued; though she had known the pains of tyranny, of ridicule, and neglect, yet almost every recurrence of either had led to some- thing consolatory: her aunt Bertram had spoken for her, or Miss Lee had been encouraging, or, what was yet more frequent or more dear, Edmund had been her champion and her friend: he had supported her cause or explained her meaning, he had told her not to cry, or had given her some proof of affection which made her tears delightful; and the whole was now so blended together, so harmonised by distance, that every former affliction had its charm. The room was most dear to her, and she would not have changed its furniture for the handsomest in the house, though what had been originally plain had suffered all the ill-usage of children; and its greatest elegancies and ornaments were a faded footstool of Julia's work, too ill done for the drawing-room, three transparencies, made in a rage for transparencies, for the three lower panes of one window, where Tintern Abbey held its station between a cave in Italy and a moonlight lake in Cumberland, a collection of family profiles, thought unworthy of being anywhere else, over the mantelpiece, and by their side, and pinned against the wall, a small sketch of a ship sent four years ago from the Mediterranean by William, with H.M.S. *Antwerp* at the bottom, in letters as tall as the mainmast.

To this nest of comforts Fanny now walked down to try its influence on an agitated, doubting spirit, to see if by looking at Edmund's profile she could catch any of his counsel, or by giving air to her geraniums she might inhale a breeze of mental strength herself.

By telling readers that it is the East room, Jane Austen ensured that we would know the sort of light and warmth that it had. Mrs Norris makes sure that Fanny doesn't have a fire, so it would often have been chilly. Later in the novel Fanny's uncle discovers this and sets things right. This discovery is a small incident but is significant in alerting Sir Thomas to how badly Fanny has been treated by Mrs Norris. Important scenes take place in this room, and when they do, we feel that Fanny is under attack. In Chapter 16 the theatricals which precipitate so much are only just beginning. Jane Austen doesn't often write about particular objects, so when she does the reader takes notice. The footstool made by Julia that wouldn't be given space anywhere else and Fanny's geraniums add a splash of colour to the picture readers are given. We are also told, very concisely, about the objects that Fanny treasures: her books, the picture sent by William and the picture of Edmund. It's touching that Fanny has the 'collection of family profiles, thought unworthy of being anywhere else'. Most of these people aren't even nice to her! I hope there wasn't one of Mrs Norris. Fanny would probably have been too polite not to have it up with the others although hardly anybody else came into the room.

EXERCISES

1. *Light your story.* Think about how your story is going to be lit. Novelists and short-story writers can learn much from filmmakers, painters and photographers here. How warm/cold/hot, bright/dim/hazy are the different places your characters inhabit? Think about indoors and outdoors. How do the lighting and temperature change during the day and according to the time of year? What will a character be able to

see at night? Does light come in from the outside? What colour is it? Do street lamps or lights from other buildings shine through the windows? What are the windows like? Are they dirty or clean? What shape are they? What are the curtains or blinds like? Are there lamps, candles or mirrors? Think about the details you will use to communicate the light to the reader without writing great long passages of description. Avoid telling readers that a character wakes to see dust motes dancing in the sunbeams – editors read that too many times.

Now look back through the scenes you have written so far to see if you have lit them well. Are you consistent and do you show how places change according to the time of day or year? What colours have you told the reader about? What might particular characters coming into a room notice first? What do you want the reader to notice first? What you tell us about will depend on the point of view you are using and what you are trying to set up.

Add or subtract details to light and colour your scenes better.

2. *Create rooms or private spaces for your characters.* These might be places in the present time of your novel or places that characters remember; they might be bedrooms, offices, kitchens, studies, sheds or the interiors of cars. Some characters might have almost nowhere to call their own or just a locker or rucksack. Look back at the description of the

East room and think about the things that each of your characters keeps in their space. Don't forget heating and lighting but also think about smells, possible dust and grime, sounds and textures and so on. Fanny Price's room may have smelt of her geraniums. Without a fire it would often have been very cold. What can be seen from the window(s) of your rooms? Are there secret spaces within the spaces? Use carefully chosen details. A character's space might extend into cyberspace. What apps do they have on their phone? What do they search for on Spotify?

Create rooms or private spaces for each of your characters. These may or may not appear in your finished work, but even if they don't this exercise will help ensure that you know your characters well.

3. *Think about the writers you love and the places they were inspired by.* Try to visit these places and follow in your favourite writers' footsteps. Writers almost always use spaces they know in their work, either in totality or taking aspects of different ones to create the spaces they need. Gather photographs, maps, guidebooks, leaflets, local papers, etc.

For Jane Austen, visit Jane Austen's House Museum in Chawton, Hampshire. After visiting the museum walk along the road to Chawton House Library, which was formerly one home of Edward Austen, Jane's lucky brother, who inherited a fortune. Walking around the gardens here and at the museum will help you understand Jane's work. Edward Austen's other grand house, Godmersham Park in Kent, where Jane and Cassandra often stayed, is also well worth visiting, as is The Vyne, a National Trust property near Basingstoke. The Austens were friends of the Chute family, who owned it. One of the Chutes' cousins (a poor relation) was brought to live with the family. Might this child's story have inspired Jane? There are dozens of articles about 'the real Pemberley' and 'the real Mansfield Park', and you might also like to visit the houses they discuss.

Many of Jane's letters were written from Godmersham. They give us useful insights into the life of the house, and it's clear that staying there influenced her. Jane included details about particular people – for example, she knew that her father would want to know how Edward's farming concerns were going. Jane and Cassandra had the same experience at Godmersham – visiting impecunious aunts – and Jane mentions to Cassandra how much she paid for having her hair done before a ball, an amount that shows the hairdresser was likely aware of Jane's straitened circumstances.

Mr Hall walked off this morning to Ospringe, with no inconsiderable booty. He charged Elizabeth 5s. for every time of dressing her hair, and 5s. for every lesson to Sace, allowing nothing for the pleasures of his visit here, for meat, drink, and lodging, the benefit of country air, and the charms of Mrs Salkeld's and Mrs Sace's society. Towards me he was as considerate as I had hoped for from my relationship to you, charging me only 2*s*. 6*d*. for cutting my hair, though it was as thoroughly dressed after being cut for Eastwell as it had been for the Ashford assembly. He certainly respects either our youth or our poverty.[5]

Bath and Lyme Regis are other must-see destinations for Janeites, but don't have the interiors that we know she inhabited, so will inspire you in different ways. The houses that we know Jane lived in or visited must have influenced her work, but we know that she also did her research, writing to Cassandra and Martha Lloyd when she was writing *Mansfield Park*, 'If you could discover whether Northamptonshire is a County of Hedgerows, I should be glad again,'[6] and, 'I am obliged to you for your enquiries about Northamptonshire but do not wish you to renew them, as I am sure of getting the intelligence I want from Henry, to whom I can apply at some convenient moment "sans peur et sans reproche".'[7]

Writers have to be resourceful, gleaning information where they can.

A fine pair of eyes

Point of view

'Point of view . . . is the window that takes you to the story. You can't see the window unless you are standing in the right place, once you find the right place the story can almost write itself.'

Maureen Freely[1]

Jane Austen was a pioneer in the way that she handled point of view and experimented with telling stories. Point of view is everything.

EXERCISE: THE IMPORTANCE
OF POINT OF VIEW

This is a fun exercise for a group of writers. Choose a setting that everybody knows. At Jane Austen's House Museum I have used the museum as the setting, but with university students I usually use a branch of Costa Coffee or McDonald's or the students' union shop or bar.

You need lots of folded slips of paper, each bearing a very brief character outline. Have a range of characters of different ages and backgrounds, for example a lost child, somebody who is stoned, a health and safety inspector, a pickpocket, someone who has just fallen in love, an artist, a blind person, somebody with a broken leg, a carer having a break from the person they look after, someone who has come about a job, a mother with three under-fives. Each member of the group takes a slip of paper and must not let anybody else see what's written on it. If people don't like the character they've chosen let them choose another one; this means having lots of spare character slips.

The characters (for whatever reason) arrive at the venue. They go in and up to the counter or just wander about, depending on your chosen location. What do they notice? How does the place make them feel? Each group member writes from their character's point of view. Writing in the first person is preferable as it means having to concentrate on the character's voice

134

and what they would notice. Using the present tense may also help each writer to inhabit the character and the moment. People shouldn't spell out who their character is: don't say, 'Well here I am to do the health and safety inspection.' After about fifteen minutes people read out their accounts. Compare them. If the point of view is handled well, people should be able to guess the character.[2]

FREE INDIRECT NARRATION OR DISCOURSE, ONE OF JANE AUSTEN'S MOST IMPORTANT STYLISTIC INNOVATIONS

Jane Austen didn't invent free indirect narration but was the first person to use it so extensively and effectively. Free indirect narration gives the writer the advantages of using the first person as well as the freedoms of using the third person. You can switch between points of view and effectively convey the thoughts and feelings of individual characters as your story unfolds.

Characteristics of free indirect narration

1. The language used is subjective and indicates the character's opinion.

2. Exclamations and questions may feature in the narration.

3. It pins the scene in place and time from the character's perspective.

4. There's often no need to label who thoughts belong to – readers will understand.

5. There's plenty of potential for humour, irony and misunderstandings.

Here's an example from *Emma*, Chapter 10. Emma is trying to engineer an opportunity for Mr Elton to declare his love to Harriet Smith.

Mr Elton was still talking, still engaged in some interesting detail; and Emma experienced some disappointment when she found that he was only giving his fair companion an account of the yesterday's party at his friend Cole's, and that she was come in herself for the Stilton cheese, the north Wiltshire, the butter, the celery, the beetroot and all the dessert.

'This would soon have led to something better of course,' was her consoling reflection; 'any thing interests between those who love; and any thing will serve as introduction to what is near the heart. If I could but have kept longer away!'

They now walked on together quietly, till within view of the vicarage pales, when a sudden resolution, of at least getting Harriet into the house, made her again find something very much amiss about her boot, and fall behind to arrange it once more. She then broke the lace off short, and dexterously throwing it into a ditch, was presently obliged to entreat them to stop, and acknowledge her inability to put herself to rights so as to be able to walk home in tolerable comfort.

'Part of my lace is gone,' said she, 'and I do not know how I am to contrive. I really am a most troublesome companion to you both, but I hope I am not often so ill-equipped. Mr Elton, I must beg leave to stop at your house, and ask your housekeeper for a bit of riband or string, or any thing just to keep my boot on.'

Mr Elton looked all happiness at this proposition; and nothing could exceed his alertness and attention in conducting them into his house and endeavouring to make everything appear to advantage. The room they were taken into was the one he chiefly occupied, and looking forwards; behind it was another with which it immediately communicated; the door between them was open, and Emma passed into it with the housekeeper to receive her assistance in the most comfortable manner. She was obliged to leave the door ajar as she found it; but she fully intended that Mr Elton should close it. It was not closed, however, it still remained ajar; but by engaging the housekeeper in incessant conversation, she hoped to make it practicable for him to chuse his own subject in the adjoining room. For ten minutes she could hear nothing but herself. It could be protracted no longer. She was then obliged to be finished, and make her appearance.

The lovers were standing together at one of the windows. It had a most favourable aspect; and, for half a minute, Emma felt the glory of having schemed successfully. But it would not do; he had not come to the point. He had been most agreeable, most delightful; he had told Harriet that he had seen them go by, and had purposely followed them; other little gallantries and allusions had been dropt, but nothing serious.

EXERCISES

1. Write using free indirect narration. You might like to try giving an account of a time when you or one of your characters got something very wrong. There is no need to reveal the truth in your account; just inhabit the moment. If you are writing autobiographically use the third person for this exercise.

2. Practise inhabiting a character to get the point of view right. This is an exercise that uses objects to help writers get into the minds of their characters. There is a handling collection at Jane Austen's House Museum which is perfect for this, but you can use any object that interests you. If you are in a writing group, ask everybody to bring in a few things they have found in charity shops or that have been passed down to them.

   First choose an object to work with. Sometimes objects that are less obviously appealing will provoke the most imaginative and surprising responses because we have to think harder about them. The objects don't have to be very old, but they must have had at least one owner.

   Then, using all your senses, examine your object carefully and ask yourself questions about it, for example:

   - What is it? Who made it? How?
   - What does it look/feel like?
   - Where did it come from? Who might it have belonged to?
   - How did they feel about it? Did they like it or dislike it?

- Did they use it? Did they treasure it? Did they throw it away? Might they have lost it?
- Why has it survived to be part of a museum collection/ended up in a charity shop/been passed down in a family?
- Do you have anything like it?
- What does it remind you of? Does it spark any memories?

Write down your answers. Don't censor yourself or worry that you might be getting things wrong. Don't strain for exquisite phrases – just keep writing. Don't worry if what you write is personal or might seem eccentric. Spend about ten minutes on this.

Now look back through what you have written and use your notes and thoughts to create a character inspired by or somehow connected to your object. Your character could be from the same period as the object, somebody who lived later, a person who is alive today or someone in the future. They could be an owner of the object, somebody who finds it, looks after it, hates it, steals it or . . . It's up to you.

Then write a quick sketch of your character. Use the third person. Include your character's name, age, occupation, who they live with, the things they care most about, details or quirks about their appearance, something that they long for . . . Spend about ten minutes on this.

Finally write an internal monologue for your character or practise writing using free indirect narration. Try to capture the character's voice. They could be talking/thinking about the object or about something else entirely. For example, if you chose a glove, the internal monologue might begin: 'My new gloves are here. I can't wait for tomorrow evening, when . . .' or: 'The new gloves had arrived. She couldn't wait for the evening, when . . .' Or, if you chose a candlestick: 'I hate having to polish these. My hands ache; I've been up since before dawn, and however long I spend on them Lady Catherine won't think it's enough . . .' or: 'She hated having to polish them. Her hands ached. She'd been up since before dawn and knew that however long she spent on them Lady Catherine would find something to criticize . . .' Spend about fifteen minutes on this, but then carry on if you want to. You could use it as the starting point for a poem or story.[3]

Your character's view of their world

Think about your character's way of looking at their world. Show us what they see. You might like to show them looking out of a window, looking across their office, walking to work ... This need not be a passive scene; you can make something happen. Look at the scene where Emma gazes out of the window at Ford's (p. 203) and at the following scene from *Persuasion* (Chapter 14) where Anne Elliot and Lady Russell look out at Bath.

Everybody has their taste in noises as well as in other matters; and sounds are quite innoxious, or most distressing, by their sort rather than their quantity. When Lady Russell not long afterwards, was entering Bath on a wet afternoon, and driving through the long course of streets from the Old Bridge to Camden Place, amidst the dash of other carriages, the heavy rumble of carts and drays, the bawling of newspapermen, muffin-men, and milkmen, and the ceaseless clink of pattens, she made no complaint. No, these were noises which belonged to the winter pleasures; her spirits rose under their influence; and like Mrs Musgrove, she was feeling, though not saying, that after being long in the country, nothing could be so good for her as a little quiet cheerfulness.

Anne did not share these feelings. She persisted in a very determined, though very silent disinclination for Bath; caught the first dim view of the extensive buildings, smoking in rain, without any wish of seeing them better; felt their progress through the streets to be, however disagreeable, yet too rapid; for who would be glad to see her when she arrived? And looked back, with fond regret, to the bustles of Uppercross and the seclusion of Kellynch.

EXPERIMENTING WITH OTHER FORMS OF NARRATION

Just as Jane Austen experimented with different styles of narration, have a go at writing in a way that you haven't tried (or tried much) before.

Try using a sly, objective or seemingly objective narrator. Useful examples to look at include Tim O'Brien's short story 'The Things They Carried' and parts of Catherine O'Flynn's *What Was Lost*. In this novel she uses the first person, third person (with some free indirect narration), entries from a child's journal and objective narration.

Try using different modes of narration to add texture and avoid trapping the reader in a character's thoughts. You can use the second person to put the reader at the centre of the action and to create humour, irony and empathy with your protagonist. My favourite examples are Lorrie Moore's short stories in her collection *Self-Help* and Mohsin Hamid's novel *How to Get Filthy Rich in Rising Asia*.

Using the first person plural can be really effective if you are writing about people in a recognizable group situation, for example an office or a team. *Then We Came to the End* by Joshua Ferris is a notable example of how well this can work.

YOUR CHARACTERS' EYES

Think about how Jane Austen used her characters' eyes in her work and how you can utilize glances, exchanged looks and unspoken communication. What are your characters' eyes like? How do they use them? How good is their vision? What is the light like where they live and work at different times of the day? With some genres the lack of artificial light will be really important.

Here is Elizabeth in *Pride and Prejudice* (Chapter 43) visiting Pemberley and looking at a portrait of Mr Darcy.

The picture-gallery, and two or three of the principal bedrooms, were all that remained to be shewn. In the former were many good paintings; but Elizabeth knew nothing of the art; and from such as had been already visible below, she had willingly turned to look at some drawings of Miss Darcy's, in crayons, whose subjects were usually more interesting, and also more intelligible.

In the gallery there were many family portraits, but they could have little to fix the attention of a stranger. Elizabeth walked on in quest of the only face whose features would be known to her. At last it arrested her – and she beheld a striking resemblance of Mr Darcy, with such a smile over the face as she remembered to have sometimes seen when he looked at her. She stood several minutes before the picture in earnest contemplation, and returned to it again before they quitted the gallery. Mrs Reynolds informed them that it had been taken in his father's lifetime.

There was certainly at this moment, in Elizabeth's mind, a more gentle sensation towards the original than she had ever felt in the height of their acquaintance. The commendation bestowed on him by Mrs

Reynolds was of no trifling nature. What praise is more valuable than the praise of an intelligent servant? As a brother, a landlord, a master, she considered how many people's happiness were in his guardianship! – How much of pleasure or pain it was in his power to bestow! – How much of good or evil must be done by him! Every idea that had been brought forward by the housekeeper was favourable to his character, and as she stood before the canvas, on which he was represented, and fixed his eyes upon herself, she thought of his regard with a deeper sentiment of gratitude than it had ever raised before; she remembered its warmth, and softened its impropriety of expression.

Mr Darcy has certainly enjoyed looking at Elizabeth's eyes (Chapter 6).

Occupied in observing Mr Bingley's attentions to her sister, Elizabeth was far from suspecting that she was herself becoming an object of some interest in the eyes of his friend. Mr Darcy had at first scarcely allowed her to be pretty; he had looked at her without admiration at the ball; and when they next met, he looked at her only to criticise. But no sooner had he made it clear to himself and his friends that she had hardly a good feature in her face, than he began to find it was rendered uncommonly intelligent by the beautiful expression of her dark eyes. To this discovery succeeded some others equally mortifying. Though he had detected with a critical eye more than one failure of perfect symmetry in her form, he was forced to acknowledge her figure to be light and pleasing; and in spite of his asserting that her manners were not those of the fashionable world, he was caught by their easy playfulness. Of this she was perfectly unaware; – to her he was only the man who made himself agreeable no where, and who had not thought her handsome enough to dance with.

He began to wish to know more of her, and as a step towards conversing with her himself, attended to her conversation with others. His doing so drew her notice. [...]

Mr Darcy with grave propriety requested to be allowed the honour of her hand; but in vain. Elizabeth was determined; nor did Sir William at all shake her purpose by his attempt at persuasion.

'You excel so much in the dance, Miss Eliza, that it is cruel to deny me the happiness of seeing you; and though this gentleman dislikes the amusement in general, he can have no objection, I am sure, to oblige us for one half hour.'

'Mr Darcy is all politeness,' said Elizabeth, smiling.

'He is indeed – but considering the inducement, my dear Miss Eliza, we cannot wonder at his complaisance; for who would object to such a partner?'

Elizabeth looked archly, and turned away. Her resistance had not injured her with the gentleman, and he was thinking of her with some complacency, when thus accosted by Miss Bingley.

'I can guess the subject of your reverie.'

'I should imagine not.'

'You are considering how insupportable it would be to pass many evenings in this manner – in such society;

and indeed I am quite of your opinion. I was never more annoyed! The insipidity and yet the noise – the noth-ingness, and yet the self-importance of all these people! – What would I give to hear your strictures on them!'

'Your conjecture is totally wrong, I assure you. My mind was more agreeably engaged. I have been medi-tating on the very great pleasure which a pair of fine eyes in the face of a pretty woman can bestow.'

Miss Bingley immediately fixed her eyes on his face, and desired he would tell her what lady had the credit of inspiring such reflections. Mr Darcy replied with great intrepidity,

'Miss Elizabeth Bennet.'

And, in Chapter 8, in which Elizabeth has walked across the fields to Netherfield to visit Jane, Mr Darcy responds to the Bingley sisters' criticisms of Elizabeth by saying that the exercise only brightened her fine eyes.

EXERCISE

Write a scene in which you focus on or include ways that a character uses his or her eyes. What do they see? What are their eyes like?

Light, bright and sparkling

Writing dialogue

THIS WHOLE BOOK COULD be devoted to Jane Austen's use of dialogue. She uses it to develop her characters, to move the plot forward and of course for comedy and irony. As you get to know your characters, their voices will become consistent. Your readers should be able to distinguish between them by their vocabularies, the rhythm of their speech, the jokes they make, the way they interrupt other people, the things they go on about, the words they misuse, their slang and swearing (or the lack of it) and the way that they use words to bully, cajole, charm or protect themselves.

There is no substitute for reading your dialogue aloud to yourself so you can hear how naturalistic it sounds. Look critically at your work to check that individual characters' voices are distinctive. If your characters are all from the same background, of the same age and from the same area, you'll have to work hard to ensure that they don't seem like clones of each other and quite possibly just different versions of yourself.

It's impossible to mix up *Sense and Sensibility*'s Lucy and Anne Steele from their dialogue. Lucy is much cleverer and speaks in a more refined (and hatefully confiding and manipulative) way. Anne's obsession with beaux is immediately apparent, and her accent and the way she blurts things out show her lack of insight into how to play the social games of the time. Lucy often tries to shut her sister up or turn the conversation.

This is from Elinor and Marianne's first meeting with them in Chapter 21.

'I have a notion,' said Lucy, 'you think the little Middletons rather too much indulged; perhaps they may be the outside of enough; but it is so natural in Lady Middleton; and for my part, I love to see children full of life and spirits; I cannot bear them if they are tame and quiet.'

'I confess,' replied Elinor, 'that while I am at Barton Park, I never think of tame and quiet children with any abhorrence.'

A short pause succeeded this speech, which was first broken by Miss Steele, who seemed very much disposed for conversation, and who now said rather abruptly,

'And how do you like Devonshire, Miss Dashwood? I suppose you were very sorry to leave Sussex.'

In some surprise at the familiarity of this question, or at least of the manner in which it was spoken, Elinor replied that she was.

'Norland is a prodigious beautiful place, is not it?' added Miss Steele.

'We have heard Sir John admire it excessively,' said Lucy, who seemed to think some apology necessary for the freedom of her sister.

'I think every one *must* admire it,' replied Elinor, 'who ever saw the place; though it is not to be supposed that any one can estimate its beauties as we do.'

'And had you a great many smart beaux there? I suppose you have not so many in this part of the world; for my part, I think they are a vast addition always.'

'But why should you think,' said Lucy, looking ashamed of her sister, 'that there are not as many genteel young men in Devonshire as Sussex?'

'Nay, my dear, I'm sure I don't pretend to say that there an't. I'm sure there's a vast many smart beaux in Exeter; but you know, how could I tell what smart beaux there might be about Norland; and I was only afraid the Miss Dashwoods might find it dull at Barton, if they had not so many as they used to have. But perhaps you young ladies may not care about the beaux, and had as lief be without them as with them. For my part, I think they are vastly agreeable, provided they dress smart and behave civil. But I can't bear to see them dirty and nasty. Now there's Mr Rose at Exeter, a prodigious smart young man, quite a beau, clerk to

Mr Simpson, you know, and yet if you do but meet him of a morning, he is not fit to be seen. – I suppose your brother was quite a beau, Miss Dashwood, before he married, as he was so rich?'

'Upon my word,' replied Elinor, 'I cannot tell you, for I do not perfectly comprehend the meaning of the word. But this I can say, that if he ever was a beau before he married, he is one still for there is not the smallest alteration in him.'

'Oh! dear! one never thinks of married men's being beaux – they have something else to do.'

'Lord! Anne,' cried her sister, 'you can talk of nothing but beaux; – you will make Miss Dashwood believe you think of nothing else.' And then to turn the discourse, she began admiring the house and the furniture.

This specimen of the Miss Steeles was enough. The vulgar freedom and folly of the eldest left her no recommendation, and as Elinor was not blinded by the beauty, or the shrewd look of the youngest, to her want of real elegance and artlessness, she left the house without any wish of knowing them better.

Jane Austen uses the Steeles to contrast with the elder Dashwood sisters. Marianne often gushes and can talk nineteen to the dozen with Willoughby, while Elinor is very measured in what she says. Elinor can be stern, is more sensible than her own mother and, like Lucy Steele, tries to curb her sister's effusions. The speech of their little sister, Margaret, is convincingly and charmingly done; she too can't help saying what she thinks.

Here is Marianne in full flood to her mother in Chapter 3.

'Edward is very amiable, and I love him tenderly. But yet – he is not the kind of young man – there is a something wanting – his figure is not striking; it has none of that grace which I should expect in the man who could seriously attach my sister. His eyes want all that spirit, that fire, which at once announce virtue and intelligence. And besides all this, I am afraid, Mama, he has no real taste. Music seems scarcely to attract him, and though he admires Elinor's drawings very much, it is not the admiration of a person who can understand their worth. It is evident, in spite of his frequent attention to her while she draws, that in fact he knows nothing of the matter. He admires as a lover, not as a connoisseur. To satisfy me, those characters must be united. I could not be happy with a man whose taste did not in every point coincide with my own. He must enter into all my feelings; the same books, the same music must charm us both. Oh! Mama, how spiritless, how tame was Edward's manner in reading to us last night! I felt for my sister most severely. Yet she bore it with so much composure, she seemed scarcely to notice it. I could hardly keep my seat. To hear those beautiful lines which have frequently almost driven me wild, pronounced with such impenetrable calmness, such dreadful indifference!'

'He would certainly have done more justice to simple and elegant prose. I thought so at the time; but you *would* give him Cowper.'

'Nay, Mama, if he is not to be animated by Cowper! – but we must allow for difference of taste. Elinor has not my feelings, and therefore she may overlook it, and be happy with him. But it would have broken *my* heart, had I loved him, to hear him read with so little sensibility. Mama, the more I know of the world, the more am I convinced that I shall never see a man whom I can really love. I require so much! He must have all Edward's virtues, and his person and manners must ornament his goodness with every possible charm.'

Marianne is often effusive, but she can't always be bothered to talk to people and leaves Elinor to make the required social effort. It isn't just what your characters say; the times when they say very little or choose not to speak are important too.

From the moment we see John Thorpe in *Northanger Abbey* we can guess that he's a wrong 'un. He boasts and bores on about driving, routes and mileage. Catherine begins to notice that he is always contradicting himself, and this, his boasting and his swearing are all indicators to the reader that he is not to be trusted. On the other hand the lovely Henry Tilney can drive much better than John Thorpe and without any of the swearing and boasting. His conversation is always interesting.

EXERCISE: TRAPPED IN A VEHICLE

Catherine Morland is tricked into going out with John Thorpe in his gig. Emma Woodhouse gets trapped with Mr Elton on the way back from a Christmas party, and it is hard to escape his advances inside the carriage. Write a scene in which one of your characters is trapped, perhaps in a vehicle, with a person they really don't want to be with. In this exercise concentrate on the dialogue. Your characters will be doing other things too – driving, looking out of the window, checking their phones. Make sure you integrate their actions and gestures into the conversation.

Mrs Norris is the worst bully in all Jane Austen's work. She resents and tyrannizes Fanny Price, denying her heating in her room, sending her on unnecessary errands and constantly belittling her. Mrs Norris perhaps realizes that her position and Fanny's at Mansfield Park are very similar and so wants to reinforce her superiority. Fanny cannot protest – she is younger and must act respectfully and is far too frightened to speak out anyway. The slights and putdowns are incessant. Whatever Fanny does is wrong. Here (Chapter 23) Aunt Norris is in full flood when Fanny is invited to dinner by Mrs Grant. Mrs Norris gets in a criticism of the Grants and tries to dampen Fanny's spirits further by saying that it will rain and she must put up with a soaking. She wants Fanny to be always 'the lowest and last'.

'Upon my word, Fanny, you are in high luck to meet with such attention and indulgence! You ought to be very much obliged to Mrs Grant for thinking of you, and to your aunt for letting you go, and you ought to look upon it as something extraordinary; for I hope you are aware that there is no real occasion for your going into company in this sort of way, or ever dining out at all; and it is what you must not depend upon ever being repeated. Nor must you be fancying that the invitation is meant as any particular compliment to *you*; the compliment is intended to your uncle and aunt and me. Mrs Grant thinks it a civility due to *us* to take a little notice of you, or else it would never have come into her head, and you may be very certain that, if your cousin Julia had been at home, you would not have been asked at all.'

Mrs Norris had now so ingeniously done away all Mrs Grant's part of the favour, that Fanny, who found herself expected to speak, could only say that she was very much obliged to her aunt Bertram for sparing her, and that she was endeavouring to put her aunt's evening work in such a state as to prevent her being missed.

'Oh! depend upon it, your aunt can do very well without you, or you would not be allowed to go. *I* shall be here, so you may be quite easy about your aunt. And I hope you will have a very *agreeable* day, and find it all mighty *delightful*. But I must observe that five is the very awkwardest of all possible numbers to sit down to table; and I cannot but be surprised that such an *elegant* lady as Mrs Grant should not contrive better! And round their enormous great wide table, too, which fills up the room so dreadfully! Had the doctor been contented to take my dining-table when I came away, as anybody in their senses would have done, instead of having that absurd new one of his own, which is wider, literally wider than the dinner-table here, how infinitely better it would have been! and how much more he would have been respected! for people are never respected when they step out of their proper sphere. Remember that, Fanny. Five – only five to be sitting round that table. However, you will have dinner enough on it for ten, I dare say.'

Mrs Norris fetched breath, and went on again.

'The nonsense and folly of people's stepping out of their rank and trying to appear above themselves, makes me think it right to give *you* a hint, Fanny, now that you are going into company without any of us; and I do beseech and entreat you not to be putting yourself forward, and talking and giving your opinion as if you were one of your cousins – as if you were dear Mrs Rushworth or Julia. *That* will never do, believe me. Remember, wherever you are, you must be the lowest and last; and though Miss Crawford is in a manner at home at the Parsonage, you are not to be taking place of her. And as to coming away at night, you are to stay just as long as Edmund chuses. Leave him to settle *that*.'

'Yes, ma'am, I should not think of anything else.'

'And if it should rain, which I think exceedingly likely, for I never saw it more threatening for a wet evening in my life, you must manage as well as you can, and not be expecting the carriage to be sent for you. I certainly do not go home to-night, and, therefore, the carriage will not be out on my account; so you must make up your mind to what may happen, and take your things accordingly.'

Her niece thought it perfectly reasonable. She rated her own claims to comfort as low even as Mrs Norris could; and when Sir Thomas soon afterwards, just opening the door, said, 'Fanny, at what time would you have the carriage come round?' she felt a degree of astonishment which made it impossible for her to speak.

'My dear Sir Thomas!' cried Mrs Norris, red with anger, 'Fanny can walk.'

'Walk!' repeated Sir Thomas, in a tone of most unanswerable dignity, and coming farther into the room. 'My niece walk to a dinner engagement at this time of the year! Will twenty minutes after four suit you?'

'Yes, sir,' was Fanny's humble answer, given with the feelings almost of a criminal towards Mrs Norris; and not bearing to remain with her in what might seem a state of triumph, she followed her uncle out of the room, having staid behind him only long enough to hear these words spoken in angry agitation –

'Quite unnecessary! a great deal too kind! But Edmund goes; true, it is upon Edmund's account. I observed he was hoarse on Thursday night.'

But this could not impose on Fanny. She felt that the carriage was for herself, and herself alone: and her uncle's consideration of her, coming immediately after such representations from her aunt, cost her some tears of gratitude when she was alone.

Fanny Price keeps quiet about Mrs Norris's dreadful bullying, and at least Sir Thomas tries to treat her kindly, but your character may be much more at the Elizabeth

Bennet end of the spectrum. Have a look at the wonderful scene in *Pride and Prejudice* (Chapter 56) in which Lady Catherine arrives out of the blue aiming to bully Elizabeth into promising not to marry her nephew, Mr Darcy. Lady Catherine is rude to Elizabeth's mother and rude about their house. She ensures that she gets Elizabeth by herself by asking to be shown around what she calls 'a prettyish kind of a little wilderness on one side of your lawn'. It is as though the two women go out to a deserted place for a duel, a duel for which Elizabeth has had no time to prepare. We know that Lady Catherine has previously enjoyed Elizabeth's company – when she was staying with Charlotte and Mr Collins Lady Catherine even tried to make her stay longer. The situation is very different now. Lady Catherine will have heard that Jane is to marry Mr Bingley, and rumours about Elizabeth and Mr Darcy must also have reached her. They are armed with parasols and words.

> As soon as they entered the copse, Lady Catherine began in the following manner: –
> 'You can be at no loss, Miss Bennet, to understand the reason of my journey hither. Your own heart, your own conscience, must tell you why I come.'
> Elizabeth looked with unaffected astonishment.
> 'Indeed, you are mistaken, madam. I have not been at all able to account for the honour of seeing you here.'
> 'Miss Bennet,' replied her ladyship, in an angry tone, 'you ought to know that I am not to be trifled with. But, however insincere *you* may chuse to be, you shall

not find *me* so. My character has ever been celebrated for its sincerity and frankness, and in a cause of such moment as this, I shall certainly not depart from it. A report of a most alarming nature reached me two days ago. I was told that not only your sister was on the point of being most advantageously married, but that *you*, that Miss Elizabeth Bennet, would, in all likelihood, be soon afterwards united to my nephew, my own nephew, Mr Darcy. Though I *know* it must be a scandalous falsehood, though I would not injure him so much as to suppose the truth of it possible, I instantly resolved on setting off for this place, that I might make my sentiments known to you.'

'If you believed it impossible to be true,' said Elizabeth, colouring with astonishment and disdain, 'I wonder you took the trouble of coming so far. What could your ladyship propose by it?'

'At once to insist upon having such a report universally contradicted.'

'Your coming to Longbourn, to see me and my family,' said Elizabeth coolly, 'will be rather a confirmation of it; if, indeed, such a report is in existence.'

'If! Do you then pretend to be ignorant of it? Has it not been industriously circulated by yourselves? Do you not know that such a report is spread abroad?'

'I never heard that it was.'

'And can you likewise declare, that there is no *foundation* for it?'

'I do not pretend to possess equal frankness with your ladyship. *You* may ask questions which *I* shall not chuse to answer.'

'This is not to be borne. Miss Bennet, I insist on being satisfied. Has he, has my nephew, made you an offer of marriage?'

'Your ladyship has declared it to be impossible.'

'It ought to be so; it must be so, while he retains the use of his reason. But *your* arts and allurements may, in a moment of infatuation, have made him forget what he owes to himself and to all his family. You may have drawn him in.'

'If I have, I shall be the last person to confess it.'

'Miss Bennet, do you know who I am? I have not been accustomed to such language as this. I am almost the nearest relation he has in the world, and am entitled to know all his dearest concerns.'

'But you are not entitled to know *mine*; nor will such behaviour as this ever induce me to be explicit.'

'Let me be rightly understood. This match, to which you have the presumption to aspire, can never take place. No, never. Mr Darcy is engaged to *my daughter*. Now, what have you to say?'

'Only this; that if he is so, you can have no reason to suppose he will make an offer to me.'

Lady Catherine hesitated for a moment, and then replied,

'The engagement between them is of a peculiar kind. From their infancy, they have been intended for each other. It was the favourite wish of *his* mother, as well as of hers. While in their cradles, we planned the union: and now, at the moment when the wishes of both sisters would be accomplished in their marriage, to be prevented by a young woman of inferior birth, of no importance in the world, and wholly unallied to the family! Do you pay no regard to the wishes of his friends? To his tacit engagement with Miss de Bourgh? Are you lost to every feeling of propriety and delicacy? Have you not heard me say, that from his earliest hours he was destined for his cousin?'

'Yes, and I had heard it before. But what is that to me? If there is no other objection to my marrying your nephew, I shall certainly not be kept from it by knowing that his mother and aunt wished him to marry Miss de Bourgh. You both did as much as you could in planning the marriage. Its completion depended on others. If Mr Darcy is neither by honour nor inclination confined to his cousin, why is not he to make another choice? And if I am that choice, why may not I accept him?'

'Because honour, decorum, prudence, nay, interest, forbid it. Yes, Miss Bennet, interest; for do not expect to be noticed by his family or friends if you wilfully act against the inclinations of all. You will be censured, slighted, and despised, by every one connected with him. Your alliance will be a disgrace; your name will never even be mentioned by any of us.'

'These are heavy misfortunes,' replied Elizabeth. 'But the wife of Mr Darcy must have such extraordinary sources of happiness necessarily attached to her situation, that she could, upon the whole, have no cause to repine.'

'Obstinate, headstrong girl! I am ashamed of you! Is this your gratitude for my attentions to you last spring? Is nothing due to me on that score? Let us sit down. You are to understand, Miss Bennet, that I came here with the determined resolution of carrying my purpose; nor will I be dissuaded from it. I have not been used to submit to any person's whims. I have not been in the habit of brooking disappointment.'

'*That* will make your ladyship's situation at present more pitiable; but it will have no effect on *me*.'

'I will not be interrupted. Hear me in silence. My daughter and my nephew are formed for each other. They are descended, on the maternal side, from the same noble line; and on the father's, from respectable, honourable, and ancient – though untitled – families. Their fortune on both sides is splendid. They are destined for each other by the voice of every member of their respective houses; and what is to divide them? The upstart pretensions of a young woman without family, connexions, or fortune. Is this to be endured? But it must not, shall not be! If you were sensible of your own good, you would not wish to quit the sphere in which you have been brought up.'

'In marrying your nephew, I should not consider myself as quitting that sphere. He is a gentleman; I am a gentleman's daughter: so far we are equal.'

'True. You *are* a gentleman's daughter. But who was your mother? Who are your uncles and aunts? Do not imagine me ignorant of their condition.'

'Whatever my connexions may be,' said Elizabeth, 'if your nephew does not object to them, they can be nothing to *you*.'

'Tell me once for all, are you engaged to him?'

Though Elizabeth would not, for the mere purpose of obliging Lady Catherine, have answered this question, she could not but say, after a moment's deliberation, 'I am not.'

Lady Catherine seemed pleased.

'And will you promise me, never to enter into such an engagement?'

'I will make no promise of the kind.'

Lady Catherine has decided that the confrontation will take place and then arranges for them to go alone into the 'wilderness'. Her carriage and 'waiting-woman' remain at the door, as though for a quick getaway. During the conversation Elizabeth remains polite – she would lose face and moral advantage if she were deliberately rude – although her mettle is really tested, but she is able to parry all of Lady Catherine's blows and also land many real stingers of her own, pointing out the ridiculousness of what her adversary is trying to do.

There is so much to take from this scene; apart, of course, from sheer enjoyment:

1. *The words themselves.* Sparkling, complex dialogue like this takes lots of polish to get right.

2. *The differences in the way the characters speak and the length of their speeches.* Lady Catherine does not know when to stop, and her invective and bullying appeals often run on for paragraphs; Elizabeth's replies tend to be much shorter. Lady Catherine reveals herself as lonely and pompous.

Although she is really upset by what Lady Catherine says, even though it is so obviously unjust and odious, Elizabeth shows that she is a match for anyone.

3. *The pauses in the conversation.* Readers as well as characters sometimes need to take stock or catch their breath to appreciate changes that have taken place or the impact of what has been said.

4. *The stage directions we get.* These are scant during this heated conversation. We are told that they are walking around the little wood. (There would have been paths; they aren't stumbling through the undergrowth.) Lady Catherine says that they should sit down, but later it is Elizabeth who stands up and says that she wants to return to the house. There is power play in these movements too. Sometimes in conversations you need to supplement the speech with a lot of gestures or actions as your characters are not saying what they think, but here words are not spared (by Lady Catherine, anyway), and what is said communicates almost everything. In contrast, there is a scene in Chapter 34 of *Mansfield Park* in which Henry Crawford is being really quite nice, and Fanny's actions, rather than her words, speak for her. She stops what she is doing and allows herself to listen to him reading and (almost) be charmed.

The reader will feel as out of breath as Elizabeth after this encounter. Jane Austen ends the scene and chapter swiftly with Lady Catherine's carriage driving away and Elizabeth avoiding explaining anything to her mother. After such a scene of high drama you need to give the reader a moment to catch their breath and think about what has occurred. The next chapter begins with Elizabeth considering the implications of Lady Catherine's visit. She is then called to talk to her father, who has received a letter from Mr Collins. This letter concerns Jane's engagement to Mr Bingley and also warns Elizabeth against marrying Mr Darcy as this would go against Lady Catherine's wishes. Mr Bennet wants Lizzy to laugh with him at the ridiculousness of the suggestion that she and Mr Darcy might marry. They are very used to laughing together at the follies of others, but poor Elizabeth is plunged into further confusion and doubt. The chapter ends thus:

'Oh!' cried Elizabeth, 'I am excessively diverted. But it is so strange!'

'Yes; *that* is what makes it amusing. Had they fixed on any other man it would have been nothing; but *his* perfect indifference, and *your* pointed dislike, make it so delightfully absurd! Much as I abominate writing, I would not give up Mr Collins's correspondence for any consideration. Nay, when I read a letter of his, I cannot help giving him the preference even over Wickham, much as I value the impudence and hypocrisy of my son-in-law. And pray, Lizzy, what said Lady Catherine about this report? Did she call to refuse her consent?'

To this question his daughter replied only with a laugh; and as it had been asked without the least suspicion, she was not distressed by his repeating it. Elizabeth had never been more at a loss to make her feelings appear what they were not. It was necessary to laugh, when she would rather have cried. Her father had most cruelly mortified her, by what he said of Mr Darcy's indifference, and she could do nothing but wonder at such a want of penetration, or fear that perhaps, instead of his seeing too *little*, she might have fancied too *much*.

Note the way that Jane Austen shifts the mood between scenes and chapters. You may find it helpful to think of the different moods in terms of colours and imagine your pages coloured as you work. How will the mood contrasts work? Do you have enough contrasts? Once you have a draft, try drawing lines in the margins with different coloured pens to indicate different moods. Do this for your whole draft using one colour for each character so that you can see if somebody is dominating in a way you didn't intend or disappearing for so long that the reader will forget who they are. You should also use different colours for particular types of writing – dialogue, exposition, passages of description, places where you are dwelling in a character's thoughts (quite possibly for too long) and so on.

The words spoken by Jane Austen's female characters are so revealing because she was writing at a time when the way women were able to act was heavily circumscribed. Women's words therefore often had to speak louder than their actions. Of course some women – those richer, more powerful and more confident than the majority – were relatively free to do what they wanted.

Emma's rudeness to Miss Bates at the Box Hill picnic shows how she has fallen under Frank Churchill's malign influence. In *Mansfield Park*, if Edmund Bertram had paid proper attention to what the beguiling Mary Crawford said, he wouldn't have fallen so under her spell. Fanny Price would never have made risqué jokes or spoken disparagingly of the Church. It takes Edmund the whole of the novel to realize that Fanny and not Mary is right for him, although in Chapter 6 he is shocked by Mary Crawford's joke.

'Miss Price has a brother at sea,' said Edmund [. . .]
    'At sea, has she? In the king's service, of course?'
    Fanny would rather have had Edmund tell the story, but his determined silence obliged her to relate her brother's situation: her voice was animated in speaking of his profession, and the foreign stations he had been on; but she could not mention the number of years that he had been absent without tears in her eyes. Miss Crawford civilly wished him an early promotion.
    'Do you know anything of my cousin's captain?' said Edmund; 'Captain Marshall? You have a large acquaintance in the navy, I conclude?'
    'Among admirals, large enough; but,' with an air of grandeur, 'we know very little of the inferior ranks. Post-captains may be very good sort of men, but they do not belong to *us*. Of various admirals I could tell you a great deal: of them and their flags, and the gradation of their pay, and their bickerings and jealousies. But, in general, I can assure you that they are all passed over, and all very ill used. Certainly, my home at my uncle's brought me acquainted with a circle of admirals. Of *Rears* and *Vices* I saw enough. Now do not be suspecting me of a pun, I entreat.'

Edmund again felt grave, and only replied, 'It is a noble profession.'

'Yes, the profession is well enough under two circumstances: if it make the fortune, and there be discretion in spending it; but, in short, it is not a favourite profession of mine. It has never worn an amiable form to *me*.'

It isn't just *what* your characters say that's important; it's how *much* or how *little* they say. In contrast to the fine-talking Frank Churchill, who has chattered and flirted his way around Highbury, Mr Knightley finds it hard to express the depth of his love for Emma (Chapter 49).

'I cannot make speeches, Emma,' – he soon resumed; and in a tone of such sincere, decided, intelligible tenderness as was tolerably convincing. – 'If I loved you less, I might be able to talk about it more. But you know what I am. – You hear nothing but truth from me. – I have blamed you, and lectured you, and you have borne it as no other woman in England would have borne it. – Bear with the truths I would tell you now, dearest Emma, as well as you have borne with them. The manner, perhaps, may have as little to recommend them. God knows, I have been a very indifferent lover. – But you understand me. – Yes, you see, you understand my feelings – and will return them if you can. At present, I ask only to hear, once to hear your voice.'

In *Sense and Sensibility* Marianne Dashwood finds Willoughby effortless to talk to, and he seems to share all her enthusiasms and opinions. It's easy for her to get carried away, something that Elinor soon points out in Chapter 10:

'Well, Marianne,' said Elinor, as soon as he had left them, 'for *one* morning I think you have done pretty well. You have already ascertained Mr Willoughby's opinion in almost every matter of importance. You know what he thinks of Cowper and Scott; you are certain of his estimating their beauties as he ought, and you have received every assurance of his admiring Pope no more than is proper. But how is your acquaintance to be long supported, under such extraordinary despatch of every subject for discourse? You will soon have exhausted each favourite topic. Another meeting will suffice to explain his sentiments on picturesque beauty, and second marriages, and then you can have nothing farther to ask.'

In *Pride and Prejudice*, if Elizabeth Bennet had stopped to think, she would have realized that Wickham was saying too much. Only with hindsight does she see that Wickham being so keen to dish the (fictitious) dirt on Mr Darcy should have rung alarm bells. Here they are at Elizabeth's aunt's in Chapter 16. Wickham immediately begins to ingratiate himself and to gauge what is known locally of Mr Darcy and himself. Elizabeth often feels that she shouldn't ask more, that to do so would be indelicate, but whenever their conversation about Mr Darcy draws to a close, Wickham starts it up again. Elizabeth is hooked.

Mr Wickham was the happy man towards whom almost every female eye was turned, and Elizabeth was the happy woman by whom he finally seated himself; and the agreeable manner in which he immediately fell into conversation, though it was only on its being a wet night, and on the probability of a rainy season, made her feel that the commonest, dullest, most threadbare topic might be rendered interesting by the skill of the speaker.

With such rivals for the notice of the fair as Mr Wickham and the officers, Mr Collins seemed likely to sink into insignificance; to the young ladies he certainly was nothing; but he had still at intervals a kind listener in Mrs Philips, and was, by her watchfulness, most abundantly supplied with coffee and muffin.

When the card-tables were placed, he had an opportunity of obliging her in return, by sitting down to whist.

'I know little of the game at present,' said he, 'but I shall be glad to improve myself, for in my situation of life—' Mrs Philips was very thankful for his compliance, but could not wait for his reason.

Mr Wickham did not play at whist, and with ready delight was he received at the other table between Elizabeth and Lydia. At first there seemed danger of Lydia's engrossing him entirely, for she was a most determined talker; but being likewise extremely fond of lottery tickets, she soon grew too much interested in the game, too eager in making bets and exclaiming after prizes, to have attention for any one in particular. Allowing for the common demands of the game, Mr Wickham was therefore at leisure to talk to Elizabeth, and she was very willing to hear him, though what she chiefly wished to hear she could not hope to be told, the history of his acquaintance with Mr Darcy. She dared not even mention that gentleman. Her curiosity however was unexpectedly relieved. Mr Wickham began the subject himself. He inquired how far Netherfield was from Meryton; and after receiving her answer, asked in an hesitating manner how long Mr Darcy had been staying there.

'About a month,' said Elizabeth; and then, unwilling to let the subject drop, added, 'He is a man of very large property in Derbyshire, I understand.'

'Yes,' replied Wickham; – 'his estate there is a noble one. A clear ten thousand per annum. You could not have met with a person more capable of giving you certain information on that head than myself – for I have been connected with his family in a particular manner from my infancy.'

Elizabeth could not but look surprized.

'You may well be surprized, Miss Bennet, at such an assertion, after seeing, as you probably might, the very cold manner of our meeting yesterday. – Are you much acquainted with Mr Darcy?'

'As much as I ever wish to be,' cried Elizabeth warmly. – 'I have spent four days in the same house with him, and I think him very disagreeable.'

'I have no right to give *my* opinion,' said Wickham, 'as to his being agreeable or otherwise. I am not qualified to form one. I have known him too long and too well to be a fair judge. It is impossible for *me* to be impartial. But I believe your opinion of him would in general astonish – and perhaps you would not express it quite so strongly anywhere else. – Here you are in your own family.'

'Upon my word I say no more *here* than I might say in any house in the neighbourhood, except Netherfield. He is not at all liked in Hertfordshire. Every body is disgusted with his pride. You will not find him more favourably spoken of by any one.'

'I cannot pretend to be sorry,' said Wickham, after a short interruption, 'that he or that any man should not be estimated beyond their deserts; but with *him* I believe it does not often happen. The world is blinded by his fortune and consequence, or frightened by his high and imposing manners, and sees him only as he chuses to be seen.'

'I should take him, even on *my* slight acquaintance, to be an ill-tempered man.' Wickham only shook his head.

'I wonder,' said he, at the next opportunity of speaking, 'whether he is likely to be in this country much longer.'

'I do not at all know; but I heard nothing of his going away when I was at Netherfield. I hope your plans in favour of the ——shire will not be affected by his being in the neighbourhood.'

'Oh! no – it is not for *me* to be driven away by Mr Darcy. If *he* wishes to avoid seeing *me*, he must go. We are not on friendly terms, and it always gives me pain to meet him, but I have no reason for avoiding *him* but what I might proclaim to all the world; a sense of very great ill-usage, and most painful regrets at his being what he is. His father, Miss Bennet, the late Mr Darcy, was one of the best men that ever breathed, and the truest friend I ever had; and I can never be in company with this Mr Darcy without being grieved to the soul by a thousand tender recollections. His behaviour to myself has been scandalous; but I verily believe I could forgive him any thing and every thing, rather than his disappointing the hopes and disgracing the memory of his father.'

Elizabeth found the interest of the subject increase, and listened with all her heart; but the delicacy of it prevented further inquiry.

Mr Wickham began to speak on more general topics, Meryton, the neighbourhood, the society, appearing highly pleased with all that he had yet seen, and speaking of the latter especially, with gentle but very intelligible gallantry.

'It was the prospect of constant society, and good society,' he added, 'which was my chief inducement to enter the ——shire. I knew it to be a most respectable, agreeable corps, and my friend Denny tempted me farther by his account of their present quarters, and the very great attentions and excellent acquaintance Meryton had procured them. Society, I own, is necessary to me. I have been a disappointed man, and my spirits will not bear solitude. I *must* have employment and society. A military life is not what I was intended for, but circumstances have now made it eligible. The church *ought* to have been my profession – I was brought up for the church, and I should at this time have been in possession of a most valuable living, had it pleased the gentleman we were speaking of just now.'

'Indeed!'

'Yes – the late Mr Darcy bequeathed me the next presentation of the best living in his gift. He was my godfather, and excessively attached to me. I cannot do justice to his kindness. He meant to provide for me amply, and thought he had done it; but when the living fell, it was given elsewhere.'

'Good heavens!' cried Elizabeth; 'but how could *that* be? – How could his will be disregarded? – Why did not you seek legal redress?'

'There was just such an informality in the terms of the bequest as to give me no hope from law. A man of honour could not have doubted the intention, but Mr Darcy chose to doubt it – or to treat it as a merely conditional recommendation, and to assert that I had forfeited all claim to it by extravagance, imprudence, in short, any thing or nothing. Certain it is, that the living became vacant two years ago, exactly as I was of an age to hold it, and that it was given to another man; and no less certain is it, that I cannot accuse myself of having really done any thing to deserve to lose it. I have a warm, unguarded temper, and I may perhaps have sometimes spoken my opinion *of* him, and *to* him, too freely. I can recall nothing worse. But the fact is, that we are very different sorts of men, and that he hates me.'

'This is quite shocking! – He deserves to be publicly disgraced.'

'Some time or other he *will* be – but it shall not be by *me*. Till I can forget his father, I can never defy or expose *him*.'

Elizabeth honoured him for such feelings, and thought him handsomer than ever as he expressed them. [...]

'What sort of a girl is Miss Darcy?' [Elizabeth goes on to ask]

He shook his head. – 'I wish I could call her amiable. It gives me pain to speak ill of a Darcy. But she is too much like her brother – very, very proud. – As a child, she was affectionate and pleasing, and extremely fond of me; and I have devoted hours and hours to her amusement. But she is nothing to me now. She is a handsome girl, about fifteen or sixteen, and, I understand, highly accomplished. Since her father's death, her home has been London, where a lady lives with her, and superintends her education.'

This scene is so skilfully done that a lucky reader new to the novel will follow Elizabeth's point of view and very likely believe the tall tales of Mr Darcy's dastardliness. The way Wickham talks about Georgiana Darcy, whom he has just tried to seduce through what we would now call grooming and abduction, is particularly odious.

In *Sense and Sensibility* we see the same sort of manipulative confiding practised by Lucy Steele on Elinor Dashwood. Sensing that she is a threat to her hold over Edward Ferrars, Lucy tells Elinor – whom she hardly knows – about their secret engagement.

DIALOGUE, ACTION AND MISUNDERSTANDINGS

One of the key skills in writing dialogue is conveying what is understood and misinterpreted. *Emma*, with its riddles and mistakes, is Jane Austen's masterclass in this area. In Chapter 9 we learn that Harriet Smith is 'collecting and transcribing all the riddles of every sort that she could meet with, into a thin quarto of hot-pressed paper, made up by her friend, and ornamented with cyphers and trophies. In this age of literature, such collections on a very grand scale are not uncommon. Miss Nash, head-teacher at Mrs. Goddard's, had written out at least three hundred; and Harriet, who had taken the first hint of it from her, hoped, with Miss Woodhouse's help, to get a great many more.'[1]

Emma can solve the riddle that Mr Elton leaves them ('Courtship') but thinks that it is meant for Harriet and not for her. The scene where the characters look at the painting Emma has done of Harriet is excellent as a study of how to structure a scene and show the different ways that people interpret things. People very rarely do nothing when they are talking; even if it is just examining their fingernails or looking over the shoulder of the person they are meant to be listening to, they almost always do something. In one of my favourite Raymond Carver short stories, 'Boxes', the narrator is on the phone, having a difficult conversation with his mother, but all the while he is looking out of a window, watching a man up a ladder fixing telephone wires.

Think about what your characters do in each scene and how that affects their dialogue. It often helps a scene to give them some time-limited activity – anything from making an omelette to watching a football match. Jane Austen used all sorts of things to structure her scenes – dances, card games, walks, meals, carriage rides, trips to the theatre. The action and dialogue work together. In the eighteenth and nineteenth century social visits followed a strict etiquette, so her readers would have known that if a particular person came to call, they would stay for a certain amount of time.

Look at the way the characters misunderstand each other and also betray their true selves and feelings in this passage from *Emma*, Chapter 6. Emma shows Mr Elton some of the portraits she has already 'taken', ending with the one of her sister's husband, John Knightley. She explains that she had vowed to give up painting portraits as her sister was so dismissive of her efforts . . . 'But for Harriet's sake, or rather for my own, and as there are no husbands and wives in the case at present, I will break my resolution now.'

Mr Elton seizes on what she has said and takes it as encouragement repeating,

'No husbands and wives in the case *at present* indeed, as you observe. Exactly so. No husbands and wives,' with so interesting a consciousness, that Emma began to consider whether she had not better leave them together at once. But as she wanted to be drawing, the declaration must wait a little longer.

She had soon fixed on the size and sort of portrait. It was to be a whole-length in water-colours, like Mr John Knightley's, and was destined, if she could please herself, to hold a very honourable station over the mantlepiece.

The sitting began; and Harriet, smiling and blushing, and afraid of not keeping her attitude and counte-nance, presented a very sweet mixture of youthful expression to the steady eyes of the artist. But there was no doing any thing, with Mr Elton fidgetting behind her and watching every touch. She gave him credit for stationing himself where he might gaze and gaze again without offence; but was really obliged to put an end to it, and request him to place himself elsewhere. It then occurred to her to employ him in reading.

'If he would be so good as to read to them, it would be a kindness indeed! It would amuse away the difficulties of her part, and lessen the irksomeness of Miss Smith's.'

Mr Elton was only too happy. Harriet listened, and Emma drew in peace. She must allow him to be still frequently coming to look; any thing less would certainly have been too little in a lover; and he was ready at the smallest intermission of the pencil, to jump up and see the progress, and be charmed. – There was no being displeased with such an encourager, for his admiration made him discern a likeness almost before it was possible. She could not respect his eye, but his love and his complaisance were unexceptionable.

The sitting was altogether very satisfactory; she was quite enough pleased with the first day's sketch to wish to go on. There was no want of likeness, she had been fortunate in the attitude, and as she meant to throw in a little improvement to the figure, to give a little more height, and considerably more elegance, she had great confidence of its being in every way a pretty drawing at last, and of its filling its destined place with credit to them both – a standing memorial of the beauty of one, the skill of the other, and the friendship of both; with as many other agreeable associations as Mr Elton's very promising attachment was likely to add.

Harriet was to sit again the next day; and Mr Elton, just as he ought, entreated for the permission of attending and reading to them again.

'By all means. We shall be most happy to consider you as one of the party.'

The same civilities and courtesies, the same success and satisfaction, took place on the morrow, and accompanied the whole progress of the picture, which was rapid and happy. Every body who saw it was pleased, but Mr Elton was in continual raptures, and defended it through every criticism.

'Miss Woodhouse has given her friend the only beauty she wanted,' – observed Mrs Weston to him – not in the least suspecting that she was addressing a lover. – 'The expression of the eye is most correct, but Miss Smith has not those eyebrows and eyelashes. It is the fault of her face that she has them not.'

'Do you think so?' replied he. 'I cannot agree with you. It appears to me a most perfect resemblance in every feature. I never saw such a likeness in my life. We must allow for the effect of shade, you know.'

'You have made her too tall, Emma,' said Mr Knightley.

Emma knew that she had, but would not own it, and Mr Elton warmly added,

'Oh, no! certainly not too tall; not in the least too tall. Consider, she is sitting down – which naturally presents a different – which in short gives exactly the idea – and the proportions must be preserved, you know. Proportions, fore-shortening. – Oh, no! it gives one exactly the idea of such a height as Miss Smith's. Exactly so indeed!'

'It is very pretty,' said Mr Woodhouse. 'So prettily done! Just as your drawings always are, my dear. I do not know any body who draws so well as you do. The only thing I do not thoroughly like is, that she seems to be sitting out of doors, with only a little shawl over her shoulders – and it makes one think she must catch cold.'

'But, my dear papa, it is supposed to be summer; a warm day in summer. Look at the tree.'

'But it is never safe to sit out of doors, my dear.'

'You, sir, may say any thing,' cried Mr Elton, 'but I must confess that I regard it as a most happy thought, the placing of Miss Smith out of doors; and the tree is touched with such inimitable spirit! Any other situation would have been much less in character. The naïveté of Miss Smith's manners – and altogether – Oh, it is most admirable! I cannot keep my eyes from it. I never saw such a likeness.'

The next thing wanted was to get the picture framed; and here were a few difficulties. It must be done directly; it must be done in London; the order must go through the hands of some intelligent person whose taste could be depended on; and Isabella, the usual doer of all commissions, must not be applied to, because it was December, and Mr Woodhouse could not bear the idea of her stirring out of her house in the fogs of December. But no sooner was the distress known to Mr Elton, than it was removed. His gallantry was always on the alert. 'Might he be trusted with the commission, what infinite pleasure should he have in executing it! he could ride to London at any time. It was impossible to say how much he should be gratified by being employed on such an errand.'

'He was too good! – she could not endure the thought! – she would not give him such a troublesome office for the world' – brought on the desired repetition of entreaties and assurances, – and a very few minutes settled the business.

Mr Elton was to take the drawing to London, chuse the frame, and give the directions; and Emma thought she could so pack it as to ensure its safety without much incommoding him, while he seemed mostly fearful of not being incommoded enough.

'What a precious deposit!' said he with a tender sigh, as he received it.

'This man is almost too gallant to be in love,' thought Emma. 'I should say so, but that I suppose there may be a hundred different ways of being in love. He is an excellent young man, and will suit Harriet exactly; it will be an "Exactly so," as he says himself; but he does sigh and languish, and study for compliments rather more than I could endure as a principal. I come in for a pretty good share as a second. But it is his gratitude on Harriet's account.'

Sensible, tactful Mrs Weston points out that Harriet's eyebrows and eyelashes aren't quite as Emma has painted them. Mr Elton can see only perfection in Emma's painting, perfection that Emma thinks he sees in Harriet.

Mr Knightley tells Emma that she 'has made her too tall'. It is as though he is commenting on all of Emma's doings with Harriet Smith. Mr Woodhouse is worried that the Harriet in the picture will catch cold, sitting outdoors with only a little shawl over her shoulders. Given that his wife died very young, we can understand why he worries so much about everybody, but it is Mr Elton who says the most. He cannot praise the picture highly enough and offers to take the precious portrait to London to be framed. Emma can see that Mr Elton's cloying words and behaviour are 'too gallant' but is convinced that his efforts are all for Harriet.

You are a writer, of course you have a notebook, but make sure that it is always with you so that you can jot down jokes or strange/cruel/witty things that you hear or that suddenly occur to you. Perhaps Jane heard a woman suggest to her husband that their daughter stop playing the piano because she had delighted people long enough . . .

EXERCISES USING DIALOGUE

1. *Dialogue reveals.* Sometimes a person says something that we remember because it seems so revealing or significant. Try using dialogue to move your plot forward while also showing the reader exactly what your characters are like. The characters may be speaking about something seemingly trivial or insignificant or making a joke like Mary Crawford. Write

a scene where a seemingly insignificant conversation is anything but.

2. *Bullies and manipulators.* Write a scene in which a character is bullying or manipulating somebody else. Such scenes can be key in setting things up for the future and moving your plot on. Think Lucy Steele, Wickham, Lady Catherine and Mrs Norris.

3. *Saying too much, saying very little and saying without words.* Which of your characters are voluble? Which say very little? Remember that so much of a conversation is about gestures, actions and glances. Write a scene in which you pay particular attention to how much or how little is said and how meanings are conveyed in other ways.

4. Write a scene structured around a particular activity. Jane Austen often used dances, but you could have characters on a circular walk (as happens in *Persuasion*), eating a meal, making something, watching a play, film or some sport, getting their nails done . . . The possibilities are almost endless. Think about what you want to happen in the scene and what you want to be said. How will the activity affect the conversation? For example how would a 'breaking-up' conversation at a child's birthday party differ from a breaking-up conversation taking place during a walk along a windswept beach?

Secrets and suspense

Jane Austen's recipe and method for a suspenseful novel

S ECRETS ARE KEY TO Jane Austen's fiction and to driving her narratives forward. She lived in a society where life was lived very publicly, and yet true feelings and emotions were often kept hidden. In *Love and Freindship* she spoofed the cult of sensibility – the characters have constant fits of fainting, weeping and running mad – but in her mature works Jane Austen demonstrated the power of keeping characters' feelings under wraps. Mr Darcy's first proposal to Elizabeth is a wonderful example of suppressed feelings coming to the surface. In Chapter 34 of *Pride and Prejudice* he bursts out, 'In vain have I struggled. It will not do. My feelings will not be repressed. You must allow me to tell you how ardently I admire and love you,' sentences that can now be bought on tote bags and keyrings. Until this point Mr Darcy has kept his feelings hidden because he thinks that Elizabeth's family are beneath him.

In this section we'll look at secrets and suspense in fiction, at successful plotting and the use of dramatic irony – all as important in novels and stories today as they were two hundred years ago.

At Jane Austen's House Museum you can see the family recipe book kept by Jane's friend Martha Lloyd. There are recipes for everything from white soup – as enjoyed at the Netherfield Ball – to 'curry after the Indian manner', apple snow (an apple meringue pudding that sounds delicious), ink, medicinal cures and household products. There's even a pudding recipe written in rhyme by Mrs Austen. Jane was too busy writing to contribute much to the book; Cassandra and Martha saved her from many domestic chores. Here, instead, is a recipe for a suspenseful novel.

A RECIPE FOR A SUSPENSEFUL NOVEL

Backstories

You need interesting and convincing backstories for all your characters. You'll have to decide what to reveal to the reader and to other characters and when to reveal it. This is one of the ways to create suspense. It's all in the revealing – a kind of dance of the seven veils of storytelling.

Think about the things that the reader and the characters do and don't know in the early sections of your novel, and when (if ever) these things will be found out.

In *Sense and Sensibility* Elinor and Marianne never learn exactly how they were deprived of their inheritance but still have to cope with the realities of their new life, while Willoughby's backstory is revealed relatively late. In *Pride and Prejudice* Wickham's backstory is also kept from the reader until later on.

In the opening of *Mansfield Park* the backstory of the three sisters (Lady Bertram, Mrs Norris and Mrs Price) sets up the plot. This establishes the themes of the novel and sets the whole story in motion.

Subplots

You need these for texture, to help build suspense and to ensure that the narrative is interesting enough and 'works'. Think about how you are going to cut from one strand of your story to another, and how you are going to pull all the threads together at the end. Think about how you will use point of view, tenses and chronology, and how these will have an impact on the way the reader experiences your work. Subplots will sometimes be a way of solving problems in your main plot.

Think about the characters in your subplots and how they could be the characters in the main plot. *Emma* could actually have been a novel called *Jane Fairfax*.

But why doesn't she just . . . ?

Your plot must be watertight, as readers will constantly question it. There should be no easy solutions. Make sure your characters' reasons for behaving as they do are compelling. The plot of *Sense and Sensibility* relies on Lucy Steele's calculation that Elinor will not disclose her secret. In a similar way, Wickham calculates that Mr Darcy will not reveal the truth about him because of the disgrace and distress it would bring to Georgiana.

Reflections and parallels

Think about balance in your story. You can use parallel plot lines and characters to show different things and offer the reader alternative outcomes to similar situations and dilemmas. Symmetry is pleasing. Elinor and Marianne show the reader contrasting ways of viewing things and of behaving; they are paralleled by Lucy and Anne Steele. When Willoughby becomes engaged, Elinor appreciates the consequences of this for the jilted party (Marianne). Elinor wouldn't want to be the wrecker of another woman's happiness, not even the dreadful Lucy's. Edward Ferrars and his siblings, the avaricious Fanny and self-centred Robert, are also contrasted. Their attitudes to money and possessions drive the plot, and we see each character's worth. Again and again Jane Austen gives us parallel stories and characters to compare and contrast. Think about the texture of your fiction and how using parallels and reflections might enrich it.

A METHOD

Keep your characters longing, waiting, struggling . . .

Whether you are writing a siege narrative or a quest narrative,[1] you must keep cranking up the tension. Plots are driven by longing and desire. Think about what it is that your characters need and how this is made clear to the reader. Think about how needs and desires can be made more pressing as the story progresses. You may have to make cuts to make your work compelling enough. Check that each scene has a real function. Ask yourself what it will reveal about the characters and how it will develop the plot.

Jane Austen's heroines are very often found waiting for news or for the arrival of other characters, particularly men. Limitations on the freedom of women were integral to Jane Austen's plots. In *Sense and Sensibility* Marianne waits and waits for Willoughby to reply to her letters, while Elinor must endure to the end of the story before Edward is free to declare his love for her. In *Persuasion* Anne Elliot must wait to find out how Captain Wentworth feels about her and to tell him how she feels. Even after their meeting at Pemberley Mr Darcy and Lizzy have to wait to see how each other's feelings have changed; just when they seem about to get together, Lydia and Wickham's elopement derails everything. Male characters have to wait too – in *Sense and Sensibility* Colonel Brandon has to wait for Marianne to love him – but Jane Austen's main focus is on her heroines' experiences and feelings.

Too much waiting and longing can, however, become boring. Make sure that you have plenty of action, humour and constant developments to keep things moving. If the story seems to be stuck or dragging, add some sort of ticking-bomb device. In Jane's most siege-like of narratives, Captain Wentworth and Anne Elliot might marry the wrong people (Louisa Musgrove and William Elliot) if their misunderstandings continue. Something is needed to break a siege, and this something can come from the actions of one of your minor characters or from a development in one of your subplots.

Your heroines and heroes should make mistakes

To be appealing and convincing, your heroes and heroines must not be perfect; they should get things wrong from time to time. You must decide when the reader will realize that this has happened. All of Jane Austen's heroines make mistakes, even wise, reserved Elinor Dashwood. She is happy to believe that Edward has a ring containing a lock of her hair, even though she has never given him any. This is from Chapter 18 of *Sense and Sensibility*.

> Marianne remained thoughtfully silent, till a new object suddenly engaged her attention. She was sitting by Edward, and in taking his tea from Mrs Dashwood, his hand passed so directly before her, as to make a ring, with a plait of hair in the centre, very conspicuous on one of his fingers.
>
> 'I never saw you wear a ring before, Edward,' she cried. 'Is that Fanny's hair? I remember her promising to give you some. But I should have thought her hair had been darker.'
>
> Marianne spoke inconsiderately what she really felt – but when she saw how much she had pained Edward, her own vexation at her want of thought could not be surpassed by his. He coloured very deeply, and giving a momentary glance at Elinor, replied, 'Yes; it is my

sister's hair. The setting always casts a different shade on it, you know.'

Elinor had met his eye, and looked conscious likewise. That the hair was her own, she instantaneously felt as well satisfied as Marianne; the only difference in their conclusions was, that what Marianne considered as a free gift from her sister, Elinor was conscious must have been procured by some theft or contrivance unknown to herself. She was not in a humour, however, to regard it as an affront, and affecting to take no notice of what passed, by instantly talking of something else, she internally resolved henceforward to catch every opportunity of eyeing the hair, and satisfying herself, beyond all doubt, that it was exactly the shade of her own.

Elinor realizes her mistake in Chapter 22.

'Writing to each other,' said Lucy, returning the letter into her pocket, 'is the only comfort we have in such long separations. Yes, I have one other comfort in his picture; but poor Edward has not even *that*. If he had but my picture, he says he should be easy. I gave him a lock of my hair set in a ring when he was at Longstaple last, and that was some comfort to him, he said, but not equal to a picture. Perhaps you might notice the ring when you saw him?'

'I did,' said Elinor, with a composure of voice, under which was concealed an emotion and distress beyond anything she had ever felt before. She was mortified, shocked, confounded.

Secrets, irony, drama and revelations

Limiting what characters know and creating layers of irony helps to build towards dramatic scenes when things are revealed. Because Elinor is so restrained, the moments when she does reveal or discover things are particularly potent and moving. When she has the sorry task of telling Marianne that Edward and Lucy's engagement has been discovered and that they are to marry, she is provoked into finally expressing her feelings.

'For four months, Marianne, I have had all this hanging on my mind, without being at liberty to speak of it to a single creature; knowing that it would make you and my mother most unhappy whenever it were explained to you, yet unable to prepare you for it in the least. – It was told me, – it was in a manner forced on me by the very person herself, whose prior engagement ruined all my prospects; and told me, as I thought, with triumph. – This person's suspicions, therefore, I have had to oppose, by endeavouring to appear indifferent where I have been most deeply interested; – and it has not been only once; – I have had her hopes and exultation to listen to again and again. – I have known myself to be divided from Edward forever, without hearing one circumstance that could make me less desire the connection. – Nothing has proved him unworthy; nor has anything declared him indifferent to me. – I have had to contend against the unkindness of his sister, and the insolence of his mother; and have suffered the punishment of an attachment, without enjoying its advantages. – And all this has been going on at a time when, as you too well know, it has not been my only unhappiness. – If you can think me capable of ever feeling – surely you may suppose that I have suffered *now*. The composure of mind with which I have brought myself at present to consider the matter, the consolation that I have been willing to admit, have been the effect of constant and painful exertion; – they did not spring up of themselves; – they did not occur to relieve my spirits at first. – No, Marianne. *Then*, if I had not been bound to silence, perhaps nothing could have kept me entirely – not even what I owed to my dearest friends – from openly shewing that I was *very* unhappy.'

Marianne was quite subdued. –

'Oh! Elinor,' she cried, 'you have made me hate myself forever. How barbarous have I been to you! – you, who have been my only comfort, who have borne with me in all my misery, who have seemed to be only suffering for me! – Is this my gratitude! – Is this the only return I can make you? Because your merit cries out upon myself, I have been trying to do it away.'

The tenderest caresses followed this confession.

It is so typical of the unreformed Marianne that hearing of Elinor's unhappiness makes her speak more about herself. This isn't about you, Marianne! And then the irony when John Dashwood bemoans Edward's unlucky fate – being disinherited and seeing all that should be his being given to a sibling . . .

'It is a melancholy consideration. Born to the prospect of such affluence! I cannot conceive a situation more deplorable. The interest of two thousand pounds – how can a man live on it? [...]

'Can anything be more galling to the spirit of a man,' continued John, 'than to see his younger brother in possession of an estate which might have been his own? Poor Edward! I feel for him sincerely.'[2]

When it looks as though things can't get any worse, they should

Ensure that even when your hero or heroine seems to have hit rock bottom, there is still further to fall. In *Sense and Sensibility*, even when the worst has happened – Edward and Lucy's engagement is public; Edward has been disinherited in favour of his brother and is *still* too honourable to jilt Lucy – things get even worse. Colonel Brandon, acting out of kindness and thinking that he is helping a friend of Elinor's, offers Edward a living so that he and Lucy can get married. Poor Elinor has to carry news of the offer to Edward and knows that when he accepts, he and Lucy will be living very close to Barton Cottage. She will be tortured for the rest of her life.

And finally you'll need an ending

Sense and Sensibility works like a Shakespearean comedy in that everything must be untangled. Think about how loose threads are dealt with in your novel. You may want to get everybody back onstage for the penultimate or final scene.

Close to the end of *Sense and Sensibility* we discover the truth about Willoughby's feelings, why he acted as he did and what his future holds. In *Pride and Prejudice* we learn that Wickham will never be received at Pemberley; Jane and Mr Bingley will move to be nearer the Darcys, and we are shown the futures of all the other important characters. Here are parts of the final chapter.

Mr Bennet missed his second daughter exceedingly; his affection for her drew him oftener from home than any thing else could do. He delighted in going to Pemberley, especially when he was least expected. [...]

Kitty, to her very material advantage, spent the chief of her time with her two elder sisters. In society so superior to what she had generally known, her improvement was great. She was not of so ungovernable a temper as Lydia; and, removed from the influence of Lydia's example, she became, by proper attention and management, less irritable, less ignorant, and less insipid. [...]

Mary was the only daughter who remained at home; and she was necessarily drawn from the pursuit of accomplishments by Mrs Bennet's being quite unable to sit alone. Mary was obliged to mix more with the world, but she could still moralize over every morning visit; and as she was no longer mortified by comparisons between her sisters' beauty and her own, it was suspected by her father that she submitted to the change without much reluctance. [...]

Miss Bingley was very deeply mortified by Darcy's marriage; but as she thought it advisable to retain the right of visiting at Pemberley, she dropt all her resentment; was fonder than ever of Georgiana, almost as attentive to Darcy as heretofore, and paid off every arrear of civility to Elizabeth.

Pemberley was now Georgiana's home; and the attachment of the sisters was exactly what Darcy had hoped to see. [...]

Lady Catherine was extremely indignant on the marriage of her nephew; and as she gave way to all the genuine frankness of her character in her reply to the letter which announced its arrangement, she sent him language so very abusive, especially of Elizabeth, that for some time all intercourse was at an end. But at length, by Elizabeth's persuasion, he was prevailed on to overlook the offence, and seek a reconciliation; and, after a little further resistance on the part of his aunt, her resentment gave way, either to her affection for him, or her curiosity to see how his wife conducted herself; and she condescended to wait on them at Pemberley, in spite of that pollution which its woods had received, not merely from the presence of such a mistress, but the visits of her uncle and aunt from the city.

With the Gardiners, they were always on the most intimate terms. Darcy, as well as Elizabeth, really loved them; and they were both ever sensible of the warmest gratitude towards the persons who, by bringing her into Derbyshire, had been the means of uniting them.

THE END

This is from the final chapter of *Sense and Sensibility*.

Colonel Brandon was now as happy, as all those who best loved him, believed he deserved to be; – in Marianne he was consoled for every past affliction; – her regard and her society restored his mind to animation, and his spirits to cheerfulness; and that Marianne found her own happiness in forming his, was equally the persuasion and delight of each observing friend. Marianne could never love by halves; and her whole heart became, in time, as much devoted to her husband, as it had once been to Willoughby.

Willoughby could not hear of her marriage without a pang; and his punishment was soon afterwards complete in the voluntary forgiveness of Mrs Smith, who, by stating his marriage with a woman of character, as the source of her clemency, gave him reason for believing, that had he behaved with honour towards Marianne, he might at once have been happy and rich. That his repentance of misconduct, which thus brought its own punishment, was sincere, need not be doubted; – nor that he long thought of Colonel Brandon with envy, and of Marianne with regret. But that he was forever inconsolable – that he fled from society, or contracted an habitual gloom of temper, or died of a broken heart, must not be depended on – for he did neither. He lived to exert, and frequently to enjoy himself. His wife was not always out of humour, nor his home always uncomfortable; and in his breed of horses and dogs, and in sporting of every kind, he found no inconsiderable degree of domestic felicity.

For Marianne, however – in spite of his incivility in surviving her loss – he always retained that decided regard which interested him in everything that befell her, and made her his secret standard of perfection in woman;

– and many a rising beauty would be slighted by him in after-days as bearing no comparison with Mrs Brandon.

Mrs Dashwood was prudent enough to remain at the cottage, without attempting a removal to Delaford; and fortunately for Sir John and Mrs Jennings, when Marianne was taken from them, Margaret had reached an age highly suitable for dancing, and not very ineligible for being supposed to have a lover.

Between Barton and Delaford, there was that constant communication which strong family affection would naturally dictate; and among the merits and the happiness of Elinor and Marianne, let it not be ranked as the least considerable, that though sisters, and living almost within sight of each other, they could live without disagreement between themselves, or producing coolness between their husbands.

THE END

The sentence 'Marianne could never love by halves; and her whole heart became, *in time*,[3] as much devoted to her husband, as it had once been to Willoughby' is particularly interesting. The 'in time' implies volumes. Is it a disappointment that Marianne ends up with kind, devoted, rich, adoring Colonel Brandon? Has Marianne lost something by marrying him? Having a husband twenty years one's senior wasn't unusual at that time, as so many women (and first wives) died in childbirth. Marianne, like Louisa Musgrove, has emerged more sober and serious from her illness, but the ending is nuanced and leaves the reader with some interesting things to ponder.

In Jane Austen's pocket

Techniques and devices of the great author

IRONY

Irony underpins Jane Austen's work. There is irony in the tone of the narration, verbal irony, irony in the characters' situations and dramatic irony. Her use of irony builds a relationship between the author and the reader and between the reader and the characters. Jane Austen credits her readers with the intelligence to comprehend what is going on, to get the jokes and understand her characters' feelings and predicaments without things being spelled out. It makes her writing deceptively light, but the stories and the dialogue resonate. The wit, the drama and the feelings she evokes endure. This is from Chapter 14 of *Northanger Abbey*. Catherine Morland is out for a walk with the Tilneys, who are far better educated and more articulate than she is.

> The Tilneys were soon engaged in another [topic] on which she had nothing to say. They were viewing the country with the eyes of persons accustomed to drawing, and decided on its capability of being formed into pictures, with all the eagerness of real taste. Here Catherine was quite lost. She knew nothing of drawing – nothing of taste: and she listened to them with an attention which brought her little profit, for they talked in phrases which conveyed scarcely any idea to her. The little which she could understand, however, appeared to contradict the very few notions she had entertained on the matter before. It seemed as if a good view were no longer to be taken from the top of an high hill, and that a clear blue sky was no longer a proof of a fine day. She was heartily ashamed of her ignorance. A misplaced shame. Where people wish to attach, they should always be ignorant. To come with a well-informed mind is to come with an inability of administering to the vanity of others, which a sensible person would always wish to avoid. A woman especially, if she have the misfortune of knowing anything, should conceal it as well as she can.

Catherine is only seventeen and the most ignorant of Jane Austen's heroines. Of course Jane didn't really think that it was better to be ignorant or stupid than well informed and intelligent. The irony continues right to the novel's ending. Henry Tilney may be older and better educated than Catherine – he has enjoyed telling her things and generally shaping her ideas – but it is Catherine who sees the villain in his father.

Jane Austen makes great use of irony in her accounts of relationships. There are so many examples, but just think of *Persuasion*. Anne Elliot is 'only Anne', disregarded by her father and older sister, and an unpaid nurse and babysitter to her younger sister and the little Musgroves, but it is she who interests William Elliot, she who Captain Wentworth loves and she who gets the really happy ending. The whole novel is about the feelings and actions of a woman who is left behind, taken for granted and overlooked. Here are the Elliot sisters just before Sir Walter and Elizabeth depart for Bath.

Mary, often a little unwell, and always thinking a great deal of her own complaints, and always in the habit of claiming Anne when anything was the matter, was indisposed[1]; and foreseeing that she should not have a day's health all the autumn, entreated, or rather required her, for it was hardly entreaty, to come to Uppercross Cottage, and bear her company as long as she should want her, instead of going to Bath.

'I cannot possibly do without Anne,' was Mary's reasoning; and Elizabeth's reply was, 'Then I am sure Anne had better stay, for nobody will want her in Bath.'

And here is another wonderful example – from *Sense and Sensibility*, Chapter 39. Colonel Brandon has heard that Edward Ferrars has been cast off by his family because of his engagement to Lucy and wants to offer him the living of Delaford. Colonel Brandon has been impressed by Edward and wants to do something to help Elinor's friend. Not only that, he wants Elinor to be the one to tell Edward the good news. With the living, Edward will be able to marry Lucy and offer her a home. Poor Elinor can only do as she is asked, offer her thanks to Colonel Brandon and tell Edward the good news.

'I have heard,' said he [Colonel Brandon], with great compassion, 'of the injustice your friend Mr Ferrars has suffered from his family; for if I understand the matter right, he has been entirely cast off by them for persevering in his engagement with a very deserving young woman. – Have I been rightly informed? – Is it so? –'
Elinor told him that it was.
'The cruelty, the impolitic cruelty,' – he replied, with great feeling, – 'of dividing, or attempting to divide, two young people long attached to each other, is terrible. – Mrs Ferrars does not know what she may be doing – what she may drive her son to. I have seen Mr Ferrars two or three times in Harley Street, and am much pleased with him. He is not a young man with whom one can be intimately acquainted in a short time, but I have seen enough of him to wish him well for his own sake, and as a friend of yours, I wish it still more. I understand that he intends to take orders. Will you be so good as to tell him that the living of Delaford, now just vacant, as I am

informed by this day's post, is his, if he think it worth his acceptance – but *that*, perhaps, so unfortunately circumstanced as he is now, it may be nonsense to appear to doubt; I only wish it were more valuable. – It is a rectory, but a small one; the late incumbent, I believe, did not make more than 200 pounds per annum, and though it is certainly capable of improvement, I fear, not to such an amount as to afford him a very comfortable income. Such as it is, however, my pleasure in presenting him to it, will be very great. Pray assure him of it.'

Elinor's astonishment at this commission could hardly have been greater [...] The preferment, which only two days before she had considered as hopeless for Edward, was already provided to enable him to marry; – and *she*, of all people in the world, was fixed on to bestow it!

Elinor hopes she can get away with just writing to Edward, but then he calls and she must tell him face to face; things just get more and more excruciating for her.

Skilful use of irony brings home the desperation of your characters' situations. Readers will cringe at the horror and cruelty of their predicaments.

EXERCISES

1. Using irony:
   - Write a scene in which at least one of your characters doesn't know everything that has gone on or is going on. You may find it useful to structure this around an activity, for example a game of

some sort, a circular walk, a visit somewhere. Use plenty of dialogue.

- Put one of your characters in an excruciating situation. Only the character and the reader should know how uncomfortable things really are.
- Write a scene in which somebody blunders on. Think of Mrs Bennet being rude to Mr Darcy, not knowing that he is the one who rescued Lydia.

2. Print out a copy of whatever you are working on. Look through it and ask yourself these questions:
   - Where can I be more subtle?
   - Where can I be more sly?
   - Am I happy with the tone?
   - Does it plod anywhere?
   - Am I crediting my readers with enough intelligence?
   - Can I make things more excruciating for my characters?
   - Am I giving away too much to the reader or to individual characters?
   - Can it be funnier?

Write notes in the margins and then go back through your manuscript revising accordingly. This may take some time. Be half novelist, half fox.

HANDLING TIME

If you are writing a novel for adults you have anything between 50,000 words (very short) and a few hundred thousand words (extremely long) to play with. A typical novel is around 70,000 or 80,000 words. How are you going to use all those words? And how do you decide how much time to cover? Will it be just one day? A hundred years? Five generations of a family? Time is something that writers can handle, stretch out or compact; as David Tennant's Doctor Who put it, 'People assume that time is a strict progression of cause to effect, but *actually* from a non-linear, non-subjective viewpoint it's more like a big ball of wibbly wobbly, timey wimey . . . stuff.'[2] The key thing for a writer to know is that they must exercise conscious control over time in their work. This is exactly what Jane Austen did.

This passage from *Emma* Chapter 27 is one of my favourites in all Austen's work.

Harriet had business at Ford's. – Emma thought it most prudent to go with her. Another accidental meeting with the Martins was possible, and, in her present state, would be dangerous.

Harriet, tempted by every thing and swayed by half a word, was always very long at a purchase; and while she was still hanging over muslins and changing her mind, Emma went to the door for amusement. – Much could not be hoped from the traffic of even the busiest part of Highbury; – Mr Perry walking hastily by, Mr William Cox letting himself in at the office door, Mr Cole's carriage horses returning from exercise, or a stray letter-boy on an obstinate mule, were the liveliest objects she could presume to expect; and when her eyes fell only on the butcher with his tray, a tidy old woman travelling homewards from shop with her full basket, two curs quarrelling over a dirty bone, and a string of dawdling children round the baker's little bow-window eyeing the gingerbread, she knew she had no reason to complain, and was amused enough; quite enough still to stand at the door. A mind lively and at ease, can do with seeing nothing, and can see nothing that does not answer.

She looked down the Randalls road. The scene enlarged; two persons appeared; Mrs Weston and her son-in-law; they were walking into Highbury; – to Hartfield of course. They were stopping, however, in the first place at Mrs Bates's; whose house was a little nearer Randalls than Ford's; and had all but knocked, when Emma caught their eye. – Immediately they crossed the road and came forward to her; and the agreeableness of yesterday's engagement seemed to give fresh pleasure to the present meeting. Mrs Weston informed her that she was going to call on the Bateses, in order to hear the new instrument.

I love the way we see the world through Emma's eyes and the glimpse this passage gives us into the very real and functioning village of Highbury. I love the details that Emma's (and so the reader's) eye lingers on. I always think of this passage when I'm at Jane Austen's House Museum and looking out of the window beside her writing table, even though Highbury wasn't modelled on Chawton. In Jane Austen's letters we get little details like the ones she uses here, for instance in this letter to Cassandra, written from Chawton on 23 June 1814.

Mrs Driver, &c., are off by Collier,[3] but so near being too late that she had not time to call and leave the keys herself. I have them, however. I suppose one is the key of the linen-press, but I do not know what to guess the other.

The coach was stopped at the blacksmith's, and they came running down with Triggs and Browning, and trunks, and birdcages. Quite amusing.

My mother desires her love, and hopes to hear from you.

Yours very affectionately,
J. AUSTEN

In the passage from *Emma* we are given Emma's assumption that Frank Churchill is on his way to visit her, *of course*. It doesn't occur to her that Frank wants to see Jane Fairfax and hear her play the piano he has given her. This might seem like a static passage, but it isn't. Although Emma is just standing and looking, our understanding of her and the setting is being developed, and the action speeds up with the arrival of Frank and Mrs Weston. Harriet is there in the background, and Emma is about to step in to tell her what she should choose. Any quietness in this scene is swiftly replaced with Miss Bates's chatter and Jane Fairfax's piano playing as the chapter continues.

EXERCISE: SLOW DOWN TIME

Allow your 'camera' to linger on a character in a particular scene. Write from that character's point of view so we see what they see and gain their impressions of it.

Use evocative details, but don't go on and on. Follow Jane Austen's example by ending your scene of quiet observation with movement and dialogue.

Sometimes when you slow things down because the moment is important and you want readers to appreciate it, it helps to give them a particular image to focus on. You can do this with a piece of music or a song (think of Jane Austen's characters sitting at the piano) or with another piece of literature (Henry Crawford reads aloud and Fanny is almost swayed) or with a painting, such as the one Emma does of Harriet Smith.

In *Sense and Sensibility* Chapter 22, when Lucy Steele shows Elinor the miniature she has of Edward, there can be no doubt that Lucy is telling the truth and that it is Elinor's Edward she is engaged to.

'Good heavens!' cried Elinor, 'what do you mean? Are you acquainted with Mr Robert Ferrars? Can you be?' And she did not feel much delighted with the idea of such a sister-in-law.

'No,' replied Lucy, 'not to Mr *Robert* Ferrars – I never saw him in my life; but,' fixing her eyes upon Elinor, 'to his elder brother.'

What felt Elinor at that moment? Astonishment, that would have been as painful as it was strong, had not an immediate disbelief of the assertion attended it. She turned towards Lucy in silent amazement, unable to divine the reason or object of such a declaration; and though her complexion varied, she stood firm in incredulity, and felt in no danger of an hysterical fit, or a swoon.

'You may well be surprised,' continued Lucy; 'for to be sure you could have had no idea of it before; for I dare say he never dropped the smallest hint of it to you or any of your family; because it was always meant to be a great secret, and I am sure has been faithfully kept so by me to this hour. Not a soul of all my relations know of it but Anne, and I never should have mentioned it to you, if I had not felt the greatest dependance in the world upon your secrecy; and I really thought my behaviour in asking so many questions about Mrs Ferrars must seem so odd, that it ought to be explained. And I do not think Mr Ferrars can be displeased, when he knows I have trusted you, because I know he has the highest opinion in the world of all your family, and looks upon yourself and the other Miss Dashwoods quite as his own sisters.' – She paused.

Elinor for a few moments remained silent. Her astonishment at what she heard was at first too great for words; but at length forcing herself to speak, and to speak cautiously, she said, with calmness of manner, which tolerably well concealed her surprise and solicitude – 'May I ask if your engagement is of long standing?'

'We have been engaged these four years.'

'Four years!'

'Yes.'

Elinor, though greatly shocked, still felt unable to believe it.

'I did not know,' said she, 'that you were even acquainted till the other day.'

'Our acquaintance, however, is of many years' date. He was under my uncle's care, you know, a considerable while.'

'Your uncle!'

'Yes; Mr Pratt. Did you never hear him talk of Mr Pratt?'

'I think I have,' replied Elinor, with an exertion of spirits, which increased with her increase of emotion.

'He was four years with my uncle, who lives at Longstaple, near Plymouth. It was there our acquaintance begun, for my sister and me was often staying with my uncle, and it was there our engagement was formed, though not till a year after he had quitted as a pupil; but he was almost always with us afterwards. I was very unwilling to enter into it, as you may imagine, without the knowledge and approbation of his mother; but I was too young, and loved him too well, to be so prudent as I ought to have been. – Though you do not know him so well as me, Miss Dashwood, you must have seen enough of him to be sensible he is very capable of making a woman sincerely attached to him.'

'Certainly,' answered Elinor, without knowing what she said; but after a moment's reflection, she added, with revived security of Edward's honour and love, and her companion's falsehood – 'Engaged to Mr Edward Ferrars! – I confess myself so totally surprised at what you tell me, that really – I beg your pardon; but surely there must be some mistake of person or name. We cannot mean the same Mr Ferrars.'

'We can mean no other,' cried Lucy smiling. 'Mr Edward Ferrars, the eldest son of Mrs Ferrars of Park Street, and brother of your sister-in-law, Mrs John Dashwood, is the person I mean; you must allow that *I* am not likely to be deceived as to the name of the man on who all my happiness depends.'

'It is strange,' replied Elinor, in a most painful perplexity, 'that I should never have heard him even mention your name.'

'No; considering our situation, it was not strange. Our first care has been to keep the matter secret. – You knew nothing of me, or my family, and, therefore, there could be no *occasion* for ever mentioning my name to you; and, as he was always particularly afraid of his sister's suspecting anything, *that* was reason enough for his not mentioning it.'

She was silent. – Elinor's security sunk; but her self-command did not sink with it.

'Four years you have been engaged,' said she with a firm voice.

'Yes; and heaven knows how much longer we may have to wait. Poor Edward! It puts him quite out of heart.' Then taking a small miniature from her pocket, she added, 'To prevent the possibility of mistake, be so good as to look at this face. It does not do him justice, to be sure, but yet I think you cannot be deceived as to the person it was drew for. – I have had it above these three years.'

She put it into her hands as she spoke; and when Elinor saw the painting, whatever other doubts her fear of a too hasty decision, or her wish of detecting false-hood might suffer to linger in her mind, she could have none of its being Edward's face. She returned it almost instantly, acknowledging the likeness.

In a much happier moment, in *Pride and Prejudice* Chapter 43, Elizabeth Bennet stops to gaze upon a portrait of Mr Darcy. Have a look at that scene too for inspiration. I have quoted from it on page 143.

The rendering of a piece of music or another artwork in words is known as ekphrasis.[4]

EXERCISE: EKPHRASIS

Use a work of art in your writing. This could be anything from a poster in somebody's bedroom to a concert, but it must be something that the character(s) would own or come across naturally. They don't need to like it. You can use the ekphrasis to add texture to your work, make it more visual or give it a soundtrack. By making readers consider something along with the character(s) you can slow things down and help them appreciate the signifi-cance of a moment and any change that is occurring. In the examples I've given you there isn't any lingering on brush strokes or colours, but you may want to use those sorts of details if they are things that your character(s) would notice.

A LITTLE MORE ON DIALOGUE

There will be significant conversations that you need your characters to have, and perhaps other characters to overhear. Jane Austen uses dialogue as a key method of progressing her plots. Sometimes the conversations are ones that the whole novel has been building up to – marriage proposals for example – but sometimes they will be seemingly trivial pieces of dialogue that later prove to be significant. In *Persuasion*, for example, there are discussions of whether long or short engagements are better and whether women or men's feelings endure the longest, and these prove crucial in reuniting Anne and Captain Wentworth.

Jane Austen's quiet heroines, particularly Fanny Price and Anne Elliot, are often placed in situations where others are talking and they are listening. In *Mansfield Park* and *Persuasion* Jane Austen made use of hedges so that her heroines could accidentally overhear what other people were discussing. You can employ hedges, screens in open-plan offices, baby monitors left on or any number of other devices to achieve the same thing.

In Chapter 10 of *Persuasion*, Anne Elliot overhears Captain Wentworth's thoughts on people who are too easily persuaded.

The brow of the hill, where they remained, was a cheerful spot: Louisa returned; and Mary, finding a comfortable seat for herself on the step of a stile, was very well satisfied so long as the others all stood about her; but when Louisa drew Captain Wentworth away, to try for a gleaning of nuts in an adjoining hedge-row, and they were gone by degrees quite out of sight and sound, Mary was happy no longer; she quarrelled with her own seat, was sure Louisa had got a much better somewhere, and nothing could prevent her from going to look for a better also. She turned through the same gate, but could not see them. Anne found a nice seat for her, on a dry sunny bank, under the hedge-row, in which she had no doubt of their still being, in some spot or other. Mary sat down for a moment, but it would not do; she was sure Louisa had found a better seat somewhere else, and she would go on till she over-took her.

Anne, really tired herself, was glad to sit down; and she very soon heard Captain Wentworth and Louisa in the hedge-row, behind her, as if making their way back along the rough, wild sort of channel, down the centre. They were speaking as they drew near. Louisa's voice was the first distinguished. She seemed to be in the middle of some eager speech. What Anne first heard was –

'And so, I made her go. I could not bear that she should be frightened from the visit by such nonsense. What! would I be turned back from doing a thing that I had determined to do, and that I knew to be right, by the airs and interference of such a person, or of any person I may say? No, I have no idea of being so easily persuaded. When I have made up my mind, I have made it; and Henrietta seemed entirely to have made up hers to call at Winthrop today; and yet, she was as near giving it up out of nonsensical complaisance!'

'She would have turned back, then, but for you?'

'She would, indeed. I am almost ashamed to say it.'

'Happy for her, to have such a mind as yours at hand! After the hints you gave just now, which did but confirm my own observations, the last time I was in company with him, I need not affect to have no comprehension of what is going on. I see that more than a mere dutiful morning visit to your aunt was in question; and woe betide him, and her too, when it comes to things of consequence, when they are placed in circumstances requiring fortitude and strength of mind, if she have not resolution enough to resist idle interference in such a trifle as this. Your sister is an amiable creature; but yours is the character of decision and firmness, I see. If you value her conduct or happiness, infuse as much of your own spirit into her as you can. But this, no doubt, you have been always doing. It is the worst evil of too yielding and indecisive a character, that no influence over it can be depended on. You are never sure of a good impression being durable; everybody may sway it. Let those who would be happy be firm. Here is a nut,' said he, catching one down from an upper bough, 'to exemplify: a beautiful glossy nut, which, blessed with original strength, has outlived all the storms of autumn. Not a puncture, not a weak spot any where. This nut,' he continued, with playful solemnity, 'while so many of its brethren have fallen and been trodden under foot, is still in possession of all the happiness that a hazel nut can be supposed capable of.' Then returning to his former earnest tone – 'My first wish for all whom I am interested in, is that they should be firm. If Louisa Musgrove would be beautiful and happy in her November of life, she will cherish all her present powers of mind.'

He had done, and was unanswered. It would have surprised Anne if Louisa could have readily answered such a speech: words of such interest, spoken with such serious warmth! She could imagine what Louisa was feeling. For herself, she feared to move, lest she should be seen. While she remained, a bush of low rambling holly protected her, and they were moving on. Before they were beyond her hearing, however, Louisa spoke again.

'Mary is good-natured enough in many respects,' said she; 'but she does sometimes provoke me excessively, by her nonsense and her pride – the Elliot pride. She has a great deal too much of the Elliot pride. We do so wish that Charles had married Anne instead. I suppose you know he wanted to marry Anne?'

After a moment's pause, Captain Wentworth said –

'Do you mean that she refused him?'

'Oh! yes; certainly.'

'When did that happen?'

'I do not exactly know, for Henrietta and I were at school at the time; but I believe about a year before he married Mary. I wish she had accepted him. We should all have liked her a great deal better; and papa and mamma always think it was her great friend Lady Russell's doing, that she did not. They think Charles might not be learned and bookish enough to please Lady Russell, and that therefore, she persuaded Anne to refuse him.'

The sounds were retreating, and Anne distinguished no more. Her own emotions still kept her fixed. She had much to recover from, before she could move. The listener's proverbial fate was not absolutely hers; she had heard no evil of herself, but she had heard a great deal of very painful import. She saw how her own character was considered by Captain Wentworth, and there had been just that degree of feeling and curiosity about her in his manner which must give her extreme agitation.

As soon as she could, she went after Mary, and having found, and walked back with her to their former station, by the stile, felt some comfort in their whole party being immediately afterwards collected, and once more in motion together. Her spirits wanted the solitude and silence which only numbers could give.

EXERCISE: INVISIBLE CONVERSATIONS

Sometimes you need only summarise a conversation, devoting just a line or two to it, but others are worth expanding so that the reader can see things unfolding. Write a conversation, but do it from the point of view of a character who can hear what is going on but not necessarily see the speakers or be involved. This is a useful exercise, not just for focusing your point of view, but for choreographing your characters and ensuring that you have their voices right.

SPEEDING THINGS UP

There are lots of instances of Jane Austen spending just a few words on things where lesser writers might spend pages. She does this when she needs to progress the plot and doesn't want to waste words.

Look at this passage from *Pride and Prejudice* Chapter 42, which gets Elizabeth from Longbourn to Lambton with wit and economy, evoking in our minds the places she visits on the way without the need to describe them and making sure that we understand enough of what the Gardiners are like as travelling companions.

The Gardiners staid only one night at Longbourn, and set off the next morning with Elizabeth in pursuit of novelty and amusement. One enjoyment was certain – that of suitableness as companions; a suitableness which comprehended health and temper to bear inconveniences – cheerfulness to enhance every pleasure – and affection and intelligence, which might supply it among themselves if there were disappointments abroad.

It is not the object of this work to give a description of Derbyshire, nor of any of the remarkable places through which their route thither lay; Oxford, Blenheim, Warwick, Kenelworth, Birmingham, &c., are sufficiently known. A small part of Derbyshire is all the present concern. To the little town of Lambton, the scene of Mrs Gardiner's former residence, and where she had lately learnt that some acquaintance still remained, they bent their steps, after having seen all the principal wonders of the country; and within five miles of Lambton, Elizabeth found from her aunt that Pemberley was situated. It was not in their direct road, nor more than a mile or two out of it. In talking over their route the evening before, Mrs Gardiner expressed an inclination to see the place again. Mr Gardiner declared his willingness, and Elizabeth was applied to for her approbation.

'My love, should not you like to see a place of which you have heard so much?' said her aunt. 'A place too, with which so many of your acquaintance are connected. Wickham passed all his youth there, you know.'

Elizabeth was distressed. She felt that she had no business at Pemberley, and was obliged to assume a disinclination for seeing it. She must own that she was tired of great houses; after going over so many, she really had no pleasure in fine carpets or satin curtains.

Sometimes it is worth spending words on a journey or a conversation or something that may seem trivial but is really significant. For instance we get lots of Miss Bates's seemingly inconsequential chatter as we need to know what she is like, how people react to her and to understand Highbury. It's important to the novel so Jane Austen includes it. Her conversation is funny and sad by turns, but it isn't there as filler.

EXERCISE: NIFTY AND THRIFTY

This exercise is an editing one. Have a look through a piece of your work, something that you feel is close to being finished. For every passage and scene ask, 'Does this develop the characters and progress the plot? Could my work be more economical?' Think of each word you use as a pound coin or dollar bill and ask whether it is worth spending.

Choose a passage or scene that now seems like filler or could be told in a punchier, smarter or more amusing way. Make drastic cuts and rewrite it. Succinct and efficient is good. Remember that boring readers is the worst thing you can do.

'And what is fifty miles of good road?'

Making use of journeys (and staying at home) in your work

'And what is fifty miles of good road? Little more than half a day's journey. Yes, I call it a *very* easy distance.'
Mr Darcy, Chapter 32, *Pride and Prejudice*

As I MENTIONED IN 'Building the village of your story', the axiom that all great literature is one of two stories – a man goes on a journey or a stranger comes to town – certainly seems true of Jane Austen's work. In *Pride and Prejudice* Mr Bingley and Mr Darcy come to town and Elizabeth goes on a journey. Frank Churchill comes to town in *Emma*, and the arrivals of Jane Fairfax and Mrs Elton act to propel the plot further. Henry and Mary Crawford are the strangers in *Mansfield Park*, while Fanny Price is sent to Portsmouth, having once been the stranger at Mansfield Park herself. Catherine Morland goes to Bath and beyond in *Northanger Abbey*; Anne Elliot goes to Lyme and Bath in *Persuasion*, and *Sanditon* was to be all about trips to the seaside.

Journeys are extremely useful to writers. By sending your characters on journeys you can make things happen in interesting and believable ways. Journeys enable you to develop your characters, to introduce new ones and to ensure that the plot doesn't stagnate. Readers like to be taken on journeys and to visit new worlds. Extraordinary things can happen in new places and prejudices can be overturned.

In contrast to a novel set in a village (of any sort), where your action will be confined to one place, perhaps giving the story a siege atmosphere (a siege that must be broken), a novel structured around a journey will probably have more of a quest or voyage-and-return sort of plot. *Northanger Abbey* is the Austen novel that follows this most. Of course not all novels conform exactly to these plot types.[1]

We frequently see Jane Austen's characters in transit. It is often when they are lifted out of their own environment that they develop, learn and change. Being in an unfamiliar place and out of their 'comfort zone' (horrible phrase!) means that the characters experience things in different ways, see the world with fresh eyes and become more vulnerable to falling in love, being seduced or behaving badly.

In Chapter 1 of *Northanger Abbey* Jane Austen sends her heroine out into the world on a life-changing journey.

> She had reached the age of seventeen, without having seen one amiable youth who could call forth her sensibility, without having inspired one real passion, and without having excited even any admiration but what was very moderate and very transient. This was strange indeed! But strange things may be generally accounted for if their cause be fairly searched out. There was not one lord in the neighbourhood; no – not even a baronet. There was not one family among their acquaintance who had reared and supported a boy accidentally found at their door – not one young man whose origin was unknown. Her father had no ward, and the squire of the parish no children.
>
> But when a young lady is to be a heroine, the perverseness of forty surrounding families cannot prevent her. Something must and will happen to throw a hero in her way.
>
> Mr Allen, who owned the chief of the property about Fullerton, the village in Wiltshire where the Morlands lived, was ordered to Bath for the benefit of a gouty constitution – and his lady, a good-humoured woman, fond of Miss Morland, and probably aware that if adventures will not befall a young lady in her

own village, she must seek them abroad, invited her to go with them. Mr and Mrs Morland were all compliance, and Catherine all happiness.

And so the tone of the novel is established and Catherine Morland is on her way.

When Mr Darcy says 'And what is fifty miles of good road? Little more than half a day's journey. Yes, I call it a *very* easy distance' he shows how free he is to travel and do as he pleases. He has a younger sister to care for and the responsibility of Pemberley but, unlike Elizabeth, he can go where he wants when he wants. Jane Austen travelled but often had to wait to be accompanied, usually by a brother. We frequently see her heroines waiting, looking out of windows, while other people – richer or male – come and go as they please. Even rich Emma Woodhouse is kept at home by the need to look after her father. Think about the constraints that might or might not be on your characters. With hindsight, Elizabeth and the reader may realize that Mr Darcy was sounding her out about moving away from her family. Think about the assumptions that your travellers will make. Are they happy and able to travel alone? Where can they afford to stay? Are they confident travellers? What will they worry about? Where will they eat? Are they compelled to take a packed lunch?

When you use journeys in your writing you can bring all the emotions associated with departing, travelling and arriving into your work. A journey can energize your plot. We'll start with setting out.

EMBARKING ON A JOURNEY

This could be used at the beginning, somewhere in the middle or as a very good ending for your story. In *Pride and Prejudice* Elizabeth is delighted at the prospect of a trip with Mr and Mrs Gardiner. She has already been to stay with Charlotte Lucas (now Collins), spending time with Mr Darcy and Colonel Fitzwilliam at Rosings, the home of Lady Catherine. She has turned down Mr Darcy's proposal but learned the truth about Wickham, while Jane has been disappointed by Mr Bingley. Elizabeth is thoroughly fed up with the whole business of men and the marriage market. No wonder she prefers the idea of rocks and mountains to men (Chapter 27).

Before they were separated by the conclusion of the play, she had the unexpected happiness of an invitation to accompany her uncle and aunt in a tour of pleasure which they proposed taking in the summer.

'We have not quite determined how far it shall carry us,' said Mrs Gardiner, 'but perhaps to the Lakes.'

No scheme could have been more agreeable to Elizabeth, and her acceptance of the invitation was most ready and grateful. 'My dear, dear aunt,' she rapturously cried, 'what delight! what felicity! You give me fresh life and vigour. Adieu to disappointment and spleen. What are men to rocks and mountains? Oh! what hours of transport we shall spend! And when we *do* return, it shall not be like other travellers, without being able to give one accurate idea of any thing. We *will* know where we have gone – we *will* recollect what we have seen. Lakes, mountains, and rivers shall not be jumbled together in our imaginations; nor, when we attempt to describe any particular scene, will we begin quarrelling about its relative situation. Let *our* first effusions be less insupportable than those of the generality of travellers.'

A little later on, in Chapter 41, Lydia is equally delighted about going to Brighton, but for rather different reasons.

But the gloom of Lydia's prospect was shortly cleared away; for she received an invitation from Mrs Forster, the wife of the Colonel of the regiment, to accompany her to Brighton. This invaluable friend was a very young woman, and very lately married. A resemblance in good humour and good spirits had recommended her and Lydia to each other, and out of their *three* months' acquaintance they had been intimate *two*.

The rapture of Lydia on this occasion, her adoration of Mrs Forster, the delight of Mrs Bennet, and the mortification of Kitty, are scarcely to be described. Wholly inattentive to her sister's feelings, Lydia flew about the house in restless ecstacy, calling for everyone's congratulations, and laughing and talking with more violence than ever; whilst the luckless Kitty continued in the parlour repining at her fate in terms as unreasonable as her accent was peevish.

'I cannot see why Mrs Forster should not ask *me* as well as Lydia,' said she, 'though I am *not* her particular friend. I have just as much right to be asked as she has, and more too, for I am two years older.' [. . .]

In Lydia's imagination, a visit to Brighton comprised every possibility of earthly happiness. She saw, with the creative eye of fancy, the streets of that gay bathing place covered with officers. She saw herself the object of attention, to tens and to scores of them at present unknown. She saw all the glories of the camp; its tents stretched forth in beauteous uniformity of lines, crowded with the young and the gay, and dazzling with scarlet; and to complete the view, she saw herself seated beneath a tent, tenderly flirting with at least six officers at once. [...]

When the party broke up, Lydia returned with Mrs Forster to Meryton, from whence they were to set out early the next morning. The separation between her and her family was rather noisy than pathetic. Kitty was the only one who shed tears; but she did weep from vexation and envy. Mrs Bennet was diffuse in her good wishes for the felicity of her daughter, and impressive in her injunctions that she would not miss the opportunity of enjoying herself as much as possible; advice, which there was every reason to believe would be attended to; and in the clamorous happiness of Lydia herself in bidding farewell, the more gentle adieus of her sisters were uttered without being heard.

EXERCISE

Write about somebody setting out on a journey. You might like to describe other people's reactions to this event too. Seeing a character embark on a journey makes a very good ending, as not only can you utilize the emotions associated with departures, your story will end with the sense that life for your characters goes on after the last page – and you even set up a sequel.

CREATING PLACES

Writers needn't restrict themselves to places that they have visited. We know that Jane Austen used places she knew well in her work, but she wasn't afraid to imagine and invent locations for her stories – sometimes from places glimpsed from a carriage window, sometimes from what people told her and sometimes from intelligent guesswork and research.

The Watsons and *Emma* are both set in Surrey, which Jane Austen must have often travelled through on her journeys between Hampshire and Edward's home, Godmersham, in Kent, where she often stayed. She also visited relatives in Great Bookham, close to Box Hill, which was a popular place for day trippers. If you visit it (or just look at photographs of it) you'll see just why she wanted to send the party from Highbury there. Used to a village and more rolling, wooded countryside and lanes, suddenly being so high and able to see for miles would have had quite an impact on Emma – as it doubtless did on Jane herself. There is a sense of the characters being lifted up and put onto a high stage.

You could do a similar thing by sending your characters to another summit/peak/hilltop or up a tower or to the top of a skyscraper or a Ferris wheel, which might get stuck. Jane Austen, even in *Emma*, the most geographically contained of her novels, makes great use of different locations, of the changing seasons and the weather: the snow on the night of the Westons' party results in Emma travelling alone in a carriage with Mr Elton; Jane Fairfax is spotted going to the post office in the rain and then flees the strawberry-picking party on a swelteringly hot day. The characters journey through the year and the changing seasons in a way that Jane Austen worked out meticulously.

We can see how Jane built the worlds of her novels around the glimpses and memories of places she visited and read about as well as the ones that she knew intimately.[2]

EXERCISE: IS IT A COUNTY OF HEDGEROWS?

It's so easy now to research places without actually going to them, but don't be lazy. Even if you look at a place using maps or satellite photographs, the reality will still be different from how you imagined it. Make sure that you collect enough information about the places you are using in your story, whether real or imagined. Pin things above your desk to inspire you or keep a file of things you find out.

Choose an important location in your story. Research the history of the place. What is beneath your characters' feet? How has the place changed over the years? What vestiges are there of the place's past? Draw a map of it. What infrastructure is there? Where do people eat/ shop/relax? What trees, plants, animals and birds live there? Are there points of tension or places to avoid?

Do worlds collide? Collect postcards, photos, leaflets, local newsletters, press cuttings, information about the natural world, menus, etc. etc.

ARRIVAL

Think about somebody arriving somewhere. They may be seeing the place for the first time or have been there before. How will arriving at this place affect your character? What will their impressions tell readers about the place and themselves? How might the preconceptions of the characters and your readers be overturned? Here, Elizabeth arrives at Pemberley in Chapter 43 of *Pride and Prejudice.*

Elizabeth, as they drove along, watched for the first appearance of Pemberley Woods with some perturbation; and when at length they turned in at the lodge, her spirits were in a high flutter.

The park was very large, and contained great variety of ground. They entered it in one of its lowest points, and drove for some time through a beautiful wood, stretching over a wide extent.

Elizabeth's mind was too full for conversation, but she saw and admired every remarkable spot and point of view. They gradually ascended for half a mile, and then found themselves at the top of a considerable eminence, where the wood ceased, and the eye was instantly caught by Pemberley House, situated on the opposite side of a valley, into which the road, with some abruptness, wound. It was a large, handsome, stone building, standing well on rising ground, and backed by a ridge of high woody hills; – and in front, a stream of some natural importance was swelled into greater, but without any artificial appearance. Its banks were neither formal, nor falsely adorned. Elizabeth was delighted. She had never seen a place for which nature had done more, or where natural beauty had been so little counteracted by an awkward taste. They were all of them warm in their admiration; and at that moment she felt that to be mistress of Pemberley might be something!

They descended the hill, crossed the bridge, and drove to the door; and, while examining the nearer aspect of the house, all her apprehensions of meeting its owner returned. She dreaded lest the chambermaid had been mistaken. On applying to see the place, they were admitted into the hall; and Elizabeth, as they waited for the housekeeper, had leisure to wonder at her being where she was.

EXERCISE

Write about somebody arriving somewhere. They might be happy, sad, scared, reluctant, in for a surprise . . . The place doesn't have to be their final destination. Set up what will happen next in the plot, or use the feelings that your character has about the place to provide some tension. Be ready to surprise the reader.

Elizabeth has no idea that she'll be seeing so much of Mr Darcy while she's staying with Charlotte and

Mr Collins at Hunsford or that they will meet again at Pemberley. In *Persuasion* Anne Elliot doesn't know that she and Captain Wentworth will finally be reunited in Bath. In *Sense and Sensibility* Marianne is excited about seeing Willoughby again in London.

THE JOURNEY ITSELF

Travelling could be dangerous in Jane Austen's time; even a short journey could end in tragedy. Jane Austen's cousin Jane Cooper was killed in a carriage accident. Such accidents weren't always fatal, though, and a mishap is the inciting incident in *Sanditon*, described in the opening of the novel.

A gentleman and lady travelling from Tunbridge towards that part of the Sussex coast which lies between Hastings and Eastbourne, being induced by business to quit the high road and attempt a very rough lane, were overturned in toiling up its long ascent, half rock, half sand. The accident happened just beyond the only gentleman's house near the lane ... The severity of the fall was broken by their slow pace and the narrowness of the lane; and the gentleman having scrambled out and helped out his companion, they neither of them at first felt more than shaken and bruised. But the gentleman had, in the course of the extrication, sprained his foot; and soon becoming sensible of it, was obliged in a few moments to cut short both his remonstrances to the driver and his congratulations to his wife and himself and sit down on the bank, unable to stand.

Mr Thomas Parker being tipped out of his carriage and spraining his foot makes a perfect opening. There is the drama verging on comedy of the accident, and one of the themes of the novel, illness and doctors, is introduced. The possible folly of Mr Parker's actions in working so hard on Sanditon, the seaside town he is trying to develop, is also set up. This is a plainly written episode and might put readers in mind of a fable or a parable.

And here is Marianne being self-centered and rude, in *Sense and Sensibility* (Chapter 26), leaving Elinor to be polite to Mrs Jennings – who is being her unfailingly jovial and well-meaning self – as they travel to London.

They were three days on their journey, and Marianne's behaviour as they travelled was a happy specimen of what future complaisance and companionableness to Mrs Jennings might be expected to be. She sat in silence almost all the way, wrapt in her own meditations, and scarcely ever voluntarily speaking, except when any object of picturesque beauty within their view drew from her an exclamation of delight exclusively addressed to her sister. To atone for this conduct therefore, Elinor took immediate possession of the post of civility which she had assigned herself, behaved with the greatest attention to Mrs Jennings, talked with her, laughed with her, and listened to her whenever she could; and Mrs Jennings on her side treated them both with all possible kindness, was solicitous on every occasion for their ease and enjoyment, and only disturbed that she could not make them choose their own dinners at the inn, nor extort a confession of their preferring salmon to cod, or boiled fowls to veal cutlets.

As well as advancing the plot, you can reveal much about your characters by showing them in transit. How do they behave? Are they rude? Do they get road or airport rage? Do they mislay their tickets or get lost? The uncertainty of travelling also gives you opportunities to introduce new characters or send the plot in new directions in a plausible way.

In *Northanger Abbey* when Catherine Morland is driven by Henry Tilney she (and thus the reader) compares him to the boorish John Thorpe (Chapter 20):

> Much was Catherine then surprised by the general's proposal of her taking his place in his son's curricle for the rest of the journey: 'the day was fine, and he was anxious for her seeing as much of the country as possible.'
>
> The remembrance of Mr Allen's opinion, respecting young men's open carriages, made her blush at the mention of such a plan, and her first thought was to decline it; but her second was of greater deference for General Tilney's judgment; he could not propose anything improper for her; and, in the course of a few minutes, she found herself with Henry in the curricle, as happy a being as ever existed. A very short trial convinced her that a curricle was the prettiest equipage in the world; the chaise and four wheeled off with some grandeur, to be sure, but it was a heavy and troublesome business, and she could not easily forget its having stopped two hours at Petty France. Half the time would have been enough for the curricle, and so nimbly were the light horses disposed to move, that, had not the general chosen to have his own carriage lead the way,

they could have passed it with ease in half a minute. But the merit of the curricle did not all belong to the horses; Henry drove so well – so quietly – without making any disturbance, without parading to her, or swearing at them: so different from the only gentleman-coachman whom it was in her power to compare him with! And then his hat sat so well, and the innumerable capes of his greatcoat looked so becomingly important! To be driven by him, next to being dancing with him, was certainly the greatest happiness in the world.

EXERCISE: WHO IS DRIVING AND WHAT DOES THEIR
DRIVING SAY ABOUT THEM?

Write a scene in which one of your characters is driving. How do they behave behind the wheel? What is their vehicle like? Do they listen to music? Get distracted? Might their passenger view them the way that Catherine Morland does Henry Tilney?

'TO PEMBERLEY, THEREFORE, THEY WERE TO GO' –
JOURNEYS AND PLOTTING

In *The Creative Writing Coursebook* Patricia Duncker distinguishes between siege narratives and quest narratives. What sort of story are you writing? Emma Woodhouse stays at home, but *Emma* isn't really a siege narrative because it's about her journey of self-discovery. Despite this, the fact that she hardly goes anywhere is interesting; only at the end is she going to leave Highbury for a trip to the seaside.

Journeys are key to the narrative in *Pride and Prejudice*. We can imagine how Jane Austen plotted, probably making notes and consulting maps, carefully working out journey times and routes, such as the one she describes when Elizabeth and the Gardiners travel north in Chapter 42. This is another quest narrative.

Jane Austen's description of the route to Pemberley is evocative but economical. Remember where your hero or heroine must go and get them there; you don't have to show everything that happens along the way. You will also have to decide if your character will be going home again. You might like to think of your narrative as being a quest, but it may be one of 'voyage and return'.[3]

EXERCISES: GOING HOME OR STAYING HOME

1. Does your hero or heroine have to return home or perhaps find a new one? Write about coming home or finding a home. Ruby slippers are optional.

2. Write about a character who has to stay at home while others go on journeys. I often think about how Jane and Cassandra Austen and their parents had to wait for news of Frank and Charles when they were away at sea. In *Mansfield Park* Fanny Price was in the same situation with her brother William. Cassandra's fiancé, Thomas Fowle, was a ship's chaplain and died of yellow fever in the West Indies. It was several months before the heartbreaking news reached England.

'You know how interesting the purchase of a sponge-cake is to me[1]

Using food and meals in your writing

JANE AUSTEN MADE CLEVER use of food and meals in her novels. She also often commented in her letters on menus and what was going on in the kitchen. Depending on your potential readers, you will have plenty of scope to do likewise. Is there a child who wouldn't want to join

Ratty and Mole on their picnic in *The Wind in the Willows* by Kenneth Grahame?

> The Mole waggled his toes from sheer happiness, spread his chest with a sigh of full contentment, and leaned back blissfully into the soft cushions. 'WHAT a day I'm having!' he said. 'Let us start at once!'
>
> 'Hold hard a minute, then!' said the Rat. He looped the painter through a ring in his landing-stage, climbed up into his hole above, and after a short interval reappeared staggering under a fat, wicker luncheon-basket.
>
> 'Shove that under your feet,' he observed to the Mole, as he passed it down into the boat. Then he untied the painter and took the sculls again.
>
> 'What's inside it?' asked the Mole, wriggling with curiosity.
>
> 'There's cold chicken inside it,' replied the Rat briefly; 'coldtonguecoldhamcoldbeefpickledgherkinssalad-frenchrollscresssandwichespottedmeatgingerbeerlem-onadesodawater—'
>
> 'O stop, stop,' cried the Mole in ecstacies: 'This is too much!'
>
> 'Do you really think so?' enquired the Rat seriously. 'It's only what I always take on these little excursions; and the other animals are always telling me that I'm a mean beast and cut it VERY fine!'

USING FOOD TO PIN YOUR WORK IN PLACE AND TIME

Read this piece by Josh Sutton. It appeared in the *Guardian* on 18 April 2012.[2]

Blyton wrote twenty-one *Famous Five* books; the first, *Five on a Treasure Island*, was published in 1942. As Dr Joan Ransley, Honorary Lecturer in Human Nutrition at the University of Leeds, notes: 'The food eaten in the books anchors the Famous Five to a definite period in dietary history. During and immediately after the Second World War British children ate well but austerely and Blyton is true to this.' In other words, they ate healthily but not heartily. Well over half of the books were written during food rationing. Perhaps Blyton is consciously enticing her readers with elaborate descriptions of foods way beyond the ration book allowance.

In that first book, a simple spread of cold ham, salad, bacon and eggs, plums and a ginger cake fuelled the discovery of gold ingots on Kirrin Island. But over the years, as the five go off in a caravan, or camping on Billycock Hill, the author has discovered the importance of food in recounting a good yarn: 'A large ham sat on the table, and there were crusty loaves of new bread. Crisp lettuces, dewy and cool, and red radishes were side by side in a big glass dish, great slabs of butter and jugs of creamy milk' – simple descriptive skills which make the food hugely appealing. Menu writers take note.

Jane Austen sends the characters in *Emma* on a picnic to Box Hill, but perhaps because she wasn't writing for children she doesn't say much about the actual food. The servants on the trip are invisible, and it's interesting to speculate what the day must have been like for them.

The characters also go strawberry picking at Donwell Abbey. Picnics and outdoor events are excellent ways of getting your characters together.

EXERCISE: SEND YOUR CHARACTERS
OUT ON A PICNIC

The event might be romantic, funny, disastrous or surreal. Who brings the food? What do they bring? What does that tell the reader?

FOOD AND CHARACTER

Jane Austen loved to use food as an indicator of character. Mr Woodhouse is such a worrier that his guests at Hartfield in Chapter 3 of *Emma* are in danger of going hungry if his daughter doesn't intervene.

She [Emma] was so busy in admiring those soft blue eyes [Harriet Smith's], in talking and listening, and forming all these schemes in the in-betweens, that the evening flew away at a very unusual rate; and the supper-table, which always closed such parties, and for which she had been used to sit and watch the due time, was all set out and ready, and moved forwards to the fire, before she was aware. With an alacrity beyond the common impulse of a spirit which yet was never indifferent to the credit of doing every thing well and attentively, with the real good-will of a mind delighted with its own ideas, did she then do all the honours of the meal, and help and recommend the minced chicken and scalloped oysters with an urgency which she knew would be acceptable to the early hours and civil scruples of their guests.

Upon such occasions poor Mr Woodhouse's feelings were in sad warfare. He loved to have the cloth laid, because it had been the fashion of his youth, but his conviction of suppers being very unwholesome made him rather sorry to see anything put on it; and while his hospitality would have welcomed his visitors to every thing, his care for their health made him grieve that they would eat.

Such another small basin of thin gruel as his own, was all that he could, with thorough self-approbation, recommend; though he might constrain himself, while the ladies were comfortably clearing the nicer things, to say:

'Mrs Bates, let me propose your venturing on one of these eggs. An egg boiled very soft is not unwholesome. Serle understands boiling an egg better than any body. I would not recommend an egg boiled by any body else; but you need not be afraid, they are very small, you see – one of our small eggs will not hurt you. Miss Bates, let Emma help you to a *little* bit of tart – a *very* little bit. Ours are all apple tarts. You need not be afraid of unwholesome preserves here. I do not advise the custard. Mrs Goddard, what say you to *half* a glass of wine? A *small* half glass, put into a tumbler of water? I do not think it could disagree with you.'

Emma allowed her father to talk – but supplied her visitors in a much more satisfactory style, and on the present evening had particular pleasure in sending them away happy. The happiness of Miss Smith was quite equal to her intentions. Miss Woodhouse was so great a personage in Highbury, that the prospect of the introduction had given as much panic as pleasure; but the humble, grateful little girl went off with highly gratified feelings, delighted with the affability with which Miss Woodhouse had treated her all the evening, and actually shaken hands with her at last!

In *Mansfield Park* Dr Grant dies after overindulging – 'Dr Grant had brought on apoplexy and death, by three great institutionary dinners in one week' (Chapter 48) – and Mrs Norris is adept at scrounging and sponging, while in *Pride and Prejudice* (Chapter 8) Mr Hurst loses interest in Lizzy Bennet when he discovers she prefers plain sauces. Perhaps Jane is being patriotic here – Elizabeth is expressing a preference for English food during the Napoleonic Wars – but she is definitely showing us how greedy Mr Hurst is.

At five o'clock the two ladies retired to dress, and at half-past six Elizabeth was summoned to dinner. To the civil enquiries which then poured in, and, among which she had the pleasure of distinguishing the much superior solicitude of Mr Bingley's, she could not make a very favourable answer. Jane was by no means better. The sisters, on hearing this, repeated three or four times how much they were grieved, how shocking it was to have a bad cold, and how excessively they disliked being ill themselves, and then thought no more of the matter;

and their indifference towards Jane, when not immediately before them, restored Elizabeth to the enjoyment
of all her original dislike.

Their brother, indeed, was the only one of the party
whom she could regard with any complacency. His anxiety for Jane was evident, and his attentions to herself
most pleasing, and they prevented her feeling herself so
much an intruder as she believed she was considered by
the others. She had very little notice from any but him.
Miss Bingley was engrossed by Mr Darcy, her sister
scarcely less so; and as for Mr Hurst, by whom Elizabeth
sat, he was an indolent man, who lived only to eat, drink,
and play at cards, who, when he found her prefer a plain
dish to a ragout, had nothing to say to her.

In 'The Beautifull Cassandra', which was written when
Jane Austen was very young, her rebellious heroine devours
six ices, refuses to pay for them, and escapes.

Even when her own health was failing, Jane Austen
could poke fun at fussiness as well as overindulgence. Here
is an evening with the Parkers in *Sanditon*.

'If I were bilious,' he continued, 'you know, wine would
disagree with me, but it always does me good. The more
wine I drink – in moderation – the better I am. I am
always best of an evening. If you had seen me today
before dinner, you would have thought me a very poor
creature.'

Charlotte could believe it. She kept her countenance, however, and said, 'As far as I can understand

what nervous complaints are, I have a great idea of the efficacy of air and exercise for them – daily, regular exercise – and I should recommend rather more of it to you than I suspect you are in the habit of taking.'

'Oh, I am very fond of exercise myself,' he replied, 'and I mean to walk a great deal while I am here, if the weather is temperate. I shall be out every morning before breakfast and take several turns upon the Terrace, and you will often see me at Trafalgar House.'

'But you do not call a walk to Trafalgar House much exercise?'

'Not as to mere distance, but the hill is so steep! Walking up that hill, in the middle of the day, would throw me into such a perspiration! You would see me all in a bath by the time I got there! I am very subject to perspiration, and there cannot be a surer sign of nervousness.'

They were now advancing so deep in physics that Charlotte viewed the entrance of the servant with the tea things as a very fortunate interruption. It produced a great and immediate change. The young man's attentions were instantly lost. He took his own cocoa from the tray, which seemed provided with almost as many teapots as there were persons in company – Miss Parker drinking one sort of herb tea and Miss Diana another – and turning completely to the fire, sat coddling and cooking it to his own satisfaction and toasting some slices of bread, brought up ready-prepared in the toast rack; and till it was all done, she heard nothing of his voice but the murmuring of a few broken sentences of self-approbation and success.

When his toils were over, however, he moved back his chair into as gallant a line as ever, and proved that he had not been working only for himself by his earnest invitation to her to take both cocoa and toast. She was already helped to tea – which surprised him, so totally self-engrossed had he been.

'I thought I should have been in time,' said he, 'but cocoa takes a great deal of boiling.'

'I am much obliged to you,' replied Charlotte. 'But I prefer tea.'

'Then I will help myself,' said he. 'A large dish of rather weak cocoa every evening agrees with me better than anything.'

It struck her, however, as he poured out this rather weak cocoa, that it came forth in a very fine, dark-coloured stream; and at the same moment, his sisters both crying out, 'Oh, Arthur, you get your cocoa stronger and stronger every evening,' with Arthur's somewhat conscious reply of 'Tis rather stronger than it should be tonight,' convinced her that Arthur was by no means so fond of being starved as they could desire or as he felt proper himself. He was certainly very happy to turn the conversation on dry toast and hear no more of his sisters.

'I hope you will eat some of this toast,' said he. 'I reckon myself a very good toaster. I never burn my toasts, I never put them too near the fire at first. And yet, you see, there is not a corner but what is well browned. I hope you like dry toast.'

'With a reasonable quantity of butter spread over it, very much,' said Charlotte, 'but not otherwise.'

'No more do I,' said he, exceedingly pleased. 'We think quite alike there. So far from dry toast being wholesome, I think it a very bad thing for the stomach. Without a little butter to soften it, it hurts the coats of the stomach. I am sure it does. I will have the pleasure of spreading some for you directly, and afterwards I will spread some for myself. Very bad indeed for the coats of the stomach – but there is no convincing some people. It irritates and acts like a nutmeg grater.'

He could not get command of the butter, however, without a struggle; his sisters accusing him of eating a great deal too much and declaring he was not to be trusted, and he maintaining that he only ate enough to secure the coats of his stomach, and besides, he only wanted it now for Miss Heywood.

Such a plea must prevail. He got the butter and spread away for her with an accuracy of judgement which at least delighted himself. But when her toast was done and he took his own in hand, Charlotte could hardly contain herself as she saw him watching his sisters while he scrupulously scraped off almost as much butter as he put on, and then seizing an odd moment for adding a great dab just before it went into his mouth. Certainly, Mr Arthur Parker's enjoyments in invalidism were very different from his sisters' – by no means so spiritualized. A good deal of earthy dross hung about him. Charlotte could not but suspect him of adopting that line of life principally for the indulgence of an indolent temper, and to be determined on having no disorders but such as called for warm rooms and good nourishment.

In one particular, however, she soon found that he had caught something from them. 'What!' said he. 'Do you venture upon two dishes of strong green tea in one evening? What nerves you must have! How I envy you. Now, if I were to swallow only one such dish, what do you think its effect would be upon me?'

'Keep you awake perhaps all night,' replied Charlotte, meaning to overthrow his attempts at surprise by the grandeur of her own conceptions.

'Oh, if that were all!' he exclaimed. 'No. It acts on me like poison and would entirely take away the use of my right side before I had swallowed it five minutes. It sounds almost incredible, but it has happened to me so often that I cannot doubt it. The use of my right side is entirely taken away for several hours!'

'It sounds rather odd to be sure,' answered Charlotte coolly, 'but I dare say it would be proved to be the simplest thing in the world by those who have studied right sides and green tea scientifically and thoroughly understand all the possibilities of their action on each other.'

EXERCISE

Write a scene or scenes in which your characters' food choices communicate more than a hill of beans to the reader. Of course not everybody can choose or afford what they would really like to eat.

SYMBOLIC FOOD

Jane Austen understood very well the sensual and symbolic importance of food. At Pemberley Georgiana's shyness is demonstrated by her lack of prowess with the tea things, while exotic and seasonal fruits show Lizzy how sweet life with Mr Darcy would be (*Pride and Prejudice*, Chapter 45).

Convinced as Elizabeth now was that Miss Bingley's dislike of her had originated in jealousy, she could not help feeling how very unwelcome her appearance at Pemberley must be to her, and was curious to know with how much civility on that lady's side, the acquaintance would now be renewed.

On reaching the house, they were shewn through the hall into the saloon, whose northern aspect rendered it delightful for summer. Its windows, opening to the ground, admitted a most refreshing view of the high woody hills behind the house, and of the beautiful oaks and Spanish chesnuts which were scattered over the intermediate lawn.

In this room they were received by Miss Darcy, who was sitting there with Mrs Hurst and Miss Bingley, and the lady with whom she lived in London. Georgiana's reception of them was very civil; but attended with all that embarrassment which, though proceeding from shyness and the fear of doing wrong, would easily give to those who felt themselves inferior the belief of her being proud and reserved. Mrs Gardiner and her niece, however, did her justice, and pitied her.

By Mrs Hurst and Miss Bingley, they were noticed only by a curtsey; and, on their being seated, a pause, awkward as such pauses must always be, succeeded for a few moments. It was first broken by Mrs Annesley, a genteel, agreeable-looking woman, whose endeavour to introduce some kind of discourse proved her to be more truly well bred than either of the others; and between her and Mrs Gardiner, with occasional help from Elizabeth, the conversation was carried on. Miss Darcy looked as if she wished for courage enough to join in it; and sometimes did venture a short sentence, when there was least danger of its being heard.

Elizabeth soon saw that she was herself closely watched by Miss Bingley, and that she could not speak a word, especially to Miss Darcy, without calling her attention. This observation would not have prevented her from trying to talk to the latter, had they not been seated at an inconvenient distance; but she was not sorry to be spared the necessity of saying much. Her own thoughts were employing her. She expected every moment that some of the gentlemen would enter the room. She wished, she feared that the master of the house might be amongst them; and whether she wished or feared it most, she could scarcely determine. After sitting in this manner a quarter of an hour without hearing Miss Bingley's voice, Elizabeth was roused by receiving from her a cold enquiry after the health of her family. She answered with equal indifference and brevity, and the other said no more.

The next variation which their visit afforded was produced by the entrance of servants with cold meat, cake, and a variety of all the finest fruits in season; but this did not take place till after many a significant look and smile from Mrs Annesley to Miss Darcy had been given, to remind her of her post. There was now employment for the whole party; for though they could not all talk, they could all eat; and the beautiful pyramids of grapes, nectarines, and peaches soon collected them round the table.

While thus engaged, Elizabeth had a fair opportunity of deciding whether she most feared or wished for the appearance of Mr Darcy, by the feelings which prevailed on his entering the room; and then, though but a moment before she had believed her wishes to predominate, she began to regret that he came.

In *Emma* Robert Martin offers good things to Harriet Smith and will work hard to get them for her, something that Emma doesn't appreciate (Chapter 4).

With this inspiriting notion, her questions increased in number and meaning; and she particularly led Harriet to talk more of Mr Martin, and there was evidently no dislike to it. Harriet was very ready to speak of the share he had had in their moonlight walks and merry evening games; and dwelt a good deal upon his being so very good-humoured and obliging. He had gone three miles round one day, in order to bring her some walnuts, because she had said how fond she was of them, and in every thing else he was so very obliging. 'He had his shepherd's son into the parlour one night on purpose to sing to her. She was very fond of singing.

He could sing a little himself. She believed he was very clever, and understood every thing. He had a very fine flock, and, while she was with them, he had been bid more for his wool than any body in the country. She believed every body spoke well of him. His mother and sisters were very fond of him. Mrs Martin had told her one day (and there was a blush as she said it) that it was impossible for any body to be a better son, and therefore she was sure, whenever he married, he would make a good husband. Not that she *wanted* him to marry. She was in no hurry at all.'

EXERCISE

Write a scene in which you utilize the symbolic or sensual qualities of food. How might a character use food as a gift? Will the intended recipient accept it?

SET PIECES – WAYS OF GETTING EVERYBODY ONSTAGE

Meals and parties are so useful to writers. You can get lots of people onstage and have them interact in new and unexpected ways with endless potential for drama and comedy. Here is *Pride and Prejudice*, Chapter 13.

Mr Collins was punctual to his time, and was received with great politeness by the whole family. Mr Bennet, indeed, said little; but the ladies were ready enough to talk, and Mr Collins seemed neither in need of encouragement, nor inclined to be silent himself. He was a tall, heavy-looking young man of five-and-twenty. His air was grave and stately, and his manners were very formal. He had not been long seated before he complimented Mrs Bennet on having so fine a family of daughters; said he had heard much of their beauty, but that, in this instance, fame had fallen short of the truth; and added, that he did not doubt her seeing them all in due time well disposed of in marriage. This gallantry was not much to the taste of some of his hearers, but Mrs Bennet, who quarrelled with no compliments, answered most readily,

'You are very kind, sir, I am sure; and I wish with all my heart it may prove so; for else they will be destitute enough. Things are settled so oddly.'

'You allude, perhaps, to the entail of this estate.'

'Ah! sir, I do indeed. It is a grievous affair to my poor girls, you must confess. Not that I mean to find fault with *you*, for such things, I know, are all chance in this world. There is no knowing how estates will go when once they come to be entailed.'

'I am very sensible, madam, of the hardship to my fair cousins, – and could say much on the subject, but that I am cautious of appearing forward and precipitate. But I can assure the young ladies that I come prepared to admire them. At present I will not say more, but perhaps when we are better acquainted—'

He was interrupted by a summons to dinner; and the girls smiled on each other. They were not the only objects of Mr Collins's admiration. The hall, the dining-room, and all its furniture, were examined and praised; and his commendation of every thing would have touched Mrs Bennet's heart, but for the mortifying supposition of his viewing it all as his own future property. The dinner too, in its turn, was highly admired; and he begged to know to which of his fair cousins the excellence of its cookery was owing. But here he was set right by Mrs Bennet, who assured him with some asperity that they were very well able to keep a good cook, and that her daughters had nothing to do in the kitchen. He begged pardon for having displeased her. In a softened tone she declared herself not at all offended; but he continued to apologise for about a quarter of an hour.

EXERCISE

This is an exercise for once you have got to know your characters. Write a set-piece scene such as a dinner party. The food and drink are props; concentrate on dialogue, comedy, drama and showing the reader how your characters and the plot are developing.

Joints of mutton and doses of rhubarb

About the writing life, not food

WHEN YOU FEEL DISCOURAGED, which will be a lot of the time, remind yourself that Jane Austen was serious about writing and had been working hard at her craft for around twenty years before *Sense and Sensibility* was published. She had complete belief in what she was doing from a very young age. I hope this chapter will help you to hang on in there as a writer and that by using Jane's practical methods you will be able to arm yourself against adversity and get your projects finished and out into the world.

Here is Jane Austen's defence of the novel as a form of writing from *Northanger Abbey*, Chapter 5. It explains why she kept going and why you should too. Writing is difficult but worthwhile. Aim high, but even if your efforts aren't rewarded with praise and a fortune, you will have become smarter, have created something, and if you are in a good writing group you will have the same pleasures and sense of belonging that members of a choir enjoy.

I will not adopt that ungenerous and impolitic custom so common with novel-writers, of degrading by their contemptuous censure the very performances, to the number of which they are themselves adding – joining with their greatest enemies in bestowing the harshest epithets on such works, and scarcely ever permitting them to be read by their own heroine, who, if she accidentally take up a novel, is sure to turn over its insipid pages with disgust. Alas! If the heroine of one novel be not patronized by the heroine of another, from whom can she expect protection and regard? I cannot approve of it. Let us leave it to the reviewers to abuse such effusions of fancy at their leisure, and over every new novel to talk in threadbare strains of the trash with which the press now groans. Let us not desert one another; we are an injured body. Although our productions have afforded more extensive and unaffected pleasure than those of any other literary corporation in the world, no species of composition has been so much decried. From pride, ignorance, or fashion, our foes are almost as many as our readers. And while the abilities of the nine-hundredth abridger of the History of England, or of the man who collects and publishes in a volume some dozen lines of Milton, Pope, and Prior, with a paper from the *Spectator*, and a chapter from Sterne, are eulogized by a thousand pens – there seems almost a general wish of decrying the capacity and undervaluing the labour of the novelist, and of slighting the performances which have only genius, wit, and taste to recommend them. 'I am no novel-reader – I seldom look into novels – Do not imagine that I often read novels – It is really very well for a novel.' Such is the common cant. 'And what are you reading, Miss ——?' 'Oh! It is only a novel!' replies the young lady, while she lays down her book with affected indifference, or momentary shame. 'It is only *Cecilia*, or *Camilla*, or *Belinda*'; or, in short, only some work in which the greatest powers of the mind are displayed, in which the most thorough knowledge of human nature, the happiest delineation of its varieties, the liveliest effusions of wit and humour, are conveyed to the world in the best-chosen language.

A FIRST FORAY

This is probably Jane's first foray into print – a letter in the *Loiterer* (a magazine run by her brothers at Oxford) on Saturday 28 March 1789. Jane was fourteen when this was published. She may well have collaborated with Cassandra, but it seems to be vintage Jane – glorying in the absurd. The author was something of a Lizzy Bennet – 'Follies and nonsense, whims and inconsistencies, *do* divert me, I own, and I laugh at them whenever I can.'[1] The author of the letter is somebody who loves reading and thinking about books, publishing, audience and genre. I love the line 'Only conceive, in eight papers, not one sentimental story about love and honour, and all that.' And who but a sister would sign off with 'If you think fit to comply with this my injunction, you may expect to hear from me again, and perhaps I may even give you a little assistance: – but, if not – may your work be condemned to the pastry-cook's shop, and may you always continue a bachelor, and be plagued with a maiden sister to keep house for you.'

The editors (her brothers) introduced the letter like this:

> The following letter was brought us the last week, while we were deliberating on a proper subject for the Loiterer; and as it is the first favour of the kind we have ever received from the fair sex (I mean in our capacity of authors) we take the earliest opportunity of laying it before our readers, and hope the fair writer of it will consider our present eagerness to comply with her commands as some expiation for our past neglect, and will no longer condemn our paper as a pedantic performance, or set its authors down for old bachelors.

To the AUTHOR *of the* LOITERER.

Sir,

I write this to inform you that you are very much out of my good graces, and that, if you do not mend your manners, I shall soon drop your acquaintance. You must know, Sir, I am a great reader, and not to mention some hundred volumes of Novels and Plays, have, in the last two summers, actually got through all the entertaining papers of our most celebrated periodical writers, from the Tatler and Spectator to the Microcosm and the Olla Podrida. Indeed I love a periodical work beyond any thing, especially those in which one meets with a great many stories, and where the papers are not too long. I assure you my heart beat with joy when I first heard of your publication, which I immediately sent for, and have taken in ever since.

I am sorry, however, to say it, but really, Sir, I think it the stupidest work of the kind I ever saw: not but that some of the papers are well written; but then your subjects are so badly chosen, that they never interest one. – Only conceive, in eight papers, not one sentimental story about love and honour, and all that. – Not one Eastern Tale full of Bashas and Hermits, Pyramids and Mosques – no, not even an allegory or dream have yet made their appearance in the Loiterer. Why, my dear Sir – what do you think we care about the way in which Oxford men spend their time and money – we, who have enough to do to spend our own. For my part, I never, but once, was at Oxford in my life, and I am sure I never wish to go there again – They dragged me through so many dismal chapels, dusty libraries, and greasy halls, that it gave me the vapours for two days afterwards. As for your last paper, indeed, the story was good enough, but there was no love, and no lady in it, at least no young lady; and I wonder how you could be guilty of such an omission, especially when it could have been so easily avoided. Instead of retiring to Yorkshire, he might have fled into France, and there, you know, you might have made him fall in love with a French Paysanne, who might have turned out to be some great person. Or you might have let him set fire to a convent, and carry off a nun, whom he might afterwards have converted, or any thing of that kind, just to have created a little bustle, and made the story more interesting. In short, you have never yet dedicated any one number to the amusement of our sex, and have taken no more notice of us, than if you thought, like the Turks, we had no souls. From all which I do conclude, that you are neither more nor less than some old Fellow of a College, who never saw any thing of the world beyond the limits of the University, and never conversed with a female, except your bed-maker and laundress. I therefore give you this advice, which you will follow as you value our favour, or your own reputation. – Let us hear no more of your Oxford Journals, your Homelys and Cockney: but send them about their business, and get a new set of correspondents, from among the young of both sexes, but particularly ours; and let us see some nice affecting stories, relating the misfortunes of two lovers, who died suddenly, just as they were going to church. Let the lover be killed in a duel, or lost at sea, or you may make him shoot himself, just as you please; and as for his mistress, she will of course go mad; or if you will, you may kill the lady, and let the lover run mad; only remember, whatever you do, that your hero and heroine must possess a great deal of feeling, and have very pretty names. If you think fit to comply with this my injunction, you may expect to hear from me again, and perhaps I may even give you a little assistance: – but, if not – may your work be condemned to the pastry-cook's shop, and may you always continue a bachelor, and be plagued with a maiden sister to keep house for you.

Your's, as you behave,
SOPHIA SENTIMENT[2]

STARTING SMALL

Most writers' first novels are not actually their first novels. Almost all authors have some unfinished and some completed stories, false starts and often boxes of manuscripts stashed away. This was certainly the case with Jane Austen. Even she couldn't come up with *Sense and Sensibility* or *Pride and Prejudice* as a first attempt. Expect to serve your apprenticeship as a writer. People who sign up for an adult education art class don't ask the tutor for information about art dealers and London galleries on their second week, but for some reason the thoughts of those who have just started writing often centre on book deals and prizes.

Aim, first of all, to finish something, whether a short story, a flash fiction or a poem. Don't expect fame and wealth from your first efforts. People didn't talk about flash fictions in the late eighteenth century when Jane was first writing, but at 378 words we could apply the term to 'The Beautifull Cassandra', written for her sister and preserved with other early efforts in Jane's *Volume the First*:

The Beautifull Cassandra
A Novel in Twelve Chapters
dedicated by permission to Miss Austen.

Dedication:
Madam

You are a Phoenix. Your taste is refined, your Sentiments are noble, & your Virtues innumerable. Your Person is lovely, your Figure, elegant, & your Form, magestic. Your Manners are polished, your Conversation is rational & your appearance singular. If, therefore, the following Tale will afford one moment's amusement to you, every wish will be gratified of
Your most obedient
humble servant
The author

Chapter the First
Cassandra was the Daughter & the only Daughter of a celebrated Millener in Bond Street. Her father was of noble Birth, being the near relation of the Dutchess of ——'s Butler.

Chapter the 2d
When Cassandra had attained her 16th year, she was lovely & amiable, & chancing to fall in love with an elegant Bonnet her Mother had just compleated, bespoke by the Countess of ——, she placed it on her gentle Head & walked from her Mother's shop to make her Fortune.

Chapter the 3d
The first person she met, was the Viscount of ——, a young Man, no less celebrated for his Accomplishments

& Virtues, than for his Elegance & Beauty. She curt-seyed & walked on.

Chapter the 4th
She then proceeded to a Pastry-cook's, where she devoured six ices, refused to pay for them, knocked down the Pastry Cook & walked away.

Chapter the 5th
She next ascended a Hackney Coach & ordered it to Hampstead, where she was no sooner arrived than she ordered the Coachman to turn round & drive her back again.

Chapter the 6th
Being returned to the same spot of the same Street she had set out from, the Coachman demanded his Pay.

Chapter the 7th
She searched her pockets over again & again; but every search was unsuccessfull. No money could she find. The man grew peremptory. She placed her bonnet on his head & ran away.

Chapter the 8th
Thro' many a street she then proceeded & met in none the least Adventure, till on turning a Corner of Bloomsbury Square, she met Maria.

Chapter the 9th
Cassandra started & Maria seemed surprised; they trembled, blushed, turned pale & passed each other in a mutual silence.

Chapter the 10th
Cassandra was next accosted by her friend the Widow, who squeezing out her little Head thro' her less window, asked her how she did? Cassandra curtseyed & went on.

Chapter the 11th
A quarter of a mile brought her to her paternal roof in Bond Street, from which she had now been absent nearly 7 hours.

Chapter the 12th
She entered it & was pressed to her Mother's bosom by that worthy Woman. Cassandra smiled & whispered to herself 'This is a day well spent.'

Finis

EXERCISE

Write a story in the spirit of 'The Beautifull Cassandra' that is just a page long. If you wish, borrow from its circular structure – your character sets out, things happen and then they return home. You could base your character on somebody you know, though you may be better off keeping the story to yourself if you do. 'The Beautifull Cassandra' is one sister's affectionate and silly gift to another, but the characters and setting are established; things occur; there is dialogue and action; there are jokes, and at the end we have the sense that the story is complete and that the central character and our understanding of her are changed.

You could make your story about a person who covets and steals something: 'chancing to fall in love with an elegant Bonnet her Mother had just compleated, bespoke by the Countess of ——, she placed it on her gentle Head & walked from her Mother's shop to make her Fortune'. What will they do with the stolen item? Or somebody who satisfies a craving: 'She then proceeded to a Pastry-cook's, where she devoured six ices, refused to pay for them, knocked down the Pastry Cook & walked away.' Or somebody who keeps quiet about how they spend a day out. When the beautiful Cassandra gets home, she is 'pressed to her Mother's bosom by that worthy Woman', but she doesn't mention what she has been up to: 'Cassandra smiled & whispered to herself "This is a day well spent." '

Don't worry if your story seems silly or inconsequential. The most important thing is to finish it. For now keep it to one page long; if you want to expand it afterwards you can.

EXPERIMENTING WITH GENRE AND SUBJECT MATTER

Some of Jane Austen's juvenilia can seem a little impenetrable at first. Early sketches and fragments were often written for family members as responses to what she had been reading; some of the jokes we will never get and others are very much of their time. We see Jane experimenting and finding her voice in the way that every writer, even one of genius must. In *Catharine or The Bower* found in *Volume the Third* we have the opening of a novel that is an obvious precursor to her mature work. In other works she writes with freedom and irreverence. *Volume the First* and *Volume the Second* are the work of a clever teenager in the late eighteenth century; the jokes and sensibilities are very much of that period rather than of the generally more restrained nineteenth century.

Jane Austen perceived the changes taking place in the literary landscape, and in her six major novels she works with the marriage plot, which had become popular. Of course she brought her own genius to this, illuminating the inner lives of her characters and tackling big themes with humour, wit and subtlety.

When starting out as a writer it's tempting to try to go straight to your magnum opus. Instead it's important to experiment to find what it is you really want to write and where your skills lie.

EXERCISES: EXPERIMENT!

1. Try writing about a character who definitely isn't you, somebody who behaves in a way that you never

would. In *Love and Freindship* Jane Austen created two deeply silly and selfish characters in a tale of crazy coincidences. In *Lady Susan* she created a character who today would be considered a psychopath, someone manipulative and unconcerned about the feelings or welfare of others. Both stories are told through letters.

2. Think about something that you love reading, even if it isn't considered great literature. In *Northanger Abbey*, a funny, intelligent novel about novels, Jane Austen namechecks not just some of her favourite contemporary novels, but also some which we can guess she would have enjoyed even though she might have considered them trashy. Take your cue from a book that you really enjoyed and start writing. You might want to start with a character reading that book and go from there.

BE PREPARED FOR THINGS TO TAKE A LONG TIME

Jane Austen was serious about writing from a very early age. In January 1796 she wrote to Cassandra, joking, 'I am very much flattered by your commendation of my last letter, for I write only for fame, and without any view to pecuniary emolument.' She dedicated herself to her craft and clearly understood that she was talented. The restrictions of the time meant that she couldn't approach publishers directly. Some women novelists of the period were public figures, but Jane, as the daughter of a clergyman and not wanting to attract public attention and possible disapproval, had to rely on her father and later her brother Henry to act for her. How frustrating that must have been.

We know that in 1797 Jane's father tried to interest the publishers Cadell and Davis in *First Impressions* but they sent the manuscript back unopened; we don't know who else the novel that was to become *Pride and Prejudice* may have been submitted to. She had already written *Lady Susan* and *Elinor and Marianne* (later *Sense and Sensibility*). Over the next few years Jane kept working. She had to move from the family home that she loved in Steventon, Hampshire, when her father decided to retire. Her brother James took over the living and the house, an event that we seem to see echoes of in the opening of *Sense and Sensibility*. She was horrified at first at the thought of moving to Bath; perhaps her parents were hoping that she and Cassandra (whose fiancé had died) would find husbands there. Her distaste for Bath can be seen in Anne Elliot's initial attitude towards it in *Persuasion* and in the way it is critiqued in *Northanger Abbey*.

Jane's father died suddenly in Bath in early 1805, and his pension went with him. Jane, Cassandra and their mother then began a difficult semi-nomadic period, making long visits to relatives and moving between apartments, each a little cheaper and less pleasant than the last, until in 1807 they moved to Southampton to share a house with Jane's brother Frank and his family, and though we don't have exact details of what she was working on in Bath and Southampton, we know that in 1803 the manuscript of what was to become *Northanger Abbey* was sold to the publishers Crosby & Co. and that during this period she also began

The Watsons, one of her two unfinished novels, so she never gave up writing, even during these difficult times.

Jane must have been so excited when *Northanger Abbey* (then called *Susan*) was accepted, but even though the novel was advertised, it didn't appear. She had no idea why. Perhaps Crosby & Co. thought that it was too much of a satire of other works in their catalogue, or perhaps there were difficulties or personnel changes within the company. Jane had to buy the manuscript back years later, when she could finally afford to. We can imagine how embarrassed and disappointed she must have felt, but she carried on writing. It wasn't until 1811 that *Sense and Sensibility* was finally published and her career finally took off. She was thirty-six years old and had been serious about writing for at least twenty years.

FIND YOURSELF A MARTHA LLOYD OR A WHOLE GANG OF THEM

Martha and Cassandra were Jane's supporters and confidantes throughout her life. These friendships were key to Jane's happiness. Here is the young Jane writing to Cassandra on 9 January 1799 about a sleepover with Martha: 'I did not return home that night or the next, as Martha kindly made room for me in her bed, which was the shut up one in the new nursery. Nurse and the child slept on the floor; & there we all were in some confusion & great comfort; the bed did exceedingly well for us, both to lie awake in and talk till two o'clock, & to sleep in the rest of the night. I love Martha better than ever.' I hope the nurse and child were equally comfortable.

She got on well with her brothers too. Henry tried to help her in her work and retrieved the manuscript of what was to be *Northanger Abbey* from the dreadful Crosby & Co., encouraging her and giving her a base in London when she was working with publishers later on. We know from Jane's surviving letters that she sent copies of her books to her brothers as soon as she could and recorded their thoughts. Her relationship with James, the eldest, was sometimes more problematic. She had loved the theatricals he orchestrated when she was little and enjoyed the *Loiterer*. Assuming the Sophia Sentiment letter was from Jane (and it's hard to believe it wasn't), it shows the warmth of their relationship and how they must have talked and joked about novels. But a few lines in a letter written from Southampton on 9 February 1807 that escaped Cassandra's scissors[3] show how Jane sometimes felt about James later on:

I should not be surprised if we were to be visited by James again this week; he gave us reason to expect him soon ... I am sorry & angry that his Visits should not give one more pleasure;– the company of so good & so clever a Man ought to be gratifying in itself but his Chat seems all forced, his Opinions on many points too much copied from his Wife's, & his time here is spent I think in walking about the House & banging the Doors, or ringing the Bell for a glass of Water.

Jane had other significant friends. Anne Sharp, the governess of her brother Edward's children, was also important to her. It seems typical of Jane that she formed a close bond with Anne Sharp, rather than Elizabeth Knight, Edward's wife. After Jane died, Cassandra wrote to Anne Sharp and sent her a lock of Jane's hair. But Martha and Cassandra were Jane's most important friends. Cassandra took on more than her fair share of domestic duties to give Jane time to write, and the sisters seem to have decided that after Mr Austen's death their mother would always have one of them with her. Jane and Cassandra, as maiden aunts, were also often called on to help with nephews and nieces. Jane clearly missed her sister and all she did when Cassandra was away. We see evidence of this again and again in Jane's letters to Cassandra, right up to the last surviving one:

> I enjoyed Edward's company very much, as I said before, and yet I was not sorry when Friday came. It had been a busy week, and I wanted a few days quiet and exemption from the thought and contrivancy which any sort of company gives. I often wonder how *you* can find time for what you do, in addition to the care of the house; and how good Mrs West could have written such books and collected so many hard works, with all her family cares, is still more a matter of astonishment. Composition seems to me impossible with a head full of joints of mutton and doses of rhubarb.

As for Martha, she knew Jane's work so well that Jane joked that she might publish it from memory. Martha must have read the manuscript of *First Impressions* many times and been privy to the search for a publisher. Here is Jane writing to Cassandra on 11 June 1799 about Martha's knowledge of her unpublished novel: 'I would not let

Martha read *First Impressions* again upon any account, & am very glad that I did not leave it in your power. She is very cunning, but I see through her design; she means to publish it from memory & one more perusal will enable her to do it.'

This is particularly significant as only those closest to Jane knew about her ambitions. Even some of her favourite nephews and nieces read *Sense and Sensibility* and *Pride and Prejudice* without knowing who the books' anonymous author was. Cultivate your own Martha and Cassandra and try to be a Martha or Cassandra to your writer friends. Writing is a lonely business, and we all need a little help.

MAKE SURE THAT THOSE CLOSEST TO YOU UNDERSTAND YOUR COMPULSION

Although Jane was quite private about her literary ambitions, her parents and siblings knew and understood how serious she was about writing. In 1794 Jane's father bought her a lovely portable writing box (the equivalent of a laptop), probably as a birthday present. It's in the British Library now, along with her spectacles. The gift seems to show that her parents understood what Jane was all about and how important her writing was to her.

However, her parents were still concerned about her future. She had to rely on her family for money; the pressure on young women to marry well is something that she explores again and again in her work. Jane could flirt and dance with the best of them, but she was sparky and determined and perhaps a bit of an odd stick. Cassandra was engaged and Jane a very marriageable twenty years old when her mother wrote to James's future wife Mary Lloyd on 30 November 1796, 'I look forward to you as a real comfort to me in my old age, when Cassandra has gone to Shropshire, and Jane – the Lord knows where.'

FIND YOURSELF A CHAWTON COTTAGE – ACTUAL OR MENTAL

Jane Austen found her childhood home, Steventon Rectory, very conducive to work and creativity, but her years in Bath and then Southampton and the uncertainty of having no permanent home much less so. It was when she knew that she was to have a permanent home again in the Hampshire countryside that she seems to have properly got back to work again. Just before she left Southampton for Chawton she wrote her famous M.A.D. letter to Crosby and Co. for the return of the manuscript of what was to become *Northanger Abbey*. She really was mad at the publishers.

April 5, 1809

Gentlemen

In the spring of the year of 1803, a MS Novel in 2 vol. entitled Susan was sold to you by a Gentleman of the name of Seymour, & the purchase money £10 rec'd at the same time. Six years have since passed, & this work of which I am myself the Authoress, has never to the best of my knowledge, appeared in print, tho' an early publication was stipulated for at the time of sale. I can only account for such an extraordinary circumstance by supposing the MS by some carelessness to have been lost; & if that was the case, am willing to supply you with another copy if you are disposed to avail yourselves of it, & will engage for no farther delay when it comes into your hands. It will not be in my power from particular circumstances to command this copy before the Month of August, but then, if you accept my proposal, you may depend on receiving it. Be so good as to send me a Line in answer as soon as possible, as my stay in this place will not exceed a few days. Should no notice be taken of this address, I shall feel myself at liberty to secure the publication of my work, by applying elsewhere. I am Gentleman &c. &c.

M.A.D.
Direct to Mrs Ashton Dennis
Post Office, Southampton

It seems Jane knew that with peace and stability she would be able to resume serious writing, and she was right. The home in Chawton given to her, Cassandra, Mrs Austen and Martha Lloyd was where she revised *Sense and Sensibility* and *Pride and Prejudice* and saw them published, and where she wrote *Mansfield Park*, *Emma* and *Persuasion*. Only illness forced her final move to Winchester and the cessation of work on *Sanditon*. She wrote a letter in verse to Frank on 26 July 1809, a few weeks after they had moved into Chawton.

My dearest Frank, I wish you joy
Of Mary's safety with a Boy,

Whose birth has given little pain
Compared with that of Mary Jane.
[...]
　　　As for ourselves, we're very well,
As unaffected prose will tell.
Cassandra's pen will give our state
The many comforts that await
Our Chawton home – how much we find
Already in it, to our mind,
And how convinced that when complete,
It will all other Houses beat
That ever have been made or mended,
With rooms concise, or rooms distended.
　　　You'll find us very snug next year;
Perhaps with Charles & Fanny near
For now it often does delight us
To fancy them just over-right us.

Sadly we can't all live at Chawton (even the writer-in-residence there doesn't get to stay the night), but we can try to create similar spaces for ourselves whether real or mental. Put up beautiful and inspiring things in the place where you work so that your eye has something gorgeous to rest on each time you glance up. Postcards, photos and maps of places you are using will help. (I'm not sure how this applies to crime writers. Would you want autopsy shots? Perhaps noir-ish photos of your settings would be better.) Artefacts are helpful too. Keep your workspace clear of things that will depress or distract you and that aren't to do with your writing. Don't keep bank statements and bills anywhere near the place you like to write; if you're living in just one room or a shared space, put them in a box where you can't see them. I often light a scented candle when I'm working. (A Muji log fire one right now which smells like bonfires. It's autumn.)

KNOW THAT NO EFFORT OR EXPERIMENT IS WASTED

Jane Austen abandoned *The Watsons*, which was started during a very difficult period. Perhaps, as Edith Hubback speculated in the introduction to her continuation of *The Watsons*,[4] moving in with her brother and his wife in Southampton made Jane Austen feel that the novel was too close to her current situation. Perhaps Jane decided that she didn't want to write about somebody in as precarious a situation as Emma Watson. Perhaps she just got sick of the characters and felt that her other ideas were stronger. Writers frequently have false starts and ideas that don't come to fruition. After Jane moved to Chawton she revised *First Impressions* and *Elinor and Marianne* instead of continuing with *The Watsons*, and then, in her period of greatest creativity and productivity, wrote *Mansfield Park*, *Emma* and *Persuasion* in quick succession. I expect the new ideas she had for those novels were just more appealing than the one she'd had for *The Watsons* some years before.

The effort expended on *The Watsons* wasn't wasted, though. We all learn from things that don't work out. Maybe *The Watsons* made Jane feel she would be better off setting her novels in more elevated circles, or perhaps she wanted more comedy in her work. *The Watsons* really is pretty bleak, and the surviving manuscript shows how she scratched out words to make it seem even bleaker. Echoes of themes and characters in *The Watsons* can be seen in her other works: we have Emma Woodhouse rather than Emma Watson but both have ailing, elderly fathers. The theme of women needing to marry well to secure their futures is explored again and again in different ways. Jane Austen possibly intended to return to *The Watsons*. I think it's significant that she kept it.

Don't despise or discard things you don't finish; learn what you can from them and be aware of things that may be recyclable.

WHAT NOT TO WRITE

Even a genius makes the occasional mistake; this passage from *Persuasion* is borderline nasty. Mrs Musgrove is still mourning the loss of her ne'er-do-well son, who served on one of Captain Wentworth's ships.

> They [Anne Elliot and Captain Wentworth] were actually on the same sofa, for Mrs Musgrove had most readily made room for him; they were divided only by Mrs Musgrove. It was no insignificant barrier, indeed. Mrs Musgrove was of a comfortable, substantial size, infinitely more fitted by nature to express good cheer and good humour, than tenderness and sentiment; and while the agitations of Anne's slender form, and pensive face, may be considered as very completely screened, Captain Wentworth should be allowed some credit for the self-command with which he attended to her large fat sighings over the destiny of a son, whom alive nobody had cared for.

Personal size and mental sorrow have certainly no necessary proportions. A large bulky figure has as good a right to be in deep affliction, as the most graceful set of limbs in the world. But, fair or not fair, there are unbecoming conjunctions, which reason will patronize in vain – which taste cannot tolerate – which ridicule will seize.

Captain Wentworth demonstrates his caring nature by being kind to Mrs Musgrove, entering 'into conversation with her, in a low voice, about her son, doing it with so much sympathy and natural grace, as shewed the kindest consideration for all that was real and unabsurd in the parent's feelings'. Jane Austen could have conveyed what Captain Wentworth was like without being snooty about fat people, but I haven't noticed any other passages like this in her novels. Her letters are a different matter, but they were never intended for publication. Here's an extract from a letter to Cassandra written on Thursday 20 November 1800.

There were very few beauties, and such as there were were not very handsome. Miss Iremonger did not look well, and Mrs Blount was the only one much admired. She appeared exactly as she did in September, with the same broad face, diamond bandeau, white shoes, pink husband, and fat neck. The two Miss Coxes were there: I traced in one the remains of the vulgar, broad-featured girl who danced at Enham eight years ago; the other is refined into a nice, composed-looking girl, like Catherine Bigg. I looked at Sir Thomas Champneys and thought of poor Rosalie; I looked at his daughter, and thought her a queer animal with a white neck. Mrs Warren, I was constrained to think, a very fine young woman, which I much regret. She . . . danced away with great activity looking by no means very large. Her husband is ugly enough, uglier even than his cousin John; but he does not look so *very* old. The Miss Maitlands are both prettyish, very like Anne, with brown skins, large dark eyes, and a good deal of nose. The General has got the gout, and Mrs Maitland the jaundice. Miss Debary, Susan, and Sally, all in black, but without any stature, made their appearance, and I was as civil to them as their bad breath would allow me.

She adds to the letter the next day, 'I had the comfort of finding out the other evening who all the fat girls with long noses were that disturbed me at the 1st H. ball. They all prove to be Miss Atkinsons of En–'

Writing to Cassandra from Steventon on 27 October 1798 Jane is unpleasant: 'Mrs Hall, of Sherborne, was brought to bed yesterday of a dead child, some weeks before she expected, owing to a fright. I suppose she happened unawares to look at her husband.' And here she is, on 1 December the same year, writing to Cassandra about their sisters-in-law.

I was at Deane yesterday morning. Mary was very well, but does not gain bodily strength very fast. When I saw her so stout on the third and sixth days, I expected to have seen her as well as ever by the end of a fortnight.

[. . .] Mary does not manage matters in such a way as to make me want to lay in myself. She is not tidy enough in her appearance; she has no dressing-gown to sit up in; her curtains are all too thin, and things are not in that comfort and style about her which are necessary to make such a situation an enviable one. Elizabeth was really a pretty object with her nice clean cap put on so tidily and her dress so uniformly white and orderly.

It is rather unfair to compare Mary, the second wife of her clergyman brother, James, to Elizabeth, Edward's wife, who lived in such luxury at the Knights' gorgeous home, Godmersham.

A few weeks later, on 18 December, Jane writes to Cassandra,

I expect a very stupid ball; there will be nobody worth dancing with, and nobody worth talking to but Catherine, for I believe Mrs Lefroy will not be there. [. . .]

People get so horridly poor and economical in this part of the world that I have no patience with them. Kent is the only place for happiness; everybody is rich there. I must do similar justice, however, to the Windsor neighbourhood. I have been forced to let James and Miss Debary have two sheets of your drawing-paper.

In this period Jane's letters often have an arch tone. She seems bored. It is no wonder that childbearing held little appeal – her letters contain frequent mentions of women who have lost their lives in childbirth. She has still not got over Tom Lefroy, whom she had fallen for and hoped to receive a proposal from in winter 1795–6, and nobody else has won her heart. On 17 November 1798 she writes to Cassandra,

> Mrs Lefroy [Tom's aunt] did come last Wednesday, and the Harwoods came likewise, but very considerately paid their visit before Mrs Lefroy's arrival, with whom, in spite of interruptions both from my father and James, I was enough alone to hear all that was interesting, which you will easily credit when I tell you that of her nephew she said nothing at all, and of her friend[5] very little. She did not once mention the name of the former to me, and I was too proud to make any inquiries; but on my father's afterwards asking where he was, I learnt that he was gone back to London in his way to Ireland, where he is called to the Bar and means to practise.

Jane didn't expect anyone but Cassandra to read her nasty comments about people or what she wrote about Tom Lefroy or the Reverend Samuel Blackall. 'Seize upon the scissors as soon as you possibly can on the receipt of this,' she tells Cassandra in a letter written on Christmas Eve 1798, but Cassandra kept her beloved sister's letters and only took the scissors to those she was going to bequeath much later on, sometimes missing things that Jane would certainly not want others to read.

The reason I reproduce these comments is to show what a great writer Jane was in ensuring that her fiction was far removed from the snide observations she often made in private. Readers often speculate about whether her characters were portraits of people she knew, but if they were she

managed to disguise them so well that they weren't recognizable. She was also careful to locate her stories in places where
she didn't live. None of her novels are set in Hampshire,
the county she knew best. She makes excellent use of Bath
and London, but that is very different from using villages
like Steventon or Chawton. It's likely she learned from the
bad example of the Austens' one-time neighbour Egerton
Brydges, whose novel *Arthur Fitz-Albini* Jane writes about
in a letter to Cassandra on Sunday 25 November 1798.

We have got 'Fitz-Albini'; my father has bought it
against my private wishes, for it does not quite satisfy
my feelings that we should purchase the only one of
Egerton's works of which his family are ashamed. That
these scruples, however, do not at all interfere with my
reading it, you will easily believe. We have neither of us
yet finished the first volume. My father is disappointed –
I am not, for I expected nothing better. Never did any
book carry more internal evidence of its author. Every
sentiment is completely Egerton's. There is very little
story, and what there is is told in a strange, unconnected
way. There are many characters introduced, apparently
merely to be delineated. We have not been able to recog-
nise any of them hitherto, except Dr and Mrs Hey and
Mr Oxenden, who is not very tenderly treated.

To her immense credit, the young Jane Austen did all
she could to ensure that her novels didn't carry any 'internal
evidence' of their author. They are proper works of fiction.
What she did do was learn from her reading, both from
the books that she admired and those that she didn't, and

utilize her experiences and the emotions that they had brought. It is easy to see how her regrets about Tom Lefroy and the way she had let her feelings for him be known might have been drawn upon in *Sense and Sensibility*, and how his family's opposition to the match might have been the grit inside the pearl that is *Pride and Prejudice*.

The mood in Jane's earliest surviving letters to Cassandra, which date from 1796, is very different from that in the letters I have quoted from above.

Steventon: Saturday January 9.

In the first place I hope you will live twenty-three years longer. Mr Tom Lefroy's birthday was yesterday, so that you are very near of an age.

After this necessary preamble I shall proceed to inform you that we had an exceeding good ball last night. You scold me so much in the nice long letter which I have this moment received from you, that I am almost afraid to tell you how my Irish friend and I behaved. Imagine to yourself everything most profligate and shocking in the way of dancing and sitting down together. I can expose myself however, only once more, because he leaves the country soon after next Friday, on which day we are to have a dance at Ashe after all. He is a very gentlemanlike, good-looking, pleasant young man, I assure you. But as to our having ever met, except at the three last balls, I cannot say much; for he is so excessively laughed at about me at Ashe, that he is ashamed of coming to Steventon, and ran away when we called on Mrs Lefroy a few days ago. [...]

After I had written the above, we received a visit from Mr Tom Lefroy and his cousin George. The latter is really very well-behaved now; and as for the other, he has but one fault, which time will, I trust, entirely remove – it is that his morning coat is a great deal too light. He is a very great admirer of Tom Jones, and therefore wears the same coloured clothes, I imagine, which he did when he was wounded.

And from the next surviving letter (Steventon, 16 January):

Our party to Ashe to-morrow night will consist of Edward Cooper, James (for a ball is nothing without him), Buller, who is now staying with us, and I look forward with great impatience to it, as I rather expect to receive an offer from my friend in the course of the evening. I shall refuse him, however, unless he promises to give away his white coat.

I am very much flattered by your commendation of my last letter, for I write only for fame, and without any view to pecuniary emolument.

Tell Mary that I make over Mr Heartley and all his estate to her for her sole use and benefit in future, and not only him, but all my other admirers into the bargain wherever she can find them, even the kiss which C. Powlett wanted to give me, as I mean to confine myself in future to Mr Tom Lefroy, for whom I don't care sixpence. [. . .]

Friday. – At length the day is come on which I am to flirt my last with Tom Lefroy, and when you receive this it will be over. My tears flow as I write at the melancholy idea. Wm. Chute called here yesterday. I wonder what he means by being so civil.

Jane might have later wished that she had been more of an Elinor and less of a Marianne. Perhaps she even worried that she had seemed like a Lydia Bennet or an Anne Steele.

The lesson here is that great fiction can be written when one draws upon one's experiences and on the emotions they have engendered; one doesn't need to copy from life. The best novels aren't autobiographies.

BUT IT'S ALL MATERIAL

You might have periods when you can't finish much. Don't worry; just keep taking notes. Jane never wanted to move to Bath, and when she left it was 'with happy feelings of escape'.[6] She may not have completed much while she was living in the city, but she was definitely observing and planning. We see Jane's knowledge of Bath, the shops and streets, the Assembly Rooms and how people spent their time there, the weather and, above all, the people and the way they behaved put to excellent use in *Northanger Abbey* and *Persuasion*. Her letters from Bath show what she was doing and noticing. Here she is writing to Cassandra on 12 May 1801 about an evening out.

After tea we cheered up; the breaking up of private parties sent some scores more to the ball, and though it was shockingly and inhumanly thin for this place, there were people enough, I suppose, to have made five or six very pretty Basingstoke assemblies.

I then got Mr Evelyn to talk to, and Miss T. to look at; and I am proud to say that I have a very good eye at an adulteress, for though repeatedly assured that another in the same party was the She, I fixed upon the right one from the first. A resemblance to Mrs L. was my guide. She is not so pretty as I expected; her face has the same defect of baldness as her sisters, and her features not so handsome; she was highly rouged, and looked rather quietly and contentedly silly than anything else.

Mrs B. and two young women were of the same party, except when Mrs B. thought herself obliged to leave them to run round the room after her drunken husband. His avoidance, and her pursuit, with the probable intoxication of both, was an amusing scene.

And here she is on 5 May 1801, writing about what she saw from the carriage window when she arrived in Bath, a memory that she utilized in *Persuasion* with Anne Elliot and Lady Russell's contrasting feelings about arriving in the city: 'The first view of Bath in fine weather does not answer my expectations; I think I see more distinctly through rain. The sun was got behind everything, and the appearance of the place from the top of Kingsdown was all vapour, shadow, smoke, and confusion.' More than two hundred years later we can still follow the routes her characters took, see where Catherine Morland was almost run over by the appalling John Thorpe and where she first danced with Henry Tilney, and where Anne Elliot walked arm in arm (at last!) with Captain Wentworth.

KEEP READING NEW THINGS – SET UP YOUR OWN CHAWTON BOOK SOCIETY

When you are feeling dull or struggling with your writing, Jane's advice would be to read more and read something new. Here she is writing to Cassandra from Chawton on 24 January 1813 about an unexpected pleasure: 'We are quite run over with books ... I am reading a Society octavo, an "Essay on the Military Police and Institutions of the British Empire" by Capt. Pasley of the Engineers, a book which I protested against at first, but which upon trial I find delightfully written and highly entertaining.'

DON'T ALLOW YOURSELF TO BECOME STAGNANT

After Fanny Price, Jane Austen created Emma Woodhouse, saying, 'I am going to take a heroine whom no one but myself will much like.' It's interesting to look at Jane's novels as a progression. She was challenging her readers as well as herself. In publication order she went from restrained Elinor Dashwood to sparkling Lizzy Bennet and then on to Fanny Price, a complete mouse in comparison; then came Emma Woodhouse, handsome, rich and clever and, unlike Fanny Price, always getting things wrong. Anne Elliot is many people's favourite, and in her Jane chose to work with an older heroine, wiser and sadder than any of the others. We should consider Catherine Morland an early creation, despite the novel not being published until after Jane's death. Catherine is open-hearted and gullible, very different from Elinor or Lizzy, whom she preceded; even before Catherine we have Jane's anti-heroine Lady Susan.

Her novels may all be about love, marriage and money, but Jane creates new characters and locations and does something very different in each one. Her death at forty-one robbed the world of so much. If she had lived to the same age as her brother Frank, who died in 1865 at the age of ninety-one, having kept all his faculties, we might have had Austen novels with heroines who lived in industrial cities and took trains and were subject to very different expectations and societal rules. Jane would also have been reading and responding to the work of a very different set of authors and poets. In *Sanditon* she seemed to be moving in a new direction with her backdrop of a growing seaside resort. Charlotte Heywood, the heroine of *Sanditon*, is a sharp observer of people and society; we can speculate, but we just don't know the direction that novel was to take.

Writers often feel that they are writing the same story again and again, but even if that is the case, we can try to do it differently every time.

EXPERIMENT WITH LANGUAGE, STYLE AND FORM

Jane Austen worked at her craft, innovating and pushing herself with each novel. The original manuscripts weren't kept, so we can't see how much she improved her writing from the late 1790s before it was published in the 1810s. However, we can see how, starting with her juvenilia, going on to her first published work, then to *Persuasion* and the first chapters of *Sanditon*, she experimented with language, style and form. Family tradition had it that *Sense and Sensibility* had been recast from a novel in letters. This seems unlikely as the principal characters are rarely apart; perhaps it was *Pride and Prejudice* that once consisted of letters. Jane and Elizabeth Bennet are often apart, and Elizabeth could also have corresponded with Mrs Gardiner and Charlotte Collins. It's fun to imagine the content of letters between Mr Darcy and Lady Catherine or Caroline Bingley and Georgiana Darcy, or from Kitty to Lydia (Lydia would not have bothered to write much back). Here she is setting off from Longbourn with Wickham in *Pride and Prejudice*, Chapter 53:

> The day of his and Lydia's departure soon came, and Mrs Bennet was forced to submit to a separation, which, as her husband by no means entered into her scheme of their all going to Newcastle, was likely to continue at least a twelvemonth.
>
> 'Oh! my dear Lydia,' she cried, 'when shall we meet again?'
>
> 'Oh, Lord! I don't know. Not these two or three years, perhaps.'
>
> 'Write to me very often, my dear.'
>
> 'As often as I can. But you know married women have never much time for writing. My sisters may write to *me*. They will have nothing else to do.'

Jane must have appreciated how a novel in letters like *Lady Susan* might be good fun, prompting readers to imagine the actual events for themselves, but this form limits the author's ability to illuminate many aspects of the story, setting and characters. Using letters or diary entries also means that the immediacy of seeing the story unfold before one's eyes is lost.

This innovative little section from *Emma* (Chapter 42) is in complete contrast to telling a story through letters. It captures exactly what it is like to be picking strawberries in the sun with Mrs Elton in the grounds of Donwell Abbey. Jane Austen focuses on the dreadful Mrs Elton, who is dominating the event. Rather than writing the whole scene, Jane just gives us what we need to know. There is no necessity to tell us what, if anything, people might say in reply to Mrs Elton as she talks on and on, contradicting herself and never pausing for breath. Jane Austen might have spent a few pages on this scene, but we get just one paragraph of prose that seems to prefigure the work of modernist writers like Virginia Woolf. At the end of the section we can understand why Emma wants to flee indoors to escape and why poor Jane Fairfax (who is in a terrible situation with Frank Churchill) has such a headache. You can see how Mrs Elton's mood deflates as the scene progresses, while the names of the strawberry varieties add veracity.

The whole party were assembled, excepting Frank Churchill, who was expected every moment from Richmond; and Mrs Elton, in all her apparatus of happiness, her large bonnet and her basket, was very ready to lead the way in gathering, accepting, or talking – strawberries, and only strawberries, could now be thought or spoken of. – 'The best fruit in England – every body's favourite – always wholesome. – These the finest beds and finest sorts. – Delightful to gather for one's self – the only way of really enjoying them. – Morning decidedly the best time – never tired – every sort good – hautboy infinitely superior – no comparison – the others hardly eatable – hautboys very scarce – Chili preferred – white wood finest flavour of all – price of strawberries in London – abundance about Bristol – Maple Grove – cultivation – beds when to be renewed – gardeners thinking exactly different – no general rule – gardeners never to be put out of their way – delicious fruit – only too rich to be eaten much of – inferior to cherries – currants more refreshing – only objection to gathering strawberries the stooping – glaring sun – tired to death – could bear it no longer – must go and sit in the shade.'

EXERCISE: CONCISION AND EXPERIMENTATION

Have a look at your work and find a scene that you feel drags or could be improved. Now rewrite it. Start from scratch; don't just edit. How concise can you make it without losing anything essential? Can you make it punchier by being more concise? Will shifting the focus to a different character help? Can you capture one or all of the voices more convincingly? Can you make it funnier?

LIMBER UP AND REMAIN FLEXIBLE

Although Jane Austen explored similar themes in the same social milieu in all her novels, she kept changing the way she did things. Look at the different ways she opens her novels and introduces her characters.

Experiment with openings and ways of introducing characters

Pride and Prejudice opens *in media res* with dialogue, and the assumptions of the world are given in that famous opening line: 'It is a truth universally acknowledged, that a single man in possession of a good fortune, must be in want of a wife.' We discover Elizabeth Bennet only once we have met her parents and understood their concerns. In *Mansfield Park* Fanny Price is introduced only after we have been told the story of how her mother and aunts married and fell out. Seeing her as a shy little girl removed from her home makes us all the more sympathetic to her. The opening of *Sense and Sensibility* shows us how the gorgeous rug is pulled from beneath the feet of Mrs Dashwood and her three daughters. The theme of money, meanness and injustice is set up straight away. With *Northanger Abbey* the author makes herself present immediately, and the tone of the book and ordinariness of the heroine are established from the first sentence. In *Emma* the introductions are upfront.

But whichever method Jane Austen uses to open her novel and introduce its characters, we always learn what their predicament is straight away. Even with Emma Woodhouse, whose life seems pretty much perfect, we learn that her mother died when she was very young and she has since lost the company of her sister and most recently that of her governess and friend, Miss Taylor.

EXERCISE

Have a critical look at an opening you've written. Is there enough there to entice people to read on? Are you starting the story in the right place? Readers today expect things to get going faster than their nineteenth-century counterparts. I'm not saying you must put down a big chunk of backstory on your first page, but suggesting that you look at Jane's different methods and think about tone, the most suitable incident to start with and the best way for readers to discover your characters and be led into their world. Think about how your themes will be introduced. You are unlikely to come up with the perfect opening first time; by the time you get to the end of your story, the thing that you planned to write will have been transformed into something else. Once you have finished a first draft you should go back and write the most effective opening for it.

Experiment with form

If a story isn't working or you have a new idea, don't assume you should revert to a formula you have already used. Not all good ideas are right for novels, and even if your idea *is* the starting point of a wonderful novel, you should think about form and the best way of telling your story. It's important to remain playful and open to new ways of doing things. Changing the form of a work or the structure of a story will transform the way the reader experiences it. Jane Austen retained her playfulness and willingness to experiment right to the end of her life. Her juvenilia includes a spoof history book, a play and many little stories and attempts at novels. She wrote rhymes and poems and included them in letters to her family. We have a prayer that she wrote, and just a few days before she died she composed this poem. It seems Cassandra wrote it down and probably changed the rhyme in line 14 from 'dead' (which would have rhymed with 'said') to 'gone'. Poor Cassandra probably couldn't bear to write the word with her beloved sister's end so imminent.

When Winchester races first took their beginning
It is said the good people forgot their old Saint
Not applying at all for the leave of Saint Swithin
And that William of Wykeham's approval was faint.

The races however were fixed and determined
The company came and the Weather was charming
The Lords and the Ladies were satine'd and ermined
And nobody saw any future alarming.–

But when the old Saint was informed of these doings
He made but one Spring from his Shrine to the Roof
Of the Palace which now lies so sadly in ruins
And then he addressed them all standing aloof.

'Oh! subjects rebellious! Oh Venta depraved
When once we are buried you think we are gone
But behold me immortal! By vice you're enslaved
You have sinned and must suffer, ten farther he said.

These races and revels and dissolute measures
With which you're debasing a neighboring Plain
Let them stand – You shall meet with your curse in
    your pleasures
Set off for your course, I'll pursue with my rain.

Ye cannot but know my command o'er July
Henceforward I'll triumph in shewing my powers
Shift your race as you will it shall never be dry
The curse upon Venta is July in showers –'.

Jane wrote poems and rhymes on many subjects, including one in memory of her dear friend Mrs Lefroy, who had died on her (Jane's) birthday, and one to Frank on the birth of his son while he was away at sea.

That poem, a whole letter in verse, goes on to tell Frank how happy she is with their new home in Chawton. There are also poems about headaches, about family and friends departing and arriving, about current events and to accompany gifts. Jane's poems are light verse, but show her capturing moments and feelings; they demonstrate the enjoyment and release she felt in putting pen to paper.

Be like Jane Austen and don't expect every bit of writing you produce to become something significant. Particularly when you're writing your first novel, don't try to fit in all your good jokes and include everything you have ever noticed. Keep doing little throwaway things, writing on whims as well as working on bigger projects. This will help you to stay playful and creative and not be too precious about your work. Not everything you write will be great art. Be like an artist in a studio – happy to do lots of little sketches and to experiment with different materials and sizes of canvas.

EXERCISES

1. *Capturing moments.* This is something that you should keep doing, not a one-off exercise. Keep a notebook that is not necessarily to do with any big project you are working on. Keep jotting down ideas that you have for stories or poems and things that you feel strongly about and want to write about, even though they probably won't fit into your current work. When the fancy takes you, develop one of them. Seizing the moment is best. It's easy to imagine how Jane's letter in verse to Frank about the birth of his son quickly developed from what had been the opening line of a regular letter – 'My dearest Frank, I wish you joy of Mary's safety with a Boy . . .'

2. *Experimenting with form.* Not every idea you have will be right for a novel; conversely, you might have an idea for a short story that develops into a novel. Have a look at a story you have started but not finished or one that you have finished but aren't happy with, or take an entirely new idea, and experiment with structure and form. Your first idea of how to tell the story won't necessarily be the best. If you have written a long prosey work, try recasting it in

a much more succinct form, or try experimenting with structure by altering the point of view or playing with the chronology. Be inspired by the variety in Jane Austen's work. Here's the opening of *Lady Susan* – you can see how different it is from Jane's other works:

Langford, December.

My dear Brother

I can no longer refuse myself the pleasure of profiting by your kind invitation, when we last parted, of spending some weeks with you at Churchill, & therefore, if quite convenient to you & Mrs Vernon to receive me at present, I shall hope within a few days to be introduced to a Sister whom I have so long desired to be acquainted with. My kind friends here are most affectionately urgent with me to prolong my stay, but their hospitable & chearful dispositions lead them too much into society for my present situation & state of mind; & I impatiently look forward to the hour when I shall be admitted into your delightful retirement. I long to be made known to your dear little children, in whose hearts I shall be very eager to secure an interest. I shall soon have need for all my fortitude, as I am on the point of separation from my own daughter. The long illness of her dear Father prevented my paying her that attention which

Duty & affection equally dictated, & I have too much reason to fear that the Governess to whose care I consigned her was unequal to the charge. I have therefore resolved on placing her at one of the best Private Schools in Town, where I shall have an opportunity of leaving her myself, in my way to you. I am determined, you see, not to be denied admittance at Churchill. It would indeed give me most painful sensations to know that it were not in your power to receive me.

Yr. most obliged & affec: Sister
S. VERNON.

3. *Enter a spiritual dimension.* Jane Austen was a clergyman's daughter, and her brothers James and Henry became clerics too. She was steeped in this world – just look at *Mansfield Park* and her quiet hero Edward Ferrars in *Sense and Sensibility.* There is also Mr Collins ... Here's a prayer written by Jane. It was probably to be spoken aloud by one person and followed by the Lord's Prayer.[7]

Give us grace, Almighty Father, so to pray, as to deserve to be heard, to address thee with our Hearts, as with our lips. Thou art every where present, from Thee no secret can be hid. May the knowledge of this, teach us to fix our Thoughts on Thee, with Reverence and Devotion that we pray not in vain.

Look with Mercy on the Sins we have this day committed, and in Mercy make us feel them deeply, that our Repentance may be sincere, & our resolutions stedfast of endeavouring against the commission of such in future. Teach us to understand the sinfulness of our own Hearts, and bring to our knowledge every fault of Temper and every evil Habit in which we have indulged to the discomfort of our fellow-creatures, and the danger of our own Souls. May we now, and on each return of night, consider how the past day has been spent by us, what have been our prevailing Thoughts, Words, and Actions during it, and how far we can acquit ourselves of Evil. Have we thought irreverently of Thee, have we disobeyed thy commandments, have we neglected any known duty, or willingly given pain to any human being? Incline us to ask our Hearts these questions Oh! God, and save us from deceiving ourselves by Pride or Vanity.

Give us a thankful sense of the Blessings in which we live, of the many comforts of our lot; that we may not deserve to lose them by Discontent or Indifference.

Be gracious to our Necessities, and guard us, and all we love, from Evil this night. May the sick and afflicted, be now, and ever thy care; and heartily do we pray for the safety of all that travel by Land or by Sea, for the comfort & protection of the Orphan and Widow and that thy pity may be shewn upon all Captives and Prisoners.

Above all other blessings Oh! God, for ourselves, and our fellow-creatures, we implore Thee to quicken our sense of thy Mercy in the redemption of the World, of the Value of that Holy Religion in which we have been brought up, that we may not, by our own neglect, throw away the salvation thou hast given us, nor be Christians only in name. Hear us Almighty God, for His sake who has redeemed us, and taught us thus to pray.[8]

Now have a go at writing a prayer, blessing, incantation, curse or spell. You could write it from your own point of view or from the point of view of one of your characters. Use it to express whatever you want – longing, remorse, joy, a wish for revenge . . . Address it to whoever you want or whoever your character would choose. This might be God or a god, a saint, the Goddess, the Green Man . . .

This exercise can be useful for getting something off your chest – sometimes we need to do that before we start a bigger project – or for capturing and crystallizing how a character feels about something. Jane Austen's prayer asks for 'the safety of all that travel by Land or by Sea', and we can imagine her thinking of her sailor brothers and of Cassandra's fiancé, who had died in the West Indies. She also talks about being thankful – 'Give us a thankful sense of the Blessings in which we live, of the many comforts of our lot; that we may not deserve to lose them by Discontent or Indifference.' My guess is that it was hard for her not to feel discontented when she had to rely so much on the males of her family; her own position and path through life must have felt so difficult, particularly compared to Edward's. This is not a private prayer, though. Imagine what one of your characters might pray for silently.

BE TRUE TO YOURSELF AND ONLY WRITE WHAT YOU WANT TO WRITE

It's important to accept constructive criticism, but writers must also stay true to themselves. There's no point trying to be the sort of writer you are not or chasing a trend – by the time your work is finished, fashion will have moved on. Beginners often wonder if the way to make a fortune is by writing something commercial rather than something they believe in, but remember that the authors of romances, horror novels or thrillers that sell by the truckload are not writing cynically. As Rebecca West put it, 'No one can write a best-seller by taking thought. The slightest touch of insincerity blurs its appeal. The writer who keeps his tongue in his cheek, who knows that he is writing for fools and that, therefore, he had better write like a fool . . . will never make the vast, the blaring, the half a million success. That comes of blended sincerity and vitality.'9

Jane Austen knew that she had to stick to what she did best and to what she really believed in and loved. She wrote to James Stanier Clarke, the Prince Regent's librarian, on 1 April 1816,

> You are very kind in your hints as to the sort of composition which might recommend me at present, and I am fully sensible that an historical romance, founded on the House of Saxe Coburg,[10] might be much more to the purpose of profit or popularity than such pictures of domestic life in country villages as I deal in. But I could no more write a romance than an epic poem. I could not sit seriously down to write a serious romance under any other motive than to save my life; and if it were indispensable for me to keep it up and never relax into laughing at myself or other people, I am sure I should be hung before I had finished the first chapter. No, I must keep to my own style and go on in my own way; and though I may never succeed again in that, I am convinced that I should totally fail in any other.

KNOW THAT THERE WILL BE TIMES WHEN YOU CANNOT WORK – ACCEPT THEM

Even a writer of Jane Austen's skill and determination sometimes just couldn't get any work done. She and Cassandra spent weeks at a time either staying with relatives, often when a new baby had been born and extra help was required, or having people to stay. Jane's letters are peppered with comments about who is arriving when, and where they will all sleep. There was also the social round of visiting, writing letters and drinking tea. The sisters looked after Mrs Austen after she was widowed, and although her mother outlived Jane and dug potatoes in the garden of the Chawton cottage well into old age, it's clear that Jane often found her trying. On 18 December 1798 (so when her mother was not yet elderly) Jane was keeping Cassandra up to date: 'My Mother continues hearty, her appetite & nights are very good, but her Bowels are still not entirely settled, & she sometimes complains of an Asthma, a Dropsy, Water in her Chest & a Liver Disorder.' The tone here is comic, but family duties clearly had an impact on Jane's ability to work.

There will be times when it is hard or even impossible to write. Jane Austen coped with these periods by throwing herself into whatever it was she had to do. Here she is writing to Cassandra from Southampton on 24 October 1808 about caring for some nephews who had just lost their mother: 'We do not want amusement: bilbocatch,[11] at which George is indefatigable; spillikins, paper ships, riddles, conundrums, and cards, with watching the flow and ebb of the river, and now and then a stroll out, keep us well employed.' But what you mustn't do is use things as excuses.

FORCE YOURSELF TO WORK

Unless you are very ill, coping with a crisis or have a *huge* gang of relatives staying, there is really no excuse not to work. Jane Austen, like so many writers, had a routine. She would get up early, before the rest of the household, to play her piano. These solitary times must have been essential to her sanity. She described herself and her best friend Martha Lloyd as being 'desperate walkers'; only the

worst weather could keep them inside. Jane did sometimes manage to write when people were staying, but she
was very private about her work. Her nephews and nieces
didn't discover until after she was published what their
aunt was doing at that tiny little table – they had thought
she was writing letters. Jane wasn't always 'in the mood'
for writing, but her solution was to work until she was: 'I
am not at all in a humour for writing; I must write on till
I am.'[12]

It may be that your head is full of joints of mutton
(ugh!) and doses of rhubarb, but if you do have time to
sit down and work, you can often still get things done.
Writing is the only profession where people talk about
being 'blocked'. It's lucky that the ambulance drivers aren't
suddenly struck down by 'paramedics' block'. You may not
be in the mood for composition and new ideas may not be
coming thick and fast, but you can still edit or make notes,
or if you really can't do any of that, you can still read or at
the very least listen to audio books.

BE A PERFECTIONIST – 'AN ARTIST CANNOT DO
ANYTHING SLOVENLY'[13]

Jane Austen knew that only perfection is good enough if
you want to be satisfied with your work. She was writing
(and joking) about something she'd made for her nephew
when she said that, but she still meant it. You may not be
writing The Greatest Novel of All Time, but you must get
your work so good that you cannot improve upon it before
you expose it to the world. The most common mistake
aspiring writers make is to send their work to potential

agents before it is ready. Get feedback from intelligent and careful readers and then make it even better before you even *think* of sending it to anybody. You *might* hang on to your work for too long, worrying that it is still not finished or ready, but in many years of teaching, running workshops and talking to other writers, I have only met one such person.

WHATEVER YOU DO, DON'T MARRY HARRIS BIGG-WITHER

Jane Austen's life could have been much easier. In 1802 she and Cassandra were staying with their good friends the Biggs at beautiful Manydown House when Harris Bigg-Wither, their friends' younger brother, asked Jane to marry him. He wasn't Jane's type at all – he was described as awkward and clumsy, certainly no Henry Tilney, Captain Wentworth, Mr Knightley or Mr Darcy – but he was extremely rich and seems to have been a good-natured fellow.

Marrying Harris would have resulted in complete financial security, not just for Jane but for her beloved sister too. They would have lived in comfort and in the same style as their brother Edward and their mother's rich relatives for the rest of their lives. Jane knew this and must have been tempted by the beautiful house and garden she would have had. She accepted Harris, and he and his sisters were delighted, but after a presumably sleep-less night had to confess she couldn't go through with it. She and Cassandra fled. Poor Harris Bigg-Wither! His sisters didn't bear a grudge against the Austens, and they remained friends.

If she had married Harris Bigg-Wither, it's highly likely that Jane would, like so many Georgian women, have died in childbirth. We know from the dimensions of her pelisse in the Hampshire Museums Collection that although she was about five foot seven, she was extremely slim, and that certainly wouldn't have helped. Even the most robust women who had borne many children often died during or after giving birth. Thank goodness she said no. It's hard to imagine a world without the six brilliant novels that have brought so much pleasure, shaped our ideas of what can be accomplished with the form, that have helped us to understand the workings of the human heart and influenced the way that we dream and fall in love.

Jane Austen knew, as her heroines always do, that one should never 'marry without affection' – she advised her niece Fanny to do anything but that. The scene in *Pride and Prejudice* in which Lizzy confesses to Jane that she and Mr Darcy are in love and engaged has even more resonance when we know about Harris Bigg-Wither. Sadly it wasn't Mr Darcy who asked Jane Austen to marry him.

At night she opened her heart to Jane. Though suspicion was very far from Miss Bennet's general habits, she was absolutely incredulous here.

'You are joking, Lizzy. This cannot be! – engaged to Mr Darcy! – No, no, you shall not deceive me. I know it to be impossible.'

'This is a wretched beginning indeed! My sole dependence was on you; and I am sure nobody else will believe me, if you do not. Yet, indeed, I am in earnest. I speak nothing but the truth. He still loves me, and we are engaged.'

Jane looked at her doubtingly. 'Oh, Lizzy! it cannot be. I know how much you dislike him.'

'You know nothing of the matter. *That* is all to be forgot. Perhaps I did not always love him so well as I do now. But in such cases as these a good memory is unpardonable. This is the last time I shall ever remember it myself.'

Miss Bennet still looked all amazement. Elizabeth again, and more seriously, assured her of its truth.

'Good Heaven! can it be really so? Yet now I must believe you,' cried Jane. 'My dear, dear Lizzy, I would – I do congratulate you – but are you certain? forgive the question – are you quite certain that you can be happy with him?'

'There can be no doubt of that. It is settled between us already, that we are to be the happiest couple in the world. But are you pleased, Jane? Shall you like to have such a brother?'

'Very, very much. Nothing could give either Bingley or myself more delight. But we considered it, we talked of it as impossible. And do you really love him quite well enough? Oh, Lizzy! do anything rather than marry without affection. Are you quite sure that you feel what you ought to do?'

'Oh, yes! You will only think I feel *more* than I ought to do, when I tell you all.'

'What do you mean?'

'Why, I must confess that I love him better than I do Bingley. I am afraid you will be angry.'

'My dearest sister, now be serious. I want to talk very seriously. Let me know every thing that I am to know without delay. Will you tell me how long you have loved him?'

'It has been coming on so gradually, that I hardly know when it began. But I believe I must date it from my first seeing his beautiful grounds at Pemberley.'

Another entreaty that she would be serious, however, produced the desired effect; and she soon satisfied Jane by her solemn assurances of attachment. When convinced on that article, Miss Bennet had nothing further to wish.

Mr Bennet raises the same objections as his eldest daughter. Elizabeth should not marry unless she really loves Mr Darcy.

Her father was walking about the room, looking grave and anxious. 'Lizzy,' said he, 'what are you doing? Are you out of your senses, to be accepting this man? Have not you always hated him?'

How earnestly did she then wish that her former opinions had been more reasonable, her expressions more moderate! It would have spared her from explanations and professions which it was exceedingly awkward to give; but they were now necessary, and she assured him, with some confusion, of her attachment to Mr Darcy.

'Or, in other words, you are determined to have him. He is rich, to be sure, and you may have more fine clothes and fine carriages than Jane. But will they make you happy?'

'Have you any other objection,' said Elizabeth, 'than your belief of my indifference?'

'None at all. We all know him to be a proud, unpleasant sort of a man; but this would be nothing if you really liked him.'

'I do, I do like him,' she replied, with tears in her eyes; 'I love him. Indeed he has no improper pride. He is perfectly amiable. You do not know what he really is; then pray do not pain me by speaking of him in such terms.'

First Impressions was completed before Harris Bigg-Wither proposed to Jane, and we don't know how this scene may have been edited or changed for *Pride and Prejudice*, but we can be in no doubt of Jane Austen's views on marrying a person one cannot love simply for convenience and security. Jane wasn't opposed to the idea of marriage for herself; she just didn't meet the right person at the right time. She might easily have married Tom Lefroy if finances had allowed, and she had to worry about money until very late in her life. We know that she had romances, and there were probably others that aren't mentioned in any of the surviving letters or family accounts. The gaps in the surviving letters may speak volumes.

Jane Austen sets us an example about being true to ourselves. You probably won't have to turn down a Harris Bigg-Wither, but dedicating yourself to writing means following a difficult path. Choosing to concentrate on writing is likely to mean that your house will be dustier and more dilapidated than other people's; the piles of books and papers will make you look like a hoarder; you won't be able to afford as many haircuts as your friends with 'proper' careers; all your free time will be spent on writing, and you will leave undone many things which you ought to do. If you are lucky enough to have days to concentrate on your writing, you will feel like Bill Murray's character in *Groundhog Day*, who says that sometimes he goes months without looking in a mirror. You will be rummaging in the bottom of your bag looking for your bus fare while friends from university are buying tracts of woodland, but it will be worth it.

REMEMBER TO HAVE FUN

Jane chose the difficult path, although perhaps it wasn't a choice but a compulsion. But being a writer didn't stop her enjoying life. She threw herself into activities with her nephews and nieces; she loved walking, dancing, jokes, being with her friends and swimming in the sea. 'The Bathing was so delightful this morning & Molly so pressing with me to enjoy myself that I believe I staid in rather too long.'[14] She loved visiting London, staying with her brother Henry, going to the theatre and to exhibitions and 'parading about London in a barouche ... I had great amusement among the pictures; and the driving about, the carriage being open, was very pleasant. I liked my solitary elegance very much, and was ready to laugh all the time at my being where I was.'[15]

NOTES

PLAN OF A NOVEL

1 You can look at the original and see the names she wrote in the margin at http://www.janeausten.ac.uk/edition/ms/PlanHeadNote.html. This wonderful website also allows you to see Jane Austen's other surviving manuscripts – so interesting for the insight they give us into her methods of composition and editing.

2 This is in the far east of Russia, i.e. very far away.

3 Letter to Anna, 23–4 August 1814.

4 Caroline Austen, *My Aunt Jane Austen: A Memoir* (1867), in James Edward Austen-Leigh, K. Sutherland (ed.), (2008).

5 Here she must mean Anna's little notebooks, which were probably the same as the ones she herself used.

6 Letter to Anna Austen, 10 August 1814.

7 Letter to Anna Austen, Chawton, 28 September 1814.

8 Letter to Cassandra, 17 November 1798.

9 A beautiful answer to the question 'It is a much quoted maxim that there are only seven stories in fiction and that all others are based on them. Is it true, and what might these seven stories be?' in the *Guardian*'s 'Notes and Queries' column (http://www.theguardian.com/notesandqueries/query/0,,-1553,00.html) which can be read in a few minutes. Christopher Booker's *The Seven Basic Plots – Why We Tell Stories*, Continuum (2004) is jolly useful and somewhat longer.

10 There is an excellent section on plotting which I draw on here in Louise Jordan's *How to Write for Children and Get Published*. It offers Catherine MacPhail's plot plan for her children's books, which could also be used for many works for adults.

11 Jane Austen's *ADVERTISEMENT BY THE AUTHORESS, TO NORTHANGER ABBEY.*

12 How like Mrs Norris to take these pheasant eggs with the plan of having one of the Mansfield Park workers put them under a hen to hatch. She says that if they do hatch she will have the chicks moved to her own garden, but Lady Bertram will benefit too. 'I shall get the dairymaid to set them under the first spare hen, and if they come to good I can have them moved to my own house and borrow a coop; and it will be a great delight to me in my lonely hours to attend to them. And if I have good luck, your mother shall have some.' I can't imagine Mrs Norris doing any of the work of looking after the pheasants, but she probably enjoyed eating them and their eggs.

13 See http://www.southampton.ac.uk/music/research/projects/austen_family_music_books.page

14 There are other Price children, of course, but the novel is not much concerned with them

'INTRICATE CHARACTERS ARE THE *MOST* AMUSING'

1 *Pride and Prejudice*, Chapter 13.

2 *Pride and Prejudice*, Chapter 1.

3 Deirdre Le Faye, *Jane Austen's 'Outlandish Cousin' – The Life and Letters of Eliza de Feuillide*, The British Library, London (2002).

4 This exercise is developed from 'People from the Past: Characters of the Future' in the indispensable Anne Bernays and Pamela Painter, *What If?*, HarperCollins, New York (2005), one of my absolute favourite creative writing books.

5 Kurt Vonnegut's *Eight Rules* appeared in the preface to his short-story collection *Bagombo Snuff Box*. See also http://www.brainpickings.org/index.php/2012/04/03/kurt-vonnegut-on-writing-stories/ and http://www.youtube.com/watch?v=nmVcIhnvSx8

6 Emma Thompson plays this beautifully in the 1995 movie. The audience experiences the huge release of tension Elinor has felt and sees the joy that follows. Of course your starting place should be the novel, but this film is my favourite of all the adaptations. It draws skilfully on Jane Austen's letters too, and I can't resist mentioning it.

7 *Persuasion*, Chapter 9.

BUILDING THE VILLAGE OF YOUR STORY

1 Letter to Anna Austen (later Lefroy), Chawton, 9 September 1814.

2 R. I. M. Dunbar, 'Neocortex size as a constraint on group size in primates', *Journal of Human Evolution* 22 (1992), p. 6.

3 Many of the exercises in this chapter were devised with my friends Carole Burns and Judith Heneghan for our presentation at the National Association of Writers in Education conference 2014. Please see our jointly authored article in the NAWE journal, *Writing in Education – Vol. 65 – NAWE Conference Collection 2014*, http://www.nawe.co.uk/DB/current-wie-edition/editions/nawe-conference-collection-2014.html

4 Inga Moore, *Six Dinner Sid*, Hodder Children's Books (2004).

5 Letter to Cassandra, Godmersham, 24 August 1805.

6 Letter to Cassandra, 29 January 1813.

7 Letter to Martha Lloyd, 16 February 1813.

A FINE PAIR OF EYES

1 Julia Bell and Paul Magrs (eds), *The Creative Writing Coursebook*, Macmillan, London (2001).

2 This exercise was inspired by one that Maureen Freely suggests in her chapter 'Punto de Vista' in *The Creative Writing Coursebook*.

3 For further information and ideas on writing using museum objects see the Victoria and Albert Museum's useful

section on creative writing: www.ram.ac.uk/content/articles/
c/creative-writing-looking

LIGHT, BRIGHT AND SPARKLING

1   *Emma*, Chapter 9.

SECRETS AND SUSPENSE

1   This is a useful way of looking at plots outlined by Patricia
Duncker in Bell and Magrs, *The Creative Writing Coursebook*.
2   *Sense and Sensibility*, Chapter 37.
3   My italics.

IN JANE AUSTEN'S POCKET

1   She's pregnant.
2   From *Doctor Who*, 'Blink', writer Stephen Moffat, direc-
tor Hettie Macdonald, season 3, episode 10, first broadcast
9 June 2007.
3   The coach.
4   For a longer example see the episode early in *Howards End*
by E.M. Forster where the characters go to hear Beethoven's
Fifth Symphony.

'AND WHAT IS FIFTY MILES OF GOOD ROAD?'

1   There's a useful discussion and a summary of different types
of plot in Bell and Magrs, *The Creative Writing Coursebook*.
2   For information on real and imagined places in Jane Austen's work see www.pemberley.com/janeinfo/ppjalmap.html#
pplace and http://ajaneaustengazetteer.com
3   Booker, *The Seven Basic Plots*.

'YOU KNOW HOW INTERESTING THE PURCHASE
OF A SPONGE-CAKE IS TO ME'

1 Letter to Cassandra, Godmersham, 15 June 1808.
2 http://www.guardian.co.uk/lifeandstyle/2012/apr/18/
famous-five-perfect-austerity-diet

JOINTS OF MUTTON AND DOSES OF RHUBARB

1 *Pride and Prejudice*, Chapter 11.
2 For more information see http://www.bl.uk/collection-
items/the-loiterer-periodical-written-and-edited-by-jane-
austens-brothers
3 After Jane's death Cassandra destroyed some letters and por-
tions of others. The letters were going to be passed on to her
nieces and nephews. It strikes me as both right and normal
for sisters to keep each other's secrets and not allow sharp
comments made about other family members to be revealed.
Of course Cassandra had no idea that the letters she kept
would be in print some two hundred years later. Who doesn't
end some emails with 'Delete this'?
4 This charming and sure-footed continuation utilizes ideas
passed down through the Austen family of how Jane
planned to finish the novel. Her *Susan Price or Resolution*
and *Margaret Dashwood or Interference* are even more delightful, though I must admit to bias as Edith is my great-
grandmother.
5 This friend of Mrs Lefroy was the Reverend Samuel Blackall, who had expressed interest in Jane. It came to nothing.
Mrs Lefroy was probably keen to promote the alliance, having seen Jane so disappointed by what happened with her
nephew.
6 Letter to Cassandra, Godmersham, 30 June 1808.
7 http://www.pemberley.com/janeinfo/ausprayr.html

8 You can see how the ending of this prayer would lead into the Lord's Prayer.

9 Rebecca West in a review of Ethel M. Dell's *Charles Rex*, in *New Statesman* (16 September 1922). This review was reprinted in West's *The Strange Necessity*, Jonathan Cape (1928) as 'The Tosh Horse'. Ethel Dell wrote dozens of hugely popular romantic novels.

10 He suggested this as it would please the royal family.

11 Bilbocatch is cup and ball. The set said to belong to Jane is on display at Jane Austen's House Museum.

12 Letter to Cassandra, Godmersham, 26 October 1813.

13 Letter to Cassandra, 17 November 1798.

14 Letter to Cassandra, Lyme, September 1804.

15 Letter to Cassandra, London, 24 May 1813.

ACKNOWLEDGEMENTS

I would like thank Alexandra Pringle, Angelique Tran Van Sang, Lucy Clayton, Francesca Sturiale, Madeleine Feeny and their colleagues at Bloomsbury London, Lea Beresford and her colleagues at Bloomsbury, New York, Sarah J Coleman for the gorgeous illustrations, Sarah Lutyens and Susannah Godman at Lutyens & Rubinstein, the staff, volunteers and trustees (past and present) at Jane Austen's House Museum, Chawton and in particular Olive Drakes, Madelaine Smith and Annalie Talent for their help in organising and running the writing workshops, Carole Burns and Judith Heneghan for their exercises in 'Building the village of your story', Hugh Davis for his excellent copyediting, Sarah-Jane Forder for her eagle-eyed proofreading – and Stephen Smith for so much else.

JANE AUSTEN'S LIFE: A TIMELINE

Dates are taken from *Jane Austen, A Family Record* by Deirdre Le Faye, Cambridge University Press, Cambridge (2004).

1764

26 April   Jane's parents, the Reverend George Austen and Cassandra Leigh, marry.

1765

13 February   Jane's brother James born in Deane, Hampshire.

1766

26 August   Jane's brother George born.

1767

7 October   Jane's brother Edward born.

1768

Summer   Austens move to Steventon, Hampshire.

1771

8 June   Jane's brother Henry Thomas born.

1773

                       The Austens supplement their income by taking boarding pupils at Steventon, which continues until 1796.

9 January   Jane's only sister, Cassandra Elizabeth, born.

23 March | The Reverend Austen becomes rector of Deane in addition to Steventon.

1774

23 April | Jane's brother Francis William (Frank) born.

1775

16 December | Jane Austen born.

1779

23 June | Jane's brother Charles John born.

1783

Edward adopted by the Knights of Godmersham, Kent.

Spring | Jane, Cassandra and their cousin Jane Cooper go away to school in Oxford. Later that year the school moves to Southampton and the girls fall ill. Jane almost dies. They return home.

1785

Spring | Jane and Cassandra go away to the Abbey School in Reading.

1786

December | Jane and Cassandra leave the Abbey School and henceforth are educated at home.

1787

Jane works on the earliest of her juvenilia. This will be collected in *Volume the First*.

1791

27 December | Edward marries Elizabeth Bridges.

1792

Cassandra becomes engaged to Tom Fowle, one of her father's former pupils.

27 March   James marries Anne Mathew.

1793

Jane begins to write a play, *Sir Charles Grandison*, a comedy.

23 January   Edward's first child, Fanny, born. She will be a favourite of Jane and Cassandra.

15 April   James's first child, Anna, born.

3 June   Jane writes her last item of juvenilia.

1794

Jane is probably writing *Lady Susan*.

1795

Jane is probably writing *Elinor and Marianne*.

3 May   James's wife dies. Little Anna sent to live with her grandparents and aunts at Steventon until January 1797.

December   Jane's flirtation with Tom Lefroy during his visit to Ashe begins (ending in January 1796).

1796

January   Tom Fowle sails for the West Indies as a ship's chaplain.

October   Jane begins writing *First Impressions*; it will become *Pride and Prejudice*.

1797

17 January   James remarries, to Mary Lloyd, sister of Jane's friend Martha.

February	Tom Fowle dies of yellow fever in San Domingo and is buried at sea.
August	Jane finishes *First Impressions*.
1 November	The Reverend Austen offers *First Impressions* to the publisher Thomas Cadell. The manuscript is returned unopened.
November	Jane begins to revise *Elinor and Marianne*; it eventually becomes *Sense and Sensibility*.
Winter	The Reverend Samuel Blackall visits Ashe and is interested in Jane.
31 December	Henry marries Eliza de Feuillide.

1798

| August | Jane (probably) begins writing *Susan*, which eventually becomes *Northanger Abbey*. |

1799

| End of June | Jane (probably) finishes *Susan*. |

1800

| December | The Reverend Austen retires. |

1801

| May | The Reverend and Mrs Austen, Cassandra and Jane leave Steventon for Bath. |
| Late May | Jane, Cassandra and their parents have a seaside holiday, most likely at Sidmouth and Colyton. Jane probably has a holiday romance with a young clergyman. |

1802

| 25 November | Jane and Cassandra visit the Biggs. |
| 2 December | Harris Bigg-Wither proposes to Jane. She accepts. |

3 December	Jane breaks off the engagement; the sisters flee to Steventon and then return to Bath.
Winter	Jane revises *Susan*.

1803

Spring	Jane sells *Susan* to Crosby and Co. for £10.
Summer	More trips to the seaside, probably Charmouth, Uplyme, and Pinny.
November	A visit to Lyme Regis.

1804

	Jane (probably) begins *The Watsons*.
25 October	Return to Bath and move to 3 Green Park Buildings East.
16 December	Jane's friend Mrs Anne Lefroy of Ashe is killed in a riding accident on Jane's birthday.

1805

21 January	The Reverend Austen dies suddenly in Bath. His pension dies with him.
25 March	Mrs Austen, Cassandra and Jane move to 25 Gay Street.
Summer	Jane possibly courted by Edward Bridges. Martha Lloyd joins the Austen household.

1806

29 January	The Austens move to yet cheaper lodgings in Trim Street, Bath.
2 July	Mrs Austen, Jane and Cassandra leave Bath, and go via Clifton to Adlestrop and later to stay with the Coopers at Hamstall Ridware.
24 July	Frank marries Mary Gibson.

October	Mrs Austen, Jane and Cassandra move to Southampton to share a house with Frank and Mary.

1807

March	The Austens move to Castle Square, Southampton.
19 May	Charles marries Fanny Palmer in Bermuda.
September	Edward arranges a family gathering at Chawton Great House, followed by other family gatherings in Southampton.

1808

10 October	Edward's wife dies after giving birth to her eleventh child. Jane looks after some of the bereaved children in Southampton.

1809

5 April	Jane writes the famous M.A.D. letter to Crosby and Co.
7 July	Jane, Cassandra, Mrs Austen and Martha Lloyd move to Chawton Cottage in Hampshire.

1810

Winter	*Sense and Sensibility* accepted for publication by Thomas Egerton.

1811

February	Jane starts planning *Mansfield Park*.
30 October	*Sense and Sensibility* 'By A Lady' is published.
Winter	Jane is revising *First Impressions*.

1812

Autumn	Jane sells the copyright of *Pride and Prejudice* to Egerton for £110.

1813

28 January   *Pride and Prejudice* 'By The Author of *Sense and Sensibility*' is published.

April   Jane goes to London to help care for Henry's wife Eliza, who nevertheless dies. Jane returns to Chawton but spends more time with Henry in May.

Summer   Jane finishes *Mansfield Park*.

November   Second editions of *Pride and Prejudice* and *Sense and Sensibility* published.

1814

21 January   Jane begins *Emma*.

9 May   *Mansfield Park* is published by Egerton.

6 September   Charles's wife, Fanny, dies after childbirth.

1815

29 March   *Emma* is finished.

8 August   Jane begins *Persuasion*.

4 October   Jane goes to London to nurse Henry.

13 November   Jane visits the Prince Regent's library at Carlton House. She is 'invited' to dedicate her next work to him.

End of December   *Emma* is published by John Murray.

1816

Spring   Jane's health begins to fail. Henry visits Crosby and Co. and, using Jane's money, buys back the manuscript of *Susan*. Jane revises *Susan* for publication.

22 May–15 June   Jane and Cassandra visit Cheltenham, seeking a cure for Jane.

6 August   *Persuasion* completed.

1817

27 January–18 March	Jane works on *Sanditon* until she abandons it, too ill to continue.
27 April	Jane makes her will.
24 May	Jane and Cassandra move to Winchester to be closer to Jane's doctor.
18 July	Jane dies, aged forty-one.
24 July	Jane buried in Winchester Cathedral.
End of December	*Northanger Abbey* and *Persuasion* published together by Murray with Henry's 'Biographical Notice of the Author'.

BIBLIOGRAPHY AND SOURCES

JANE AUSTEN

Austen, Caroline, *Reminiscences of Jane Austen's Niece*, introduced by Deirdre Le Faye, Jane Austen Society, Chawton (2004)

Austen, Jane, *Sense and Sensibility; Pride and Prejudice; Northanger Abbey; Mansfield Park; Emma; Persuasion; The Watsons, Lady Susan and Sanditon; Catherine and Other Writings*, Oxford University Press, World's Classics editions, Oxford, and Penguin English Library, Penguin Classics and Penguin Popular Classics editions, London

Austen-Leigh, James Edward, *A Memoir of Jane Austen and Other Family Recollections*, edited by Kathryn Sutherland, Oxford World Classics, Oxford (2008)

Doody, Margaret, *Jane Austen's Names: Riddles, Persons, Places*, University of Chicago Press, Chicago and London (2015)

Hill, Constance, *Jane Austen – Her Homes and Her Friends*, John Lane, London (1902). Also available from Elibron Classics Series and online.

Honan, Park, *Jane Austen – Her Life*, Phoenix, Orion Books, London (1997)

Hubback, J. H. and Edith C., *Jane Austen's Sailor Brothers*, John Lane, London (1906)

Le Faye, Deirdre, *Jane Austen's 'Outlandish Cousin' – The Life and Letters of Eliza de Feuillide*, British Library, London (2002)

Le Faye, Deirdre, *Jane Austen: A Family Record*, Cambridge University Press, Cambridge (2003)

Le Faye, Deirdre, *Jane Austen – The World of Her Novels*, Frances Lincoln Ltd, London (2003)

Le Faye, Deirdre, *Jane Austen's Letters*, Oxford University Press, Oxford (fourth edition, 2014)

Mullan, John, *What Matters in Jane Austen?: Twenty Crucial Puzzles Solved*, Bloomsbury Paperbacks, London (2013)

Ray, Joan Klingel, *Jane Austen For Dummies*, Wiley Publishing Inc., Indianapolis (2006)

Shields, Carol, *Jane Austen*, Phoenix, Orion Books, London (2001)

Smith, Rebecca, *Jane Austen's Guide to Modern Life's Dilemmas*, Ivy Press, Lewes (2012)

Sutherland, Kathryn, *Jane Austen's Textual Lives: From Aeschylus to Bollywood*, Oxford University Press, Oxford (2007)

Tomalin, Claire, *Jane Austen – A Life*, Penguin, London (2000)

Tucker, George Holbert, *A Goodly Heritage: A History of Jane Austen's Family*, Carcanet New Press, Manchester (1983)

MY FAVOURITE CREATIVE WRITING BOOKS

Bell, Julia and Magrs, Paul, *The Creative Writing Coursebook*, Macmillan, London (2001)

Bernays, Anne and Painter, Pamela, *What If?: Writing Exercises for Fiction Writers*, HarperCollins, London (2005)

Cowan, Andrew, *The Art of Writing Fiction*, Routledge, Abingdon (2013)

Jordan, Louise, *How to Write for Children and Get Published*, Piatkus Books, London (2007)

Mittelmark, Howard and Newman, Sandra, *How NOT to Write a Novel: 200 Mistakes To Avoid At All Costs if You Ever Want To Get Published*, Penguin, London (2009)

WEBSITES

Jane Austen's House Museum, Chawton
jane-austens-house-museum.org.uk

Digital collection of Jane Austen's fiction manuscripts
janeausten.ac.uk

Jane Austen's letters, first (1884) edition
pemberley.com/janeinfo/brablets.html

Republic of Pemberley
pemberley.com

Jane Austen Centre, Bath
janeausten.co.uk

Jane Austen Society of North America
jasna.org

Jane Austen Society of North America online journal
Persuasions
jasna.org/persuasions/on-line

Jane Austen Society of Australia
jasa.com.au

Jane Austen Society of Brazil
janeaustenbrasil.com.br

Jane Austen Society of the Czech Republic
empirovyden.cz/p/englis.html

Jane Austen Society of the Netherlands
janeaustensociety.nl

Jane Austen Society of the United Kingdom
janeaustensoci.freeuk.com

Digital collection of Austen family music books
archive.org/details/austenfamilymusicbooks

A guide to places associated with Jane Austen
seekingjaneausten.com

Chawton House Library
chawtonhouse.org

BLOGS AND COMMUNITY WEBSITES

austenonly.com
janeaustensworld.wordpress.com
thesecretunderstandingofthehearts.blogspot.co.uk
austenauthors.net/blog
austenprose.com
mollands.net
austenblog.com
pemberley.com

INDEX

A NOTE ON THE AUTHOR

Rebecca Smith teaches creative writing at the University of Southampton, and is the author of three novels: *The Bluebird Café*, *Happy Birthday and All That* and *A Bit of Earth* as well as a work of non-fiction, *Jane Austen's Guide to Modern Life's Dilemmas*. Her first novel for children, *Shadow Eyes*, was shortlisted for the 2012 Kelpies Prize. From 2009–2010 she was the Writer in Residence at Jane Austen's House Museum in Chawton. She lives in Hampshire.

@RMSmithAuthor

A NOTE ON THE TYPE

The text of this book is set in Adobe Caslon, named after the English punch-cutter and type-founder William Caslon I (1692–1766). Caslon's rather old-fashioned types were modelled on seventeenth-century Dutch designs, but found wide acceptance throughout the English-speaking world for much of the eighteenth century until replaced by newer types towards the end of the century. Used in 1776 to print the Declaration of Independence, they were revived in the nineteenth century and have been popular ever since, particularly amongst fine printers. There are several digital versions, of which Carol Twombly's Adobe Caslon is one.